D0404382

PUBLIC OPINION AND POLITICAL CHANGE IN CHINA

WENFANG TANG

Public Opinion and Political Change in China

STANFORD UNIVERSITY PRESS

STANFORD, CALIFORNIA 2005

Stanford University Press
Stanford, California

© 2005 by the Board of Trustees of the Leland Stanford Junior
University. All rights reserved.

No part of this book may be reproduced or transmitted in any
form or by any means, electronic or mechanical, including
photocopying and recording, or in any information storage
or retrieval system without the prior written permission of
Stanford University Press.

Printed in the United States of America on acid-free, archival-
quality paper

Library of Congress Cataloging-in-Publication Data

Tang, Wenfang, 1955–
    Public opinion and political change in China / Wenfang Tang.
        p.   cm.
    Includes bibliographical references and index.
    ISBN 0-8047-5219-2 (cloth : alk. paper)—ISBN 0-8047-5220-6
(pbk. : alk. paper)
    1. China—Politics and government—2002—Public opinion.
    2. Public opinion—China.   I. Title.

    JQ1510.T36   2005
    320.951′09′0511—dc22   2005015412

Typeset by G & S Book Services in 10/14 Janson

Original Printing 2005

Last figure below indicates year of this printing:
14   13   12   11   10   09   08   07   06   05

Library
University of Texas
at San Antonio

To Jessi and Annie

Contents

Figures

Tables

Photographs

Photo section follows page 100.

1. A wall display of its six functions (elder care, marriage counseling, public safety, public health, women's issues, and culture and education) in a Shanghai residential council in 1998. Other functions of the residential council include household registration and the implementation of government policies, such as family planning and the anti–Falun Gong campaign. In recent years, employees of the residential councils have been younger and more educated. Some of them are laid-off workers from state-owned enterprises. The most common place to draw an urban sample begins in residential councils where household registration records are kept. By Wenfang Tang.

2. Local survey team members checking household registration records with the director of a Muslim residential council in Xian. October 1999.

3. Announcement: "A training session for the 1999 urban survey will be held at 7:00 P.M. in the Office of the Student Union. Don't miss it!" Northwestern University, Xian, October 1999.

4. A project manager (standing) conducting an interviewer training session. Wuhan University, October 1999.

5. A student leader distributing to the trained student interviewers of Wuhan University the gifts for each interviewee, in this case a tablecloth. August 1999.

6. A typical Shanghai residential building where the survey interviews were conducted. August 1999.

7. Spatial sampling: (1) Randomly selected townships and city districts are divided into a number of 50 × 50 m squares using GPS. (2) A predetermined number of squares is randomly chosen. (3) A predetermined number of households is randomly selected from each square. (4) Finally, an individual is randomly selected from each household.

8. One sample township was hidden in the Taihang Mountains in Lingshou county, Hebei province. A communist base area during the anti-Japanese invasion, Lingshou is one of the poorest counties in the country to receive government subsidies.

9. The first household we located in the first randomly selected square, in Lingshou County, Hebei province, 2003.

10. All household addresses in each randomly selected spatial square are recorded. Lingshou, 2003.

11. We never knew what we would find until we got there. Sometimes the spatial square landed in an open field. Huairou, Beijing, 2003.

12. World map with earth lights at http://earthobservatory.nasa.gov/Newsroom/NewImages/Images/earth_lights_lrg.jpg (accessed March 24, 2005). Data courtesy Marc Imhoff, the Goddard Space Flight Center (GSFC), National Aeronautics and Space Administration (NASA), and Christopher Elvidge of the National Geophysical Data Center (NGDC), National Oceanic and Atmospheric Administration (NOAA). Image by Craig Mayhew and Robert Simmon, Goddard Space Flight Center, NASA.

Acknowledgments

The idea of writing this book came during my year as a national fellow at the Hoover Institution, Stanford University, in the 1997–98 academic year. There, during my many conversations with Thomas Metzger, a historian by training but with a sharp mind in contemporary issues, he encouraged me to continue my previous research on urban reform by further tackling the question of public opinion and regime legitimacy. Consequently, Thomas Metzger and Raymond Myers at Hoover were instrumental in securing partial funding of the 1999 Six-City Survey. Thomas Metzger and Alex Inkeles played an indispensable role in questionnaire design. In this survey, I was able to repeat many questions in the Chinese urban surveys from the late 1980s to the early 1990s and examine the change in public opinion over a span of thirteen years. During the 1999–2000 academic year, a teaching and research fellowship from the School of International Studies at Peking University allowed me to implement the survey. Professors Shen Mingming and Yang Ming at Peking University provided vital support for the survey. They were instrumental in every step of the survey—questionnaire design, sampling, interviewer training, survey interviews, coding, data entry, and so on. I was very impressed with the high level of professionalism of their staff at the Research Center for Contemporary China at Peking University. In 2002, a Chun Hui Teaching/Research Fellowship from Tsinghua University allowed me to spend eight months at Tsinghua and complete most of the writing. Professor Yan Xuetong at Tsinghua provided valuable academic and logistic support during this time.

Chapter 2 is based on papers presented at a survey research conference organized by Professor Steven W. Lewis at Rice University in 2000 and the

Conference on Surveying China organized by Professor Bruce Dickson at George Washington University in 2000. I would like to thank Andrew Marble at *Issues & Studies* for allowing me to republish in chapter 2 some materials from an earlier article on survey research in China. Andrew also gave me many important suggestions on making the article more readable to a general audience. The final version of chapter 2 also benefited from Professor Pierre Landry at Yale University, who, together with Professor Shen Mingming, taught me much about spatial sampling.

Chapter 4 benefited from my discussions on Chinese media with Hu Xing at the Press Office of the State Council and with Lisa Rose Weaver and Jaime FlorCruz at CNN's Beijing Bureau. Hu Xing provided valuable insights into the process of government information management. Lisa and Jaime generously shared their experience and observation of the Chinese media and provided comparative perspectives between Chinese and Western media. Lisa also patiently proofread the entire manuscript, sharpening my academic writing style with her journalistic clarity.

The Department of Political Science at the University of Pittsburgh provided me with an ideal intellectual environment in which I was compelled to compare China with other countries. Jon Hurwitz introduced me to the literature on public opinion and generously shared his insights into cross-country comparisons with the World Values Survey. Mitchell Seligson's research on the lack of trust in Latin American democracies inspired me to write chapter 5 on interpersonal trust and the lack of democracy in China. The department provided valuable research and teaching assistantship during the entire process of this project. Liying Ren and Qing Yang were particularly helpful in serving as my research and teaching assistants. They spent many hours helping me with data analysis and grading exams. Their efforts greatly shortened the time I had to spend completing the manuscript.

I would like to thank Professor Feng Tongqing, vice president of the Labor Relations College in Beijing, for generously sharing the 1997 Staff and Workers Survey data. He was also my constant consultant, patiently answering my questions during the writing of chapter 7. A Central Research Development Fund Award in 2002 from the University of Pittsburgh provided crucial financial support for field research of chapter 7. William Parish, Dali Yang, and their graduate students at the University of Chicago made valuable suggestions on chapter 7 during my presentation at their East Asian

Studies Workshop in April 2003. William Parish was also one of the first people who drew my attention to public opinion in China.

Thomas Rawski, Nicole Constable, Bell Yung, and other colleagues on the China Council of the University of Pittsburgh provided me with a wonderful intellectual community. They were also instrumental in allocating financial support during the past several years for field research and course release times. The University Center for International Studies and the Asian Studies Center at Pitt also provided several research grants during this project.

The first-generation reformers in China Yang Guansan and Wang Xiaoqing made available to me the early urban surveys conducted by the Economic System Reform Institute of China in the late 1980s and early 1990s. The comparison between these surveys and the 1999 survey gives this book a rare historical dimension.

The undergraduate and graduate students at the University of Pittsburgh, Peking University, and Tsinghua University also contributed to the improvement of the manuscript with their comments and criticism. Many ideas in this book derived from their reaction to the earlier drafts.

Finally, Stanley Rosen and Jie Chen made extremely valuable comments on the manuscript. Many of Professor Rosen's comments and suggestions are incorporated in the book, including discussions on the linkage between public opinion and policy making, the impact of protest on political change, and the limit of survey research on the study of public opinion. Professor Chen made me tighten up the chapters with more coherent themes and encouraged me to provide an overall description of the surveys used in this book. Their careful readings saved me from a number of embarrassing errors.

Wenfang Tang
Wangjing, Beijing
Summer 2004

PUBLIC OPINION AND POLITICAL CHANGE
IN CHINA

PART ONE

Background

CHAPTER ONE

The Chinese Political Environment and Public Opinion

This book is about public opinion and political behavior in China. One of its goals is to examine China's cultural and political tradition and its role in shaping public values and behavior. Another goal is to discuss the impact of market reform and economic growth on public opinion and political behavior. The final goal is to show the role of China's political system in shaping democratic values and mass political participation. This chapter will describe the cultural, ideological, economic, and political environments in which the case studies in the following chapters are embedded.

Political Tradition

As one of the world's oldest continuous political systems, China created an extremely advanced political culture, one that has guaranteed political

Confucianism

Confucius (551–479 B.C.) was one of the most influential philosophers in the Chinese political tradition. Although few Chinese today would claim to be Confucian, his thinking, recorded in the *Analects*, serves as a guide to Chinese political culture.

Confucius believed in the importance of a well-structured society and in standardizing relationships within that society. Forming the social structure are five types of relationships: between rulers and subjects, between parents and children, between husband and wife, between elder and younger brothers, and between friends. Each individual, regardless of rank, must fulfill his or her responsibilities within these relationships. The Confucian code of conduct includes loyalty (*zhong*), filial piety (*xiao*), benevolence (*ren*), righteousness and sacrifice (*yi*), ritual (*li*), and virtue (*de*). Loyalty assures the people will support the ruler even during difficult times and provides the ruler with political stability and legitimacy. Filial piety means that taking care of elderly parents is everyone's inescapable social responsibility. The Communist party promoted different versions of this concept in order to assure social welfare for the elderly. Benevolence encourages sympathy for each other and, more important, the ruler's awareness of the needs of the people. Righteous sacrifice entails a sense of justice and self-sacrifice. It encourages helping one's friends by self-sacrifice, protecting the interest of the larger group by sacrificing one's family interest, and risking one's life in order to overthrow unjust rulers. Ritual is to be used as a means to preserve and spread established values and moral principles. Finally, virtue is important in restoring the natural order linking people with the rest of the universe that operates on moral principles. Confucius believed that humans are endowed with virtues (a view diametrically opposed to the Judeo-Christian concept of original sin), and that only selfish desires and passions place people in conflict with those innate virtues. The ruler is responsible for restoring the moral order and therefore should be the most virtuous person of all. For further readings on Confucianism and Chinese political culture, see De Bary, Chan, and Watson 1960; Nathan 1973; Pye 1981; Walder 1986; Pye and Pye 1989.

control and continuity for centuries. At the center of this tradition is Confucianism (see text box). Centuries later, Mao Zedong's Communist Revolution intended to destroy the Confucian social hierarchy. Although few Chinese would claim to believe in Confucianism today, political relations between the ruler and the ruled under the Communist Party ironically often reflect Confucian values (Pye and Pye 1989; Perry 1994).

Confucian values can play a dual role in political change. On one hand, Confucianism can create several potential barriers to the development of civil society and democratic politics. The first likely barrier is group orientation. By emphasizing one's social responsibilities, individual interests become less important. Thus, the Confucian ideal of group interest can be used to justify overriding individual interest, an ideal that differs from the Western concept of the preservation of the individual's interest.

The second potential barrier to civil society is paternalistic politics (Walder 1986). The state under the virtuous ruler acts on behalf of the people; individual rights are neither guaranteed nor protected. Also, government decision making is not generally supervised until a problem becomes a crisis. This authoritarian tradition is a barrier to democratic supervision of government.

The third barrier is the tendency to look for virtuous leaders while neglecting to build political institutions. The Maoist cult of personality in the 1960s and 1970s and Mao Zedong's efforts to destroy the party and government institutions are good examples of this tendency.

But not all political traditions are top down. Indeed, other characteristics of Confucianism seem to balance the relationship between state and society. Although Confucianism is a conservative ideology, owing to its emphasis on established social and political order and on parental and male authorities, it also has a rebellious side. This tendency is rooted in the bilateral moral contract between the ruler and his subjects (Wasserstrom and Perry 1994), in which the ruled offer their loyalty only if the ruler is morally upright (Hui 2004). This moral contract therefore assures the ruler's responsiveness to public need. One example of the ruler's fear of this rebellious aspect of Confucianism is the execution of Confucian scholars and the burning of their books by China's first emperor, Qin Shi Huang Di. The other example is Mao's attempts to purge intellectuals during the 1957 anti-rightist campaign, and again during the Cultural Revolution. Others have demonstrated the similarities between Confucian ideas and the 1989 student demonstrations in Tiananmen Square (Esherick and Wasserstrom 1994).

Furthermore, the Confucian emphasis on one's social responsibilities reduces the need for the state to provide many types of social services, such as pensions, unemployment benefits, elder care, and so on. This is a great help for a communist government that is based on the idea of social equality but does not have enough resources to provide the population with necessary services. This is the reason behind the consistent government policy of encouraging one's family responsibilities in China.

Despite China's particular political history, Confucianism per se does not seem to be a barrier to democracy. After all, democracy seems to work well in other societies with Confucian influences, such as Japan, South Korea, and Taiwan. One goal of this volume is to examine whether tradition hinders or promotes democratic values and political change in China.

Official Ideologies

Confucianism explains only part of the Chinese political culture. Indeed, the Chinese Communist Party has never explicitly claimed to be a Confucian party. Rather, the party constitution states that Marxism, Leninism, and Mao Zedong Thought are the official party ideologies.

Karl Marx and Friedrich Engels are probably the most familiar Western writers in China. They argued that human history is driven by class struggle between the working class and the ruling class (historic materialism). The former represents advanced knowledge and the desire to share political power, while the latter resists any change that may threaten the status quo. Under capitalism, the working class is exploited by property owners through unjust distribution of wealth. Property owners gain huge profits through the cheap labor of the working class (surplus value), while workers are only paid barely enough to sustain themselves. Marx and Engels called for a working-class revolution to overthrow the capitalist system and establish a communist society where the means of production are publicly owned and equality replaces social polarization (Marx and Engels 1998).

One obvious problem is the fact that such a revolution never took place in European industrial capitalist societies, as Marx had predicted it would. Instead, governments in these societies have proven capable of making compromises between labor and capital. But, according to Lenin, this gray area does not mean Marx's analysis of capitalism is wrong. Lenin argued that social revolution did not take place in industrial Europe because domestic capitalists instead expanded overseas and colonized the developing world. Corporations paid off the domestic working class through exploiting colonized peoples. For Lenin, economic imperialism was the last stage of capitalism. It was the responsibility of the working people in colonies to launch an international socialist revolution and overthrow imperialism (Lenin 1987).

Lenin's theories of imperialism and socialist revolution were realized in the 1917 Russian Revolution. It also inspired the Chinese Communist leader Mao Zedong, who was at that time searching for a viable path to China's modernization. Although Mao accepted basic Marxist and Leninist ideas about capitalism, imperialism, and social revolution, the Chinese Revolution differed from Marxism and Leninism in several ways. First, because of China's weak industrial base, the Chinese Revolution was mostly a rural revolution fought by peasants rather than a working-class revolution. Second, the Chinese Revolution was a populist movement in which Mao and his comrades directly appealed to the vast majority of the poor. This aspect of the Chinese Revolution was later reflected in Mao's anti-intellectual and anti-establishment tendencies in the 1957 anti-rightist campaign and in the 1958 Great Leap Forward. Populism discourages the role played by civil servants, technology, and intermediate institutions, such as elections and rule of law, necessary elements for a civil society. The third difference between Maoism and Marxism-Leninism was the concept of "continuing revolution under the proletarian dictatorship." Mao reminded China to continue its revolution even after the Communist victory. Without continuing revolution, he warned, socialism would be eroded by capitalist and feudal ideas. The Cultural Revolution (1966–76) was therefore Mao's last effort to keep China on the socialist track by fighting against bureaucratic control (see text box on the Cultural Revolution).

Today, Mao is officially described as having been 70% a great leader and only 30% wrong in his approach, as measured by the social, economic, and political costs of his radical campaigns. The post-Mao leaders have, by contrast, adapted a pragmatic approach to ideology. While still claiming Marxism, Leninism, and Maoism as its official ideologies, the party has quietly shifted its focus from ideological campaigns to encouraging economic development and implementing market mechanisms. This pragmatism is

The Cultural Revolution

The Great Proletariat Cultural Revolution took place in China between 1966 and 1976. People all over the country, in response to the
call by Mao and other radical leaders, participated in overthrowing
party and state bureaucratic organizations at all levels. Workers, peasants, soldiers, and radical college students (Red Guards) with working-
class family backgrounds took control over political power. Intellectuals,
managers, administrators, and professionals were criticized and sent to
re-education camps. Radical egalitarian reforms were implemented in
industrial management, agricultural production, wage distribution, education, medical care, family relations, and marriage. The Cultural Revolution ended in 1976 when Mao died and the radical leaders (the Gang
of Four) were arrested. Few other events in human history involved so
many people and affected so many aspects of their lives.

For Mao and his radical followers, the purpose of the Cultural Revolution was to resist interference and keep China on the right track of
socialist revolution. Mao saw that his socialist regime was threatened
by at least three sources. The first was feudalism (traditional forces),
including beliefs in social hierarchy and obedience. The second was
capitalism (a threat from the West), which included individualism, a
money culture, exploitation, and so on. The third source was revisionism (the Soviet threat), which included Soviet-trained technocrats and
their pro-Soviet and elitist attitude. Some argue that the purpose of the
Cultural Revolution was not to achieve ideological purity, but instead to
fulfill Mao's ambition of gaining personal power. Ideological concerns
and individual power, however, cannot be easily separated.

The Cultural Revolution did not just happen due to Mao's political
maneuvering. Indeed, such a large event could never have unfolded
without the active and sincere support of ordinary Chinese people.

Many have described the Cultural Revolution as the "dark age" in
modern Chinese history. The period was an economic disaster: Mao
focused on political struggle and ignored economic growth. The re-
education of professionals and administrators was also seen as a waste of
talent. The Cultural Revolution was also a political disaster. It encouraged the worship of Mao and the development of a cult of personality. It

also bequeathed to China a mob mentality and a deep distrust of political order and political institutions. This would threaten not only China's future political stability, but also the transition from an authoritarian system based on personal rule to a democratic system in which institutions are more important than individual leaders. The Cultural Revolution left an ideological vacuum. It not only banned traditional Chinese values, Western liberal democratic ideas, and Soviet-style socialism, but also created disillusionment with socialism itself. Subsequent generations of Chinese were left with little to believe in. The Cultural Revolution was a cultural disaster as well. The Red Guards destroyed many historic landmarks, while many works of traditional art and literature were banned. Finally, the Cultural Revolution was a social disaster. Families were scattered around the country, as parents were sent to re-education camps and children were sent to factories, villages, or the military. Marriage and divorce were based on political considerations.

The official Chinese government view of the Cultural Revolution focuses on the negative results. Yet others remind us of some positive changes (Meisner 1986). One result of the Cultural Revolution, as expected, is that it did succeed in reducing the gap between the elite and the masses. The current leaders who experienced working in the fields do have a better understanding of what China is really like for the majority of people. Those workers, peasants, and soldiers who participated in management during the Cultural Revolution did gain political skills and develop a sense of political efficacy. Also, the status of women and overall levels of education and health care improved significantly in China during the Cultural Revolution. One has to realize that most of those who condemn the Cultural Revolution come from a small group of intellectual and political elites. Many ordinary people actually benefited from the Cultural Revolution.

For further reading on the Cultural Revolution, see Lee 1978; Meisner 1986; Wang 1995.

summarized in the "three representatives" of advanced productivity, advanced culture, and the common interests of the majority of people (*People's Daily*, Feb. 26, 2000). Advanced productivity requires economic growth, a market economy, and Western technology. In addition, Chinese tradition and culture, together with the advanced elements of foreign cultures, are advocated to fill the post-Mao ideological vacuum and to combat the social problems of capitalism. Presenting the "common interest" of the people is a way to maintain political legitimacy. In essence, the three representatives are similar to the reforms made by the emperor Guang Xu in 1898, when reformers advocated borrowing Western technology and management to promote economic development (*yong*) while keeping the traditional value system as a guide in life (*ti*). What is new about post-Mao pragmatism compared to the 1898 reforms is "representing the common interest of the people." This slogan has its roots in the Maoist populism. Another goal of this book is to examine the role of official ideologies in shaping public opinion.

Central Planning and Market Reform

In the early 1950s, China introduced the Stalinist centrally planned system from the Soviet Union (Stalin 1961). This system dominated China's economic life for three decades. Under it, the goal of production is to satisfy the needs of society, not to make a profit. Means of production are owned by the state. Production is administratively carried out according to need-based central plans, rather than according to profit-driven market price signals. Accordingly, prices are set by the state based on need, not on supply and demand. Income is also distributed based on need, not on meritocracy. Job security is guaranteed. Finally, the Stalinist model of economic development also emphasized a high investment rate and less consumer spending, the priority of the development of heavy industry (power, steel, infrastructure, etc.) over that of consumer industry, and the subsidizing of urban life in order to promote industrial growth, at the expense of farmers (see Lindblom 1977; Nove 1983, 1991).

As intended, central planning brought some benefits for China and other centrally planned economies (table 1.1). Partly due to the investment bias, planned economies sustained a higher rate of economic growth than market economies at parallel income levels. Planned economies also had a higher rate of labor force participation and labor productivity, particularly in the early years of socialism (Riskin 1987; Kornai 1992).

Yet in the later years of central planning, growth rates among more affluent planned economies were lower than those in market economies at comparable income levels, although China continued to grow rapidly. Labor

TABLE 1.1
Economic performance: planned vs. market

	Planned	Market
Gross Domestic Investment (1978)		
Low income	36	21
Middle income	37[a]	25
Industrialized	28	22
% employed as total population, 1985		
	47.1	35.7 (ind = 41.3
		dev = 30.1)
Annual growth rate in GDP, mean (range)		
1970–78		
Low income	6.0	3.6 (−10/7.8)
Middle income	6.9 (0.4/10.6)	5.7 (−0.8/9.7)
Industrialized	5.4 (4.7/7.0)	3.2 (0.1/5.0)
1980–87		
Low income	10.0 (China)	2.0 (−2.6/6.6)
Middle income	1.6[a] (1.5/1.7)	2.7 (−6.1/13.0)
Industrialized	2.4[b] (1.4/3.8)	2.6 (0.9/5.8)
Labor productivity		
50–62	8.7 (China)	2.4 (USA)
74–78	1.8 (China)	1.4 (USA)
Capital productivity		
74–78	−4.5 (USSR)	−.7 (USA)

SOURCES: *Investment:* Excluding OPEC countries. Low-income market countries include much of Africa and South Asia (India, Sri Lanka, and Bangladesh). Middle-income market countries include much of Latin America, Southeast Asia, and the Middle East. Industrialized countries include most of Western Europe, North America, Australia, and Japan. Low-income socialist data are for China alone. The middle-income socialist figure is based on Hungary alone. This is an unusual year in Hungary—other years were close to 30%. Industrialized socialist countries are Poland, the USSR, E. Germany, and Czechoslovakia. Source: World Bank, *World Development Report* 1980, 1989. China: *Zhongguo Guding Zichan Touzi Tongji Ziliao* 1950–85.

Employment: Planned countries include the USSR (1984), E. Germany, Czechoslovakia, Poland, Hungary, Bulgaria, and China. Industrial markets are based on the U.S., W. Germany, the United Kingdom, France (1984), Italy, Canada, and Australia. Developing markets are Indonesia (1982), the Philippines, India (1981), Egypt (1983), Brazil, and Argentina. Source: International Labor Office, *Labor Statistics Yearbook*, 1986.

GDP growth: Weighted averages, excluding OPEC countries. For countries in each income group, see notes for "investment." Middle-income planned are Hungary and Yugoslavia. Industrial planned are estimates of the 1989 GNP growth rate in Romania, Bulgaria, Czechoslovakia, and E. Germany. Sources: World Bank, *World Development Report*, 1980, 1989.

Productivity: (a) 1950–62 series from Bergson as cited in Ellman, *Socialist Planning*, 1979, 247–48; (b) 1960–78 series from Lane, *Soviet Economy and Society*, 1985, 53; (c) China from *Chinese Economic Yearbook*, 1982, VIII–20, for the time periods 1952–57, 1957–65, and 1965–81.

NOTE: Growth and productivity figures are from Parish 1989.

productivity in China dropped sharply from the golden age of socialism to the post-Mao disillusion. Capital productivity in the Soviet Union was significantly worse than in the United States in the second half of the 1970s.

Therefore, as seen in table 1.1, although central planning worked reasonably well in an early stage and at lower levels of economic development, further economic development revealed a number of problems inherent in central planning, such as difficulty in determining need and in collecting adequate information to coordinate a complex modern economy. As industrialization took place, unavoidable mistakes in the rigid planning system created constant shortages in both production materials and consumer goods. Egalitarian income distribution provided no success indicator—a deficit that, as time passed by, amounted to little labor incentive. Finally, the inability to plan, decreased incentives for labor, and low consumption led to economic inefficiency (Friedman 1962; Lindblom 1977; Nove 1983, 1991; Riskin 1987; Kornai 1980, 1992).

Market reforms were designed to solve these problems. After an initial success in rural reform in the late 1970s and early 1980s, China launched a series of urban reforms beginning in the mid-1980s in order to further address economic inefficiency. These reform programs included the retreat of the state from planning and liberalizing economic activities such as the labor market. Performance-based labor contracts replaced life tenure. Property rights were diversified, which allowed private, joint stock, and foreign joint venture and public firms to coexist. The state also terminated subsidies for many firms that were taking losses, resulting in numerous bankruptcies. Companies were no longer required to provide welfare programs, so they could focus more efficiently on making profit.

Albeit with some momentary speedups and slowdowns, market reform in China has for the most part been an incremental process, compared with that in Russia and Central and Eastern Europe. One frequently asked question is to what extent the Chinese economy operates in a market environment. This is a multifaceted question and can be measured in many different ways. One way to measure a market environment is the percentage of companies that are public, private, or joint venture entities. Another measurement is the percentage of total industrial output by firms with these different types of ownership. Yet another indicator of marketization is the percentage of workers in different ownerships.

The degree of marketization depends on which of the above three measurements we use (fig. 1.1). In terms of number of firms, although the percentage of private firms dropped from three-quarters in 1997 to half in 2001, mostly owing to consolidation, it was still higher than the percentage of public and joint venture firms. Total output by the private sector increased from 18% in 1997 to almost 50% in 2001, while by contrast the share by public firms decreased from 64% in 1997 to only 34% in 2001. Therefore, a small

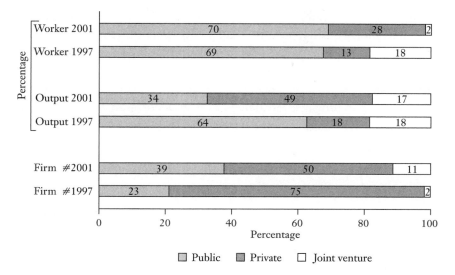

Figure 1.1   Ownership types in the Chinese economy, 1997 and 2001

SOURCES: *China Statistical Yearbook* 1998; *China Statistical Yearbook* 2001.

NOTE: For firm # and % output: public = state firms + collective firms + state companies; private = (all companies − state companies) + private firms + other firms + Hong Kong, Taiwan, and Macau firms + other foreign firms; joint venture = stock firms + jointly run firms + stock companies. For # workers: public = state units + collective units + town/township firms; private = urban non-state jointly owned companies + urban private firms + private households + Hong Kong, Taiwan, and Macau firms + other foreign firms + town/township private firms + rural private households; joint venture = stock firms + jointly run firms + joint stock companies.

number of private firms, made larger by consolidation, were the biggest contributors to the Chinese economy. However, if the focus is on the percentage of workers in different types of ownership, the public sector obviously outweighs the rest. The public sector stayed at the same high level from 1997 to 2001, and at least two out of every three wage earners still worked in the public sector. So the overall picture is a mixed one, in which the oversized public sector and the market-driven private sector are equally important.

China's economy benefited from the above reforms. Growth rates were high (table 1.1), and per capita GDP grew from $167 in 1980 to $942 in 2002 (constant 1995 US$). Adjusted for purchasing power parity, the real growth of per capita gross domestic product was more than tenfold, from $440 in 1980 to $4475 in 2002 (World Bank Group 2003). For many people, living standards, economic freedoms, and opportunities have greatly increased. Staying with a state-assigned job for life was no longer the only option for personal economic prosperity (Tang and Parish 2000).

Yet reform has created a number of problems, such as massive unemployment, income inequality, poverty, and a social safety net that had been torn apart by central planning. The third purpose of this book is to examine how the benefits and costs of market reforms shape public opinion and how the state is responding to public demands. Furthermore, two decades of urban reform have also provided researchers with an opportunity to examine how public opinion and state response have changed over time.

The Chinese Political System

According to the 1982 Constitution of the People's Republic of China (last amended in 1999), the current Chinese state was founded by the Communist Party of China, which is the leader of the Chinese people.[1] The implications of this statement are that the Communist Party is the sole party in power, and that no legitimate political opposition is allowed to challenge its leadership. Therefore, the political structure in China is a single-party state.

According to the party's 1982 constitution, last amended in 1999,[2] the party's National Congress usually meets every five years. Its delegates are indirectly elected from lower-level party committees. Normally, party committees at the work unit level and above employ full-time party officials. The party's National Congress elects the party's Central Discipline Inspection Commission and the Central Committee. The Central Committee has several hundred members, and its function is to elect the Political Bureau (Politburo), the Standing Committee of the Politburo, and the party's General Secretary. The Standing Committee nominates the members of the Secretariat (the operating body of the Politburo) and the party's Central Military Commission. The nominations are then endorsed by the Central Committee. The members of the Standing Committee represent the highest decision-making level in the party (fig. 1.2).

There were more than 66 million party members in 2002, making the Chinese Communist Party one of the largest political parties in the world

Figure 1.2 (opposite)   The Chinese party-state, 2004
NOTE: Partially from the party and state constitutions (http://www.china.org.cn/english/features/49109.htm, accessed March 28, 2005; http://www.china.org.cn/english/Political/25060.htm, accessed March 28, 2005).

THE CHINESE STATE

THE CHINESE COMMUNIST PARTY

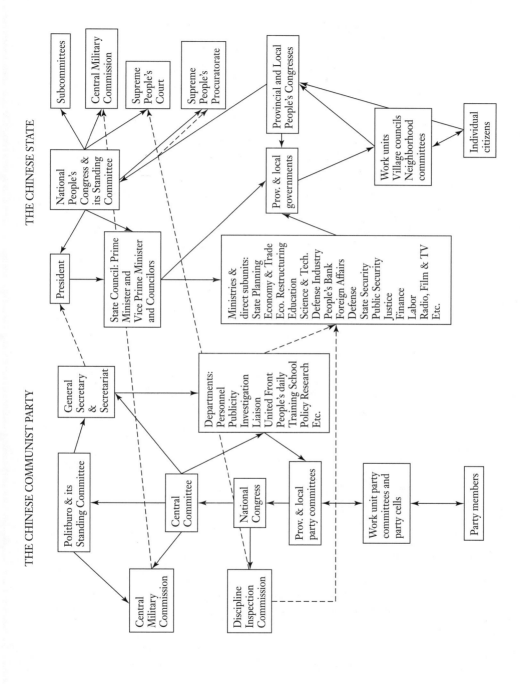

in terms of membership. But because of China's vast population, this also means that only about 5% of Chinese are party members, thus making it perhaps the smallest ruling political party in the world. Joining the party is not an easy task. One has to show political loyalty to the party over a test period that can last from several months to several years. Party membership is prestigious both in terms of material benefit and career development. However, with recent reforms providing opportunities for greater income and career advancement outside the state sector, party membership has in fact become less important as a means of career advancement.

Turning now to the state apparatus, the National People's Congress (NPC)—China's legislature—also meets every five years. As with the party's National Congress, its delegates are also indirectly elected by members of the local people's congresses. Unlike the United States, but like Great Britain prior to Tony Blair, the courts, including the Supreme Court, the middle-level courts, and the local courts, are subordinate to the legislature. The National People's Congress elects a Standing Committee which represents the NPC when it is not in session. There are nine legislative subcommittees under the NPC's Standing Committee, including the ethnic groups committee; the law committee; the finance and economics committee; the education, science, culture, and health committee; the foreign affairs committee; the overseas Chinese committee; the civil and judicial affairs committee; the environment and resources protection committee; and the agriculture and rural areas committee. According to the 1982 constitution, the president of the country is elected by the NPC for no more than two five-year terms. The NPC also elects the executive branch: the state council and the prime minister, who also cannot hold the post for more than two five-year terms. The prime minister and the state council control one of the world's largest bureaucratic machines, which employs over 11 million cadres.

Several characteristics of China's party-state system should be noted. First, although there have been experiments with local level elections, the highest-level leaders in both the party and the state are not directly elected by popular vote. The lack of free elections at the highest level is arguably the most important distinction between China's political system and a democratic one.

Second, the party exercises organizational and personnel control over the state apparatus. For example, the party's Central Military Commission also carries the same title under the NPC. The president, the prime minister, and the chairman of the NPC's Standing Committee are all members of the Standing Committee of the Politburo—key state positions with party oversight. Although the party has in recent years retreated from certain state sectors, it still has direct control over key areas such as the nomination of the highest state leaders, the legislature, the military, the courts, and the media. Although it is true that in democratic societies political parties also influence the state apparatus, the unchallenged position of the Chinese Communist Party makes such a system authoritarian by nature.

A third feature of China's party-state system is that the party has firm control over the military, upholding Mao's belief that military strength is the foundation of political power. The importance of controlling the military is illustrated by the example of Deng Xiaoping, China's powerful leader who, following Mao's death, ensured that he became the chairman of the party's Central Military Commission even though he never held the highest position in the party or the state. He was only a vice premier and a member of the Politburo Standing Committee. Following in Deng's footsteps, Jiang Zemin let Hu Jintao take over the title of the party's general secretary during the party's Sixteenth National Congress in 2002, while Jiang himself remained as the chairman of the party's Central Military Commission. In 2004, after making sure that the military continued to show its loyalty to the party and its new leadership, Jiang finally resigned and passed party control over the military to Hu Jintao.

Finally, as illustrated by the organizational chart, delegates of local People's Congresses are elected through both work units and residential committees. Traditionally, the majority of people living in urban areas participated in elections through their work units. The socialist work units in China were quite different from workplaces in a country such as the United States. The Chinese workplace not only provided a work environment, but also carried out a number of other social and political functions, such as issuing marriage permits and organizing political study meetings and elections. There are roughly four types of work units in China: state owned, collectively owned (both urban and rural), private, and joint venture. The state and collective firms, which once dominated China's economy and controlled a significant part of the lives of workers, have become less important in recent years. In contrast, private and joint venture firms are now playing an

Election Laws

The 1979 election law, further revised in 1982 and 1986, amended the original 1953 legislation to extend the direct election of deputies upward to include the 2,757 People's Congresses at the county and urban district levels (see "Election Law" in Zhang 1992, 280). Currently, urban electoral districts are subdivided by work unit for those in large work units, and by neighborhood for the nonworking and those in small work units. Each electoral district is assigned a quota of deputies to be elected. The quota system explicitly favors the urban population, because per deputy the rural population must be four times larger than the urban population. Voters, then, elect deputies from their own work unit or neighborhood. This emphasis on work units and neighborhoods increases the chances that an urban voter would know his or her potential deputy.

Before the 1979 revision of the election law, people's deputies were elected with a fixed number of candidates and an open ballot. The people's deputies would then in turn elect higher-level officials and deputies under the same rule.

The 1979 revised election law replaced the policy of one candidate for one seat by a policy allowing up to twice as many candidates as seats in a direct election. Above the local level, there can be up to 50% more candidates than seats. In practice, this leads to the nomination of up to 50% more candidates who are not officially endorsed, while the government still controls the nomination of other candidates. If there are still too many candidates, pre-elections must be held. Candidates who win more than 50% of the total votes get elected. Candidates can be nominated by any organization of ten or more individuals. The secret ballot, optional under the 1953 law, is now mandatory, and campaigning on behalf of a candidate is legal. The regulation on the length of a term is not specified in the election law, but in a separate Organizational Law of Local People's Congress and Local Government, which was passed at the same National People's Congress meeting in 1986 where the election law was passed (Zhang 1992, 292). The term for the elected deputies is five years in large cities and three years in small cities without districts. No limit is set for the total number of terms a deputy can serve. These elected local deputies in turn elect provincial and national People's Congress deputies according to similar rules. Government officials and judges at each level are also elected indirectly by the elected people's deputies at that level.

Several Web sites provide further readings on elections in China, such as China Elections and Governance (www.electionworld.org/election/china.htm [accessed March 23, 2005]); Elections around the World (www.electionworld.org/election/china.htm [accessed March 23, 2005]); and the Carter Center's China Village Election Project (www.cartercenter.org/peaceprograms/china.asp [accessed March 23, 2005]).

increasingly significant role in the economy, albeit generally without the same political and social control over the livelihoods of workers (see chap. 7).

Although China's political system lacks legitimacy in many ways, there have been some important changes in recent years. To begin with, perhaps the most meaningful and significant development in the post-Mao era has been the increasing importance of elections. Although the nomination process is still controlled from above, multi-candidacy and secret ballots now play a role, as witnessed in the elections of both the Central Committee and the Politburo since the Fourteenth National Congress in 1992. In some areas, local People's Congress elections and village council elections even permit free nominations (see text box on election laws).

Second, although decision making in the National People's Congress is still influenced by the party, the legislature has gained some degree of independence and autonomy. One example is the Legal Committee under the NPC, which has played a significant role in legislating and in limiting arbitrary interventions by the party.

Third, political and social diversity have been growing. At the highest level, since the death of Mao decision making is no longer in the hands of a single individual. Instead, members of the Politburo Standing Committee make decisions collectively. Furthermore, market reforms have been associated with a diversification of economic activities, so the state-controlled workplace has less influence over people's lives. A growing number of people are abandoning the traditional state-dependent socialist lifestyle, and the state can no longer ignore those voices that speak from outside the party-state system. Consequently, there has been greater freedom of expression than there was under Mao.

Finally, leadership succession is another area where changes have taken place. In the history of the People's Republic since 1949, political power transition has been anything but predictable and transparent. Leaders either died on the job or were expelled from their posts. The Sixteenth Party Congress in 2002 was the first time that an incumbent leader retired alive in a smooth transition and that the successor (Hu Jintao) was reasonably predictable. After becoming the Secretary General of the Communist Party in 2002, Hu Jintao also replaced Jiang Zemin and became the President of the People's Republic of China in 2003, the Chairman of the Party's Central Military Commission in 2004, and the Chairman of the Central Military Commission under the National People's Congress in 2005. These steps symbolized the completion of a relatively smooth power transition from Jiang Zemin to Hu Jintao (fig. 1.3).

Mao Zedong (1949–76), died in post

Lin Biao (1969–71), Mao's 1st chosen successor, died in a plane crash in a coup escape

Hua Guofeng (1976–81), Mao's 2nd chosen successor, purged by Deng

Deng Xiaoping, purged twice by Mao in 1966 and 1976, behind the scene leader (1981–97), died in 1997

Hu Yaobang (1981–87), Deng's 1st chosen successor, purged in 1987

Zhao Ziyang (1987–89), Deng's 2nd chosen successor, purged in 1989

Jiang Zemin (1989–2002), Deng's 3rd chosen successor

Hu Jintao (2002–). Deng's 4th chosen successor

Figure 1.3 Leadership transition in China, 1949–2002

Theories of Communist Politics

Although during the height of the cold war totalitarianism was the model most frequently used to describe communist politics, scholars have since developed several more realistic and practical theories to describe a communist political system. Similarly, in China, the party is not so much a top-down monolith as it is a main player in a political field that does challenge it. One view describes such a system as bureaucratic politics. In this view, the party's absolute authority is challenged by specialized bureaucratic organizations in a modern society. The technocrats can effectively bargain with the party by withholding crucial information for decision making. As a result of bureaucratic bargaining, the party becomes a mediator between competing bureaucratic interests (Hough 1969, 1976, 1977; Lieberthal and Oksenberg 1988; Lieberthal 1995).

Bureaucratic politics is a useful theory for predicting policy change under central planning. Its emphasis on bureaucratic organizations and their functions and interactions made important contributions to understanding the internal process of Chinese politics. As market reform continues, many bureaucratic functions have been marketized or socialized, such as medical care, pension funds, and housing. There is an additional need to look at how these new social and economic interests outside the bureaucratic system are transformed into political interests.

Corporatism is another useful concept in comparative politics for describing various top-down societies, including China. Generally speaking, there are three kinds of corporatism: societal corporatism, which is common in European democracies; plural corporatism, which is represented by the United States; and state corporatism, which is often used to describe single-party systems. According to the societal corporatist model, the state serves as the leader or mediator in a hierarchically organized and functionally differentiated society. Domestic decision making is an outcome of behind-closed-doors negotiations between the government and the "peak associations," such as those representing labor and capital. In return, the peak associations and their members offer political compliance with the government. This form of corporatism differs from American-style plural corporatism, where a diverse range of self-initiated interest groups also compete to influence policy making. Societal corporatism also differs from state corporatism with monolithic party control, such as is found in China. Under state corporatism, the lack of multiparty competition prevents the peak associations from gaining influence by supporting different political parties. Interest articulation can take place only within the narrow range recognized by the ruling party.[3]

The corporatist model has the advantage of including a broader range of political systems. Its use of peak associations goes beyond bureaucratic organizations and includes other types of social groups. One reason to expand the model is to study how interests are articulated under state corporatism by describing the interaction between the state and newly emerging social interests. Another reason to develop the corporatist theory is to study the mechanisms and conditions of the transition from state corporatism to societal and plural corporatism. Thus, the fourth goal of this book is to depict how public opinion is shaped in China's political institutions and how it affects further institutional change.

Articulation of Public Opinion

Before we address the interaction between public opinion and the political system in China, we need to briefly review the existing studies in the English-language literature on the role of public opinion in policy making and on the remaining tasks in public opinion research.

Every citizen has his or her private opinion. But until private opinions can influence policy making, they are of little interest for social science research (Stimson 1998). Much research has been devoted to show through survey data what private citizens think about various policy issues in post-socialist societies (i.e., Wyman 1997; Miller, White, and Heywood 1998) and whether there is a correlation between private opinion and policy outcome. For example, studies of public opinion in democratic countries have found a strong relationship between mass public policy preferences and policy outcome (Burnstein 1985; Eichenberg 1989; Jasper 1990; Risse-Kappen 1991; Jacobs 1993). Knowing what people think, however, provides few clues to whether they can influence policy making. The correlation between private opinion and policy outcome does not show causality between the two, nor does such correlation describe the exact mechanisms through which private opinion can influence policy making. Given these problems, researchers have called for studying the degree of responsiveness to popular opinion in a political system and the specific institutions and processes through which private opinion influences policy making (Jacobs and Shapiro 1994; Page 1994; Stimson, MacKuen, and Erikson 1994). Studying responsiveness to popular opinion is also helpful in bridging the gap between public opinion research and institutional studies and emphasizes the importance of the political elite and institutions (March and Olsen 1989, 1994; Crawford and Lijphart 1997).

Researchers have also been interested in whether public opinion can be manipulated. Page and Shapiro (1992) found that private citizens in the United States were rational actors who thought independently when choosing their policy preferences—preferences that have remained fairly stable and played an important role in American foreign and domestic policy making. In contrast to Page and Shapiro, Mayer (1992), using the General Social Survey data from 1960 to 1988, found that American public opinion in fact changed significantly, responding partly to external events (i.e., the Vietnam War), partly to the media portrayal of such events, and partly to education and generational change.

Others also found that political elites in liberal democracies can manipulate public opinion (Iyengar and Kinder 1987; Margolis and Mauser 1989; Iyengar 1991; Bartels 1993; McChesney and Nichols 2002; Goldberg 2002, 2003). According to this view, although opinion and policy are strongly linked in a democratic system, the causality is not always limited to policy that affects opinion. Public opinion can itself be manipulated and even manufactured. Therefore, there seem to be different schools of thought about whether public opinion can influence policy making unilaterally or is also itself influenced by the process of political mobilization.

The reality appears to be more multidirectional, so perhaps an interactive relationship makes more sense. Mass opinion is formulated by political socialization—itself a filter of agents such as the government, media, political parties, and interest groups of the society's dominant political and economic forces. All of these variously condition citizens in the political system. Because of the institutional arrangement of a democratic society, citizens, in turn, have the opportunity to voice their specific policy preferences through elections and other institutional and non-institutional channels. Just as political mobilization can be internalized and then transformed into autonomous political participation (Huntington and Nelson 1976), mobilized opinions can also become more individualized and hence transform into autonomous public policy choices. This is true even in a democratic system. What is important for public opinion research, however, is to state clearly the causal relationship between opinion and policy in a given study, at a given time, and on a specific policy issue, while considering the interaction between the two. It is also important to note that if private opinion in a democratic society could be partly the result of internalized political socialization, it is equally possible that private opinion could be developed in a non-democratic society sustained by political mobilization.

In a single-party authoritarian system, the lack of legitimate political competition guarantees the continued rule by the incumbent party and does not require any meaningful responsiveness to popular opinion. In China during the Mao era, the Communist Party monopolized the channels of communication and political mobilization and made decisions based on its claim of representing the interest of the vast majority of society. No difference of opinion was tolerated. In this way China was similar to the Soviet Union under Stalin, when the Communist Party laid exclusive claim to the truth and private citizens were ignorant and fearful. According to this view, public opinion simply made no impact on decision making (Crespi 1997; Wyman 1997).

In the post-Mao era, some evidence showed that the leadership continued to silence and manipulate mass opinion. Nearly a decade after the violent crackdown on the 1989 Tiananmen Square protests (see text box), the post-Deng leaders banned the religious movement known as Falun Gong (see text box), jailed unregistered Catholic priests, and put down any attempt to establish independent labor unions and opposition parties. All these were movements that arose to fill a vacuum left by the decline of the official Marxist and Leninist ideology. To counter these competing belief systems, nationalism was cultivated to provide a common foundation for public consent (Ching 1996).

Other evidence, however, showed that the post-Mao and post-Deng leaders pursued public opinion with consistency, even if policy implementation appeared authoritarian. They systematically collected popular opinion and feedback on previous policies through government policy research offices at all levels (Ketizu 2001). The National People's Congress (the lower house)

The 1989 Tiananmen Square Protests

The most serious open conflict between the Chinese government and the people since the 1949 revolution took place in the spring of 1989. On April 15, the death of the former party general secretary Hu Yaobang, a liberal leader who had been dismissed because he refused to take tough measures against student unrest a couple of years earlier, triggered memorial demonstrations by college students in Beijing, Tianjin, and other cities. Students demanding democracy, freedom, and faster political reform were soon joined by urban residents who were deeply unhappy with the consequences of rapid marketization and the resulting inflation, job insecurity, and corruption. Urban residents, ironically, demanded slower economic reform. The protesters ignored the government's demand on April 20 to end the demonstrations and instead called for the resignations of then-premier Li Peng and other leaders. On May 4, in memory of the May 4 movement seventy years earlier, a new wave of demonstrations took place and continued during Soviet President Mikhail Gorbachev's visit later that month. The Chinese government was acutely embarrassed that these student protests went on during a state visit, and on May 20, the government declared martial law. Troops were mobilized to surround the capital and to prepare to enter the city. Finally, on June 3 and 4, soldiers of the People's Liberation Army, on the orders of Deng Xiaoping, opened fire on demonstrators and took over Tiananmen Square, where students and labor protesters had their headquarters and where they had organized hunger strikes. Following the suppression, the government conducted numerous arrests and trials and strictly controlled foreign and Chinese media. Although similar protests had been quelled by governments elsewhere (for instance, in London in 1972, where a dozen protesters were shot to death; and at Kent State University in 1970, where four student demonstrators were shot to death; and in Kwangju, South Korea, in 1980, where there was a massacre), the number of fatalities involved (reportedly in the hundreds) caused widespread international condemnation of the Chinese government.

. . .

Cama Hinton's documentary *Gate of Heavenly Peace* is a good visual display of the event (http://www.pbs.org/wgbh/pages/frontline/gate [accessed March 23, 2005]). More information can also be found at the Tiananmen Web site, http://www.gwu.edu/~nsarchiv/NSAEBB/NSAEBB16 (accessed March 23, 2005; *Tiananmen Square, 1989: The Declassified History*, National Security Archive Electronic Briefing Book no. 16).

and the Chinese People's Political Consultative Conference (the upper house) played more important roles in representing different interests in legislation (O'Brien 1990). The Chinese media openly discussed their own role in reflecting mass opinion and supervising government policy and how it should be implemented. The government used public opinion polls to assist policy making in the area of economic reform (Rosen 1989, 1991). It also responded to rising nationalism in its foreign policy making (Fewsmith and Rosen 2001; Gries 2004a, 2004b). For some groups, a greater freedom of expression is allowed, such as in environment and consumer affairs (Lo and Leung 2000). In 1997 and 1998, China signed the International Covenant on Economic, Social and Cultural Rights and the International Covenant on Civil and Political Rights. These steps symbolized China's willingness to engage in the discussion of human rights with the international community (see text box on the human rights debate).

There are several possible reasons post-Mao leaders cared about public opinion even though democratic institutions were seriously underdeveloped. One is that the party's very legitimacy was challenged by the increasing number of protests by rural and urban residents owing to tax increases, unemployment, worsening work conditions, delays in salary payment, and so on. This implicit challenge existed regardless of the fact that there was no viable political opposition. It was therefore a matter of survival instinct for the party to pay attention to popular opinion.

Second, public opinion was a useful weapon in policy debate. Following a political tradition that was recorded in the late Qing dynasty in the nineteenth century (Judge 1994), politicians in contemporary China explored public opinion to formulate their own policy agenda. For example, during the 1989 urban protests, reform-minded leaders frequently cited public opinion in top-level political meetings (L. Zhang 2001). After the bombing of the

Falun Gong

In 1992 Li Hongzhi, a forty-year-old former government official now living in New York, established a sect known as the Falun Gong. It teaches a type of *qi gong* (cultivation of vital energy) based on a set of Taoist and Buddhist principles and meditations to cultivate the *falun* (wheel of law), located in the lower abdomen. The *falun* rotates constantly according to the energy in the universe and represents truth, compassion, and forbearance. The sect believes that the more energy the *falun* draws from the universe, the more unhealthy elements it draws out of the body.

By 1999 Falun Gong had attracted millions of followers in China. In April 1999 Falun Gong practitioners protested a derogatory article about the sect that had been published by a magazine for teenagers in Tianjin. Several thousand protestors surrounded the magazine's editorial building. Riot police dispersed the protesters and arrested forty-five demonstrators. Two days later, on April 24, more than 10,000 Falun Gong practitioners responded to the earlier crackdown by surrounding Zhongnanhai, the central government's compound in Beijing. On July 22 the Chinese government officially banned Falun Gong and arrested some of its leaders. For months following the ban, the government waged a campaign to eradicate Falun Gong, but its popularity continued to grow outside of China. The official media criticized its teaching, categorized it as a cult, and reported that individuals cut open their stomachs to find the wheel of law or committed suicide to find happiness. It also blocked Internet access from China to all Falun Gong–related Web sites.

Falun Gong initially gained popularity due to the side effects of market reforms, a process that had created both winners and losers. While much of the media spotlight focused on the winners in these reforms, dissatisfaction was rapidly growing among those who benefited from the old system but were now falling behind. These included state workers, party functionaries, low- and mid-level cadres, middle-aged people who lacked competitive skills, and a vast number of retirees living on pensions. These people were looking for hope, peace, and a spiritual outlet

· · ·

in the vacuum left when Deng Xiaoping downplayed ideology in order to consolidate the party's leadership during market reform. This left communism a hollow shell, and the Falun Gong was the perfect substitute. Its theory of the universe, society, and the individual, coupled with a well-developed organization, provided a sense of community and comradeship that appealed to many in uncertain times.

Further readings can be found at http://www.apologeticsindex.org/fo2.html (accessed March 23, 2005); Schechter 2000; Chan 2004.

Chinese embassy in Belgrade, Chinese leaders exploited nationalistic popular sentiment in its campaign against "American aggression." Perhaps leaders recognized that only by appealing to public sentiment could they ensure that the direction of protests remained within a controllable sphere of common interests.[4]

Furthermore, even in a single-party bureaucratic system, managing a modern economy requires specialized knowledge and extensive coordination and compromise between different bureaucratic and social interests (Hough 1976, 1977; Lieberthal 1995). Popular opinion therefore had to be taken into consideration in policy making because some of those with different opinions also possessed the specialized knowledge decision makers needed.

The final reason Chinese leaders cared about public opinion was that local elections had become a more meaningful channel for voicing public opinion (see text box on election laws). After electoral reforms, officials could only serve a fixed term and then had to face reelection. Reforms included multicandidacy (more candidates were required than the actual number of people to be elected) and secret ballot (the voter's identity could no longer be revealed by the ballot). These limited but significant freedoms in voters' choices made politicians pay more attention to voters' preferences.

This book will focus on the formation of public opinion and the articulation of interest in China's single-party system, which has inherited a paternalistic political tradition and a Marxist ideology. This system differs from totalitarianism in its intensified bureaucratic competition and marketization. In a totalitarian society, the extent to which social interests can be tolerated is dictated by the supreme leader and coordinated by a small group of subleaders at the top. As a result, the range of tolerated interests and the channels for expressing public opinion are both narrow. Such a structure of

The Human Rights Debate

There are two commonly accepted concepts of what constitutes human rights. The first is socioeconomic rights, such as food, shelter, clothing, safety, education, medical care, and so on. The second includes civil rights, such as the right to vote and to change jobs, and the freedom of speech, assembly, and religion. There is international pressure, led by the United States, on China to treat both concepts of human rights as equally important. The Chinese government argues that socioeconomic rights are the foundation of civil rights. In a country where per capita GDP is less than 5% of that in the United States, China maintains that the most important human right is for everyone to have enough to eat. Economic growth, goes the argument, will improve socioeconomic conditions. Therefore, any attempt to impede economic development should be limited, including any effort to challenge the leadership of the current regime. In recent years, China has shown some willingness to accept discussion of its civil human rights conditions in international affairs, although it traditionally maintains that human rights is a domestic affair and that no other country should interfere.

The human rights debate is best illustrated by the ongoing efforts on the part of both the United States and the Chinese governments to criticize each other's human rights violations. For example, the annual U.S. Country Reports on Human Rights Practices criticizes China for a long list of human rights violations, such as the death penalty, disappearances, torture, arbitrary arrests, the denial of fair trial, and interference with privacy. The report routinely condemns China for its lack of civil liberties, including freedom of speech, assembly, religion, and movement, and the right to select the government. It also criticizes China for its lack of government concern for human rights and its discrimination based on race, sex, disability, language, and social status. The report also cites other examples of human rights violations in China, such as forced labor, child labor, and unacceptable working conditions.

China responds each year by issuing its own white paper on human rights, which focuses on violations in the United States, such as the lack of safeguards for life and personal safety, serious rights violations by law

. . .

enforcement departments, the plight of the poor, difficult conditions for women and children, deep-rooted racial discrimination, and wanton infringement of the rights of other countries.

A final note: the issue of human rights is often used as a political weapon by different interest groups in the United States. For example, labor organizations condemn China's lack of human rights so that fewer factories will be moved to China and fewer American jobs will be lost. The business community, on the other hand, downplays the human rights problem in China so that greater profits can be made by using cheaper workers.

The U.S. State Department's Human Rights Reports on China from 1999 to 2004 can be found at www.state.gov/g/drl/rls/hrrpt (accessed April 1, 2005). The Chinese White Papers on the Human Rights Violations in the United States can be found at the following Web sites (accessed April 1, 2005): http://english.people.com.cn/200203/11/eng20020311_91880.shtml (2001), http://english.people.com.cn/200304/03/eng20030403_114520.shtml (2002), http://english.people.com.cn/200403/01/eng20040301_136190.shtml (2003), http://english.people.com.cn/200503/03/eng20050303_175406.html (2004).

interest articulation looks something like a pencil, with the sharpened tip as the supreme leader, the small sloped portion as the top aids, and the long and narrow body as the channel for expressing opinions and the range of permitted social interests. On the contrary, in a pluralistic society, the range of interests and the channels for expressing self-interest are both wide at the societal level. The top of such a system has multiple centers of power. At least in theory, most opinions can be heard through multiple channels that narrow only slightly as they reach the top. This system roughly resembles a lampshade, with a wide bottom and a slightly narrowed top. In an authoritarian market society, the top of the power center is slightly flattened due to the replacement of the supreme leader by the small group of top leaders, while the channel of interest articulation at the top remains narrow. Yet the range of societal interests at the bottom is much broader than in totalitarianism, making such a system look roughly like an upside-down funnel. This study will examine how the increased diversity of social interests affects public opinion and how public opinion in turn interacts with the political system.

This study is more about mass political attitude and behavior and less about institutional change. Although attitude and behavior are the direct results of political institutions, they are also important in interacting with and changing political institutions. Studies of democracy emphasize the importance not only of building democratic institutions, but also of creating a civil society where citizens not only possess the right to vote, as well as a sense of efficacy and the ability to influence political decision making from below (Almond and Verba 1963). Democratic values and individual political participation are thus the soil for planting democratic institutions.

Chapter Outline

The remaining chapters are case studies of public opinion and its impact on individual political behavior. Chapter 2 is on collecting public opinion. Since most of the information in this book will be drawn from eleven Chinese public opinion surveys and the World Values Survey (see appendix A), this chapter discusses the process of conducting public opinion surveys in China, including political barriers, sampling, questionnaire design, and data analysis. Chapter 3 examines regime support and approval rating and their sources by using public opinion polls covering the changes that occurred from the late 1980s to the late 1990s. Chapter 4 discusses media control and its role in shaping public opinion. The focus of this chapter is on whether the media enhance political control. Chapter 5 addresses the intriguing evidence that interpersonal trust is significantly higher in China than in democratic societies. It defines the scope of that trust and explains why it does not lead to democracy in China by comparing it with survey data from other countries. Chapter 6 describes the channels for voicing opinion and government responsiveness to public opinion in urban China. Changes from the early 1990s to the late 1990s are also examined. Chapter 7 discusses workplace politics, including the changing Chinese work environment, labor market development, changing labor-management relations, the evolving role of official labor unions, and the impact of this changing work environment on individual political behavior and attitude. Chapter 8 assesses the role of intellectuals in political reform by comparing party intellectuals and non-party intellectuals with the public. Chapter 9 returns to the questions developed in chapter 1, summarizing the findings in the previous chapters, reevaluating the impact of culture, ideology, and economic and political institutions on the formation of public opinion, and assessing the role of public opinion in policy making in an authoritarian state.

CHAPTER TWO

Collecting Public Opinion in China

A successful study of public opinion begins with the first step—collecting reliable public opinion data.[1] Since most of the empirical evidence in this study is drawn from eleven public opinion surveys conducted in urban China from 1987 to 1999 (see text box on surveys and appendix A), it is necessary to address validity and reliability up front for Western readers who constantly question the credibility of survey data coming out of China. This chapter introduces the survey process used in urban China, noting potential problems and offering useful solutions. The intention is not to provide a comprehensive discussion of all the steps necessary for undertaking survey research in China, but rather to offer an introductory overview for the nonspecialist. The five main sections of this chapter deal, respectively, with the development of survey research in post-Mao China; the political difficulties in conducting a survey and solutions for them; drawing a representative sample; quality control of the survey; and how to increase the cross-country comparability of the survey and use existing Chinese survey data in data

The Chinese Urban Surveys

This book uses data from the 1999 Six-City Survey and ten other urban surveys conducted by the Economic System Reform Institute of China in the late 1980s and early 1990s (see appendix A). The 1999 survey repeated many questions from the earlier ESRIC surveys, and the results from the 1999 survey are compared with the earlier surveys.

The 1999 Six-City Survey included Shanghai, Guangzhou, Wuhan, Chongqing, Xian, and Shenyang. The two-phase survey was conducted by this author in cooperation with the Research Center for Contemporary China at Peking University. The first phase was conducted in late August in Shanghai, Guangzhou, and Wuhan. The second was conducted in late October and early November in Chongqing, Xian, and Shenyang. The survey sample was based on a three-stage random process. First, fifteen residential councils (*ju wei hui*) were randomly selected from a complete list of residential councils in each city. Second, thirty households were randomly selected from a list of all households in each residential council. Third, an adult (sixteen or older) was randomly selected from each household. Local college students who could speak the local dialect were hired to interview the selected names. Each face-to-face interview lasted about one hour. The respondents were told that this was an academic research project on Chinese urban residents' social and political values. Each was given a small gift. The final sample contained 1820 respondents, about 300 from each city. The survey included more than 200 questions on each respondent's biographic information, family, work, income, satisfaction with reform, and many political issues, including support for the current political system, political participation, and efficacy. Questions on voicing complaints and voting were repeated from the 1987 Political Participation Survey (discussed in a later section) conducted by the Economic System Reform Institute of China. These repeated questions will provide a valuable opportunity to study the political and social trends in urban China in the past ten to fifteen years.

One obvious problem of the sample is the exclusion of migrant workers in Chinese cities who are mostly rural, less educated, and working in blue-collar and service jobs. This makes the sample's education level higher than that of the actual urban population. To solve this problem, I weight the sample by education of the urban residents in the 1990 population census. This technique will make the results from univariate analyses more similar to that of the actual population. Weighting is not used in multivariate analyses, since education will be used as an independent variable.

One other potential problem is the timing of the 1999 survey. The suppression of the Falun Gong religious movement and the heavy-handed tightening of security around the fiftieth anniversary of the founding of the People's Republic of China might have affected people's responses to politically sensitive questions. Some may therefore say that this survey was simply a snapshot of the social and political situation of a particular moment in time and is not representative of the overall political picture and long-term trends. While the survey was likely to have captured a momentary response to particular political events, these events were also quite representative of Jiang's leadership style over time.

One advantage of this book is its historical dimension. The 1999 Six-City Survey repeated many questions from the earlier urban surveys conducted by the Economic System Reform Institute of China (ESRIC). ESRIC was a government-sponsored think tank established in the mid-1980s to provide information on social reaction to reform for the purpose of government policy making. From 1987 to 1992, ESRIC conducted nine public opinion surveys on urban reaction to reform with many identical questions in forty cities in May 1987, July 1987 (an eight-city political participation survey), October 1987, May 1988, October 1988, May 1989, October 1989, November 1991, and June 1992. The random samples of the ESRIC surveys were drawn in similar ways as those of the 1999 survey. The comparisons between these surveys and the more recent 1999 survey provide a rare opportunity to examine the trends of public opinion formation in the 1980s and 1990s.

For a more detailed discussion of the ESRIC surveys, see Tang and Parish 2000. For further discussion of public opinion and survey work in China, see Rosen 1989, 1991; Nathan and Shi 1993; Manion 1994; Shi 1996; Tang 2003.

. . .

In addition to the Six-City Survey and the ESRIC surveys, this book also uses data from the 2000 World Values Survey and the 1997 [Chinese] Staff and Workers Survey. For further details of these surveys, see 2000–2001 World Values Survey Questionnaire at http://wvs.isr.umich .edu/ques4.shtml (accessed March 23, 2005), and All-China Federation of Labor Unions 1999.

comparability and analysis. Not emphasized in this chapter are such common concerns in survey research as the possible biases in designing survey questions and conducting face-to-face interviews, which can be found in standard survey handbooks.

Development of Survey Research

The pioneering efforts by American scholars in conducting survey research on China were based on interviews of Chinese immigrants in the 1970s and the early 1980s, such as William Parish and Martin Whyte's studies on rural and urban life in China (Parish and Whyte 1978; Whyte and Parish 1984) and Andrew Walder's study of Chinese factory life (1986). With the loosening of prohibitions on conducting surveys in China, an increasing number of American-based researchers have published articles and book chapters based on survey data. A few examples include Walder (1990), Whyte (1990), Logan and Bian (1993), Nathan and Shi (1993), Manion (1996, 2000), Jennings (1997), Chen (1999), and Tang (2001). Book-length studies using survey data include Keith Griffin and Renwei Zhao's study on income distribution (1993), Yanjie Bian's study on work and inequality in urban China (1994b), Deborah Davis et al.'s edited volume on various aspects of urban life (1995), Tianjian Shi's study on political participation in Beijing (1997), Wenfang Tang and William Parish's study on urban reform (2000), and Jie Chen's study on popular political support in Beijing (2004). Throughout the history of the People's Republic of China, the government has utilized systematic mechanisms to collect public opinion. Public opinion surveys, however, were rarely used to facilitate research and decision making until the mid-1980s, when survey research was introduced by such American sociologists as C. K. Yang, Nan Lin, Martin Whyte, and William Parish. Since then, China has experienced a minor explosion in survey research. Chinese sociologists began to conduct surveys for their research projects and in the late 1980s convinced then-premier Zhao Ziyang that policy making for urban reform could be made more effective via regular monitoring of public opinion. A national urban survey network (the Center for China Social Survey, formerly translated as China Social Survey Network) led by Yang Guansan was set up under the Economic System Reform Institute of China (ESRIC). Beginning in 1987, ESRIC conducted a series of urban public opinion surveys based on stratified random samples (Rosen 1991). Today Chinese government agencies and academic and commercial organizations conduct routine surveys for policy making, as well as for academic and market research.

Currently, three types of organizations conduct surveys in China: governmental and quasi-governmental units, academic institutions, and commercial organizations. Examples of governmental and quasi-governmental units include the State Statistical Bureau (SSB), ESRIC, the Ministry of Civil Affairs, labor unions, and women's and youth groups. The advantage of these organizations is that they can carry out surveys very effectively because of their vertical organizational structures and bureaucratic authority. Both SSB and ESRIC have their own survey networks of local offices staffed by full-time government employees. The State Administration of Environmental Protection, the All-China Federation of Trade Unions, the All-China Women's Federation, and the All-China Youth Federation all have their own local offices. Once the central office of any of these organizations decides to conduct a survey, this decision can be carried out as an administrative order and a budget then provided. Although these organizations are concerned about political sensitivity, they do have a certain degree of legitimacy (which other types of organizations lack) that gives them the authority to ask sensitive questions. Their disadvantage, however, is that employees of government survey organizations, being low paid, are less motivated. This lack of motivation by interviewers can often lead to reduced survey quality

Academic organizations include the Chinese Academy of Social Sciences (CASS) and its provincial affiliates, universities, and other research institutes. These organizations also have a legitimate claim to conduct surveys, yet they have neither the authority to compel people to cooperate nor adequate financial resources to carry out complex surveys. As with governmental units, their hands are tied by government regulations. They are eager, however, to cooperate with outside researchers. Another advantage of academic organizations is that, as a collaborating partner, they are more likely to be both familiar with Western social science research and more flexible in dealing with research topics and survey questions.

Finally, an increasing number of government officials and academics in the field of survey research are "jumping into the sea" (*xiahai*) of the market economy and forming private or joint venture survey companies.[2] One successful example of a commercial survey firm is Horizon (Lingdian), a private public-opinion and market-research firm. Its survey results are frequently quoted by the Chinese media in public policy discussions. Note that government and academic survey organizations sometimes form a "commercial wing" to carry out politically sensitive projects. These private survey firms are taking advantage of the freedom granted to the growing private sector. Since they do not—at least on paper—receive a budget from the government, commercial survey companies enjoy greater freedom to accept foreign contracts. Although they have the least administrative power, they are the most flexible of the three surveying bodies and can often rely more heavily on market mechanisms to implement a survey. For example, a governmental organization taking an urban household sample would order the resident committee (*juweihui*) to prepare a list of all households, but a commercial firm would pay the resident committee to do so. Once the surveyor has gained the cooperation of the resident committee, the quality of the sample and the response rate of a commercial survey is not very different from that of a governmental survey.

Thus far I have attempted to show the advantages and disadvantages of collaborating with each type of organization. Researchers have reported both successful and frustrating experiences with different types of organizations.[3] It is important to note that the actual success of a survey project depends on the compatibility of interest between the collaborators. One potential problem in a joint project between Chinese and Western researchers is that competing interests may compromise the quality of the survey. For example, Rosen and Zweig reported that in a collaborative project on Chinese scholars returning from overseas, the Chinese government officials, education specialists with an agenda of confirming government policies, did not work well with Western political economists, who wanted to challenge government policies or test their hypotheses (Rosen and Zweig 2000).

Furthermore, the success of a project may depend less on the type of collaborating organization and more on the political sensitivity of the survey, an important issue to which we now turn.

Political Difficulties and Solutions

The Chinese leadership views the 1989 Tiananmen Square protests as a result of premature liberal political reform. Consequently, the current development-oriented leadership in China considers political stability to be the precondition for economic development—and thus the party's top priority in governing. Surveys with foreign involvement and sponsorship, especially if designed to identify different opinions in the population, are often seen as a threat to stability.[4] There have been incidents where Chinese authorities have interfered with surveys conducted with the involvement of Western scholars (Whyte 2000). In 1999, the State Statistical Bureau issued a regulation ordering all "overseas-funded survey institutions or domestic survey agencies employed by foreigners" to receive approval from national or provincial statistical bureaus, and that such survey results be checked by statistical authorities before being released (State Statistical Bureau 1999). These examples seem to suggest that great barriers exist for Western researchers seeking to undertake surveys in China.

Fortunately, this is not the end of the story. Although the 1999 State Statistical Bureau regulation could be seen as a concrete step in carrying out a series of earlier efforts to curb foreign involvement in survey research, the document did not explicitly outlaw joint surveys between Chinese and foreign organizations. The approval procedure by "provincial-level statistical bureaus" and the emphasis on banning "substandard survey companies" both seem to reflect a primary concern with other surveys overlapping the bureau's own (State Statistical Bureau 1999). The emphasis on substandard and overlapping surveys in the 1999 regulation makes one suspicious that economic motivations were as strong as political concerns: if all such survey organizations conducted surveys with foreign researchers, the State Statistical Bureau would not be able to sell its own survey data to foreigners at a high price. In 2000, the State Statistical Bureau issued licenses to twenty-nine Chinese and foreign-funded companies to carry out research for overseas organizations and individuals.[5] This measure has proven to be a double-edged sword. It strengthened the position of the State Statistical Bureau by giving it further administrative authority. On the other hand, by limiting the number of licensed survey firms, it also further ensured the State Statistical Bureau's domination and profitability in a growing market of survey research.

The difficulties of collecting one's own survey data in China can be circumvented by seeking out existing survey data collected by Chinese organizations. Examples of national surveys include the State Statistical Bureau's ongoing population censuses and surveys on civil servants, industrial managers, rural and urban consumption, and many other subjects. The Center for China Social Survey under ESRIC has been conducting annual public opinion surveys since 1987 in fifty cities on such topics as reform satisfaction, housing reform, price reform, crime and safety, work and unemployment, and income (Center for China Social Survey 1996; Sun 1997). The All-China Federation of Trade Unions has carried out several national surveys on such topics as worker satisfaction, labor relations, unemployment, female workers, and rural migrant workers (All-China Federation of Trade Unions 1986, 1993, 1999, 2004). The All-China Women's Federation has conducted several national surveys on women (Tang and Parish 2000). There are also numerous single-site surveys, such as the annual Beijing Area Study by the Research Center for Contemporary China (RCCC) at Beijing University and the Beijing City Survey on Migrant Population (Beijing City Government 1995). Chinese researchers are, moreover, often willing to share their data; in exchange, the foreign collaborator can offer to organize joint research conferences, host short-term visits for Chinese researchers in a foreign country, propose joint authorship, or offer payment of research costs. According to this author's knowledge and experience, the sensitivity and political risks of data sharing are much lower than those of actually conducting the survey. At this time, there are no specific regulations against data sharing between Chinese and outside researchers.

There are, however, obvious limitations to using existing survey data. One has, for instance, no control over the design of the questionnaire or the quality of interviews and data entry. I personally have spent an entire year trying to clean up one survey data set that was plagued with errors due to sloppy data entry. I am, nevertheless, always pleasantly surprised and impressed with the amount of information in an existing survey that can be further analyzed.[6]

One potentially useful method of using existing surveys is for one to "hitch a ride" on a forthcoming or ongoing survey by adding a module of the researcher's own questions. This method has several advantages: it directly satisfies the researcher's interest, does not usually require separate approval, and—more important—can effectively cut costs.[7]

The third solution is to go through non-government channels. An increasing number of commercial firms in China accept contracts to perform surveys. These firms are politically less visible than government bodies —and are willing to take greater risks. Such companies do not have to go through as many bureaucratic hoops to get a project approved and thus can often act quickly to complete a project before the authorities even notice. Owing to these advantages, some government and academic organizations are forming commercial market-research firms as a source of additional revenue (see the earlier discussion on survey organizations).

Finally, the nature and design of survey questions can also determine the feasibility and outcome of the project. Social and economic questions are generally perceived as less threatening than political issues. Among political issues, more general questions related to the rule of law, voting and other forms of political participation, expressing dissatisfaction, attitudes toward marketization and socialism, and foreign policy issues are seen as "safer" than questions directly related to the evaluation of the current regime and leadership.

For example, a survey will draw much less attention if it does not include provocative and politically sensitive questions such as the approval rating of the Politburo, evaluation of individual leaders' qualification, or questions such as "Is the party corrupt?" or "Should China have multiparty elections?" It is helpful to state a politically sensitive question in a positive way, such as: "Is the anti-corruption campaign effective?" "Is the government (not the party) efficient?" "Is the rule of law improving?" "Are local elections meaningful in China's democratization?" "Should the system of 'multiparty cooperation under the leadership of the Communist Party' be kept or changed?" Admittedly, less risky and more politically correct questions sacrifice the very political sensitivity that many readers want to see. Yet this is better than nothing, especially if asking provocative questions does not elicit any real response because people are afraid to answer them.

Drawing a Representative Sample to Study a Population

Any researcher who claims to know what the population in a country, a city, or a village thinks based on his or her own experience is probably biased unless he or she has studied the entire population. But studying every individual in a population is too time-consuming and costly, especially if the population is in the hundreds of thousands or even millions. This is why surveys are widely used in social science research. In a survey, only a sample is drawn from the population. If the sample is drawn carefully, it can represent the population with some tolerable error. Statisticians have calculated that a sample of 2500 people can represent a population of any size ninety-five out of a hundred times with an error of ±2%, or ninety-nine out of a hundred times with an error of ±3%. For example, if the sample is 48% female, we know that 95% multiplied by the real percentage is between 46 and 50, or 99% multiplied by a number between 45 and 51 (table 2.1).

In order to achieve these levels of accuracy, however, a sample must be drawn with standard sampling techniques, including simple random, stratified random, random cluster, and systematic sampling (Fowler 1993; Fink and Kosecoff 1998). The best way to illustrate these techniques is to describe how a forty-city sample of 2640 Chinese urban residents was drawn in the

TABLE 2.1
Sample size and confidence interval

	LEVEL OF CONFIDENCE	
% Error tolerated	95%	99%
± 1	10,000	22,500
± 2	2500	5625
± 3	1111	2500
± 4	625	1406
± 5	400	900

SOURCE: Mainheim and Rich 1995, 121.

1990s by the ESRIC. Cities were classified as large, medium, or small according to population size. In addition to provincial-level cities such as Beijing, Tianjin, Shanghai, and Chongqing, thirty-six cities were randomly selected from the three categories, ranging down to the smallest municipal population of 93,800 (Zhangshu). This selection process resulted in forty cities that were scattered across twenty-three provinces.[8]

Chinese cities are organized into districts (*qu*), neighborhoods (*jiedao*), and residential councils (*juweihui*). Each city has a number of districts, each district has a number of neighborhood committees, and each neighborhood committee has a number of residential councils. The residential council (village council in rural areas) is the lowest-level government office with paid staff. It keeps the registration records of all households, including the age, gender, and family relationship of each household member.

In each city, one neighborhood is randomly selected from each of the three randomly selected districts (six each in Beijing, Shanghai, Tianjin, and Chongqing). One residential council is then randomly selected from each neighborhood. Using the household registration records kept in the residential council, twenty households are randomly chosen. One name is selected from each household using a predetermined scheme (i.e., oldest male, youngest female, oldest female, youngest male, age fifteen or older), resulting in 60 names from each city (120 in the four large cities). The final sample contains (60 × 36 cities = 2160) + (120 × 4 large cities = 480) = 2640 names and addresses (see Tang 2003 for further details).

This process is similar to the General Social Survey in the United States. In drawing a national sample, for example, the 1990 GSS included all cities and counties with at least 2000 housing units (primary sampling units). These communities were categorized by size and randomly selected in each category (100 were selected). In each community, blocks with 50 households or more were identified as the secondary sampling units, and 384 blocks were randomly selected with systematic methods. Finally, one person in each household was interviewed starting from the northwest corner of the block and going around in a fixed pattern (Davis and Smith 1991).

The difference between the GSS sample and the Chinese sample is in the method of identifying sample households. The Chinese sample relies on the administrative structure consisting of city districts, neighborhood committees within each district, residential councils within each neighborhood, and households under each residential council. The U.S. sample relies more on the natural residential dwelling environment, ranging from city level to natural dwelling blocks and then households.

The advantage of going through China's urban household registration system is obvious. This system provides an authoritative list of residents from which a reliable sample can be drawn. The problem of using the household registration system, however, is that this registry does not keep on file the growing number of rural migrants. Market reform has greatly increased population mobility. It is estimated that 120 million people have left the countryside since the late 1970s.[9] One solution is to draw a sub-sample of registered migrant workers. This information is usually kept by each neighborhood committee. But unregistered migrant workers and their families are still not included in either urban sample (the place to which they have immigrated) or a rural sample (the place they have left). A second problem associated with using the household registration system is that the bookkeeping at the residential council cannot keep up with the frequent changes in address that result from massive urban construction: sometimes the addresses obtained at the residential council cannot be found because the entire apartment building has been torn down. The third problem related to household registration–based samples is fake registration (*kong gua hu*): some people never live where their names are registered. The last two problems together can result in many names in a selected sample being incorrect or otherwise missing.

One solution is to use the GSS block-listing system, which does not depend on household registration information. Yet identifying reasonable residential blocks is a difficult task. First, it is necessary to distinguish between apartment building–based blocks and the traditional single-story-dwelling blocks. Second, residential areas are sometimes embedded inside work units, making it difficult to mix these blocks with those based on natural boundaries. Third, the GSS sample requires prior knowledge of all residential blocks of the country. Identifying all the residential blocks in China can be extremely time consuming and costly. Ideally, blocks should be identified without relying exclusively on the existing residential block boundaries, but on population density.

Professors Pierre Landry at Yale University and Mingming Shen at Peking University have made a pioneer effort to apply spatial sampling techniques in drawing a representative sample for their 2001 Beijing Area Survey (Shen 2001; Landry and Shem 2005). Simply stated, spatial sampling involve dividing Beijing (or any geographic space) into equal squares (54 × 54 m) on a map. A number of these squares are randomly selected, and members of households in each square are interviewed. Prior to the age of the Global Positioning System (GPS), it was much more difficult to physically locate geographic squares of any size by their latitude and longitude in reality than on a map. The 2001 Beijing Area Survey successfully used GPS technology to physically locate each randomly selected square from its map. The resulting spatial sample appeared to be more representative than the one using traditional household registration. For example, the 2001 spatial sample contained 25% migrant workers, 20% who did not live at the same address as their registrations, and only 55% who lived at the same address as their household registration. In other words, if the results are to be believed, the traditional household registration method can only capture 55% of the real population in Beijing. The mean age of the spatial sample was thirty-eight, as compared with forty-three in the traditional BAS samples based on household registration. Yet the mean age of the 55% registered residents in the spatial sample was also forty-three. That is to say, household registration samples overestimated the average age of the Beijing population by five years (Landry and Shen 2005). This becomes a problem if, say, older people are more likely to vote. The upwardly biased sample would generate a higher voter turnout than in the real population, where the average age is five years younger.

Although the initial results of the spatial sampling are exciting, a major difficulty is that this kind of sampling requires detailed prior knowledge of the population density in a given square. Without such information, the surveyors cannot know whether a square is empty or overcrowded. Additional squares are needed to replace the empty ones, and further random selection is needed for the overcrowded squares. For example, if the surveyor decides to randomly select twenty households from each square, a square must at least contain twenty households, or it has to be replaced. An overcrowded square may have a thousand households in ten high-rise apartment buildings. The surveyor may have to randomly select two buildings and then ten households from each building.

According to the randomization rule, each household should have an equal probability of being selected. But the process just described will change this intended probability. The probability of each household's being selected is 100% in a 20-household square but only 2% (20/1000) in a 1000-household square. With information on population density, the surveyor can stratify the squares according to population density, excluding uninhabited ones and further stratifying the overcrowded ones. One way to acquire population density information is by using satellite images of electric lights in the dark. More lights indicate greater population density. For example, using data from the Defense Meteorological Satellite Program's Operational Linescan System, NASA scientists have created satellite photos of the earth's city lights for the purpose of studying global urbanization (Weier 2000). However, obtaining detailed light imagery in 50 × 50 m squares requires much more detail than the currently available photos can provide.

Quality Control

Once the names in the sample are chosen, not all subjects will actually let you in and then sit through an entire thirty-to-sixty-minute interview. According to this author's own experience, about 50 to 90% of the interviewees are likely to be cooperative, depending on the city. It is more difficult to convince the money-driven residents of Guangzhou or the politically astute Shanghainese that the interview is worth their time; Beijing residents, in contrast, are eager to tell you what the government should or should not do.

In urban China, the response rate is also directly related to the involvement of the residential council. In some cases, employees of the residential councils will take the interviewers to each household, introduce them to the family, and explain the purpose of the survey. Without such involvement, it is much more difficult to attain the interviewee's cooperation. This is particularly true in Shanghai, where the urban residential council structure is highly effective.

Conducting household interviews is going to become more and more difficult. In some cities, the residential council will have less information and authority, given greater resident mobility and the fact that more and more people tend to live in high-security buildings. Urban residents are also becoming more aware of their privacy rights and therefore will be more likely to decline an interview. In some other cities, survey workers have reported increased difficulty working with newly recruited younger members of residential committees because they tend to be more politically wary than their predecessors (mostly retired workers).

Another quality control issue is whether the respondent is telling the truth. In China, people are often afraid of the political consequence of speaking the truth. One way to deal with this problem is to avoid asking politically sensitive questions and instead focus on various aspects of people's daily lives —such as issues related to housing, income, work, family, and so on—and then use the information to imply political and social attitudes. One example is to use reported income change to measure popular satisfaction with economic reform.

The second way to tell whether people are telling the truth is to deliberately ask politically sensitive questions, such as whether "the CCP is corrupt," "the government is inefficient," or "market reform is going too fast." If the majority of the respondents say yes, we can be more confident that people are telling the truth and are not afraid of political retribution. For example, one may be suspicious of the reliability of a May 1989 ESRIC survey owing to the low percentage (about a quarter) of urban residents expressing a desire for freedom of speech and political rights during the peak of the 1989 urban demonstrations. In the same survey, however, over three-quarters of respondents expressed dissatisfaction with the party and the government.[10] The outspokenness of the respondents suggests that an apparently weak desire for democracy was perhaps a truthful answer, rather than the result of fear of political retribution.[11]

Yet another way to test for such fear is to ask people directly in the survey whether they are afraid of being reported on by others if they criticize the government, a question posed in both the 1992 ESRIC Urban Social Survey and the 1999 urban survey. Note that 45% in 1992 and 56% in 1999 were confident that criticism of the government would not be reported by others.[12]

The fear factor is reflected less in lying outright about one's opinion and is instead more often expressed in failing to respond (Shi 2000b). For example, after the 1989 crackdown on urban protests, the percentage of "don't knows" increased between 10 and 20% for questions related to satisfaction with the party, the government, and market reform, signaling a more cautious response to sensitive questions during a period of political repression. Meanwhile, the percentage of satisfaction remained more or less the same.[13]

This example also indicates the importance of timing. Depending on the direction and strength of the political winds at the time the survey is conducted, people may be more or less likely to respond. People exhibit heightened caution in answering questions during a major national party congress than, for example, during Chinese New Year. People may be more outspoken during a public protest than they would normally. Every public opinion survey has to be aware of the volatility of the public's mood. In interpreting the survey results, one must be sensitive to the general environment in which the survey is conducted.

The third quality control issue is created by the sampling technique used in urban China. The household registration system provides the address and name of the potential interviewee; the interviewer is required to interview that exact person. This can be very difficult to accomplish: the person may not be at home, the address may be difficult to find, or the person may refuse to cooperate (a minimum of three visits should be undertaken). One time during the 1999 survey in Guangzhou, an interviewer took a bus for two hours each way to a remote neighborhood, spent six hours there, yet failed to complete even one questionnaire. This situation creates an incentive to cheat: the interviewer can, for instance, find friends to fill out questionnaires. One way to solve this problem is to require interviewers to ask for the phone numbers of their respondents, as did the 1999 urban survey. Knowing that double checking is a possibility, interviewees thus have a disincentive to cheat.

Data Comparability and Analysis

Survey designers in China often face the dilemma of whether to ask questions that are less comparable with other surveys but more suitable for China's conditions, on the one hand, or to ask questions that can easily be used in cross-national comparisons yet are unable to reflect specifics about China, on the other. For example, Jiang Zemin's new party doctrine of the "three represents" [14] is highly relevant in the Chinese context but may have little comparative value unless translated into comparable social science terms. Other questions—such as "Would you drive to work if you could take the bus" and "Would you pay taxes to support arms development or the environment"—though commonly used in Western public opinion surveys, do not fit with China's current conditions, since most people do not drive or pay taxes.

Having described the danger of finding a question that cannot travel, asking comparative questions will obviously increase the readability of China-related research among non-China specialists. To that end, one can consult the many multipurpose social surveys conducted in other societies that can be used to develop parallel questions. Examples include the biannual General Social Survey conducted by the National Opinion Research Center (NORC) at the University of Chicago (Davis, Smith, and Marsden 2003); the Taiwan Social Change Surveys conducted by the Institute of Sociology, Academia Sinica of Taiwan (Academia Sinica 2001); and the World Values Surveys (Inglehart 1997). These surveys have modules of questions on such topics as political participation, the environment, marriage and family, work, and so on. Many of these questions can be adapted for use in China.

Sometimes a survey sample is biased. For example, the less educated may be underrepresented in the sample owing to their low response rate. One way to avoid drawing incorrect conclusions due to sample bias is to exercise caution in interpreting the results. For example, if the sample error is ±3%, one should be very cautious in comparing two groups with less than 6% difference (e.g., a 50% popular approval rate for Jiang Zemin versus a 55% approval rate for Hu Jintao). Another way to deal with sample biases is to use statistical methods. Computer statistical packages include an increasing number of commands developed by researchers to deal with problems in a survey. One commonly used method is weighting: if the sample's education level is higher than the average urban education level obtained from the population census, the sample education is upwardly biased. One can weigh the sample by the actual lower levels of education in the population. This technique will display a lower percentage of voting participation than the biased sample owing to the reduced (or weighted) level of education. Another improvement is statistical methods designed to deal with missing items. For example, missing values in income can be estimated by age, education, and occupation in the sample (StataCorp 1995; Jennings 2000). Finally, as Melanie Manion correctly argues, it is often safer to study the relationship between variables than descriptive statistics about single variables (Manion 1994). For example, if the sample is biased with too many high earners, the average income level in the sample will be too high and should not be used to represent the average income of the population. However, so long as the income variable in the sample has a variation from low to high, it can still be used to examine the impact of income on, say, political participation or the divorce rate.

Conclusion

This chapter faces the question of whether public opinion surveys can be effectively used as a research tool for studying China. Unlike some human rights activists' and dissidents' claim that survey data collected in China are distorted and unreliable (He 2004), this chapter shows that survey research would not have become so popular and accepted in policy making and academic research if it was so obviously distorted. In fact, it is possible to obtain reliable survey data from China through careful design, implementation, and statistical techniques. As discussed in this chapter, several measures can by taken to ensure the reliability of survey data collected in China. The first step is to draw a representative sample through the household registration system or spatial sampling. Second, measures can be taken to check whether the sample really represents the population by comparing the basic characteristics of the sample such as age, gender, and education to those of population census results. The sample represents the population if these characteristics match. Third, if the sample does not closely represent the population characteristics, statistical techniques such as weighting can be used to correct the sample biases. Fourth, the surveyor can also ensure the reliability of survey data by carefully designed survey questions. Often a hypothetical question related to day-to-day life—for example, "What would you do if you fail to get a raise" or ". . . if your drinking water is polluted"—shows people's political attitude and behavior just as well as a general question such as "Would you criticize the government if you were dissatisfied?" Fifth, the reliability of survey data can be checked by survey results. For example, the data are likely to be reliable if they confirm common knowledge—for example, "Private entrepreneurs are more risk-taking than bureaucrats"—or if the respondents are outspoken about politically sensitive questions. Finally, potential biases in survey data can be avoided if the researcher focuses more on who wants, say, democracy and less on how much overall desire for democracy is in the sample. As long as there is variation in the desire for democracy in the sample—for example, if "a lot" = 5%, "some" = 25%, "not really" = 45%, and "not at all" = 25%—the researcher can always identify the socioeconomic and demographic characteristics in each category and tell some interesting stories, even if the overall low level of demand for democracy is questionable.

In the long run, public opinion research in China will likely be easier in some respects and more difficult in others than elsewhere. Such research will get easier as the political atmosphere becomes freer and public opinion seems less of a threat to the regime. Surveys will become more difficult, however, as social mobility and awareness of privacy and other rights further increase. By that point, survey-related problems in China will be much more similar to those in market societies.

Some of the suspicion about survey research in China is really related to the problems of survey research in general. For example, response rates tend to be low among less-educated, older, and female populations. The specific chemistry between the interviewer and the respondent tends to create inconsistencies. Politically sensitive questions that may evoke inaccurate responses also exist in democratic societies, such as race relations, abortion, and patriotism in the United States. In this sense, Chinese surveys are as reliable as surveys from any other society.

This chapter also addresses some of the broader questions raised in chapter 1, namely, the impact of the party-state and market reform on collecting public opinion. It shows the negative effect the institutional environment has on survey research in China. Political sensitivity remains a major barrier in conducting surveys. Yet political control is limited and shrinking in its scope. Surveys involving Western scholars continue to be carried out in China. For example, the World Values Surveys successfully implemented most of their survey questions in China. Only a few questions about directly challenging the government were censored from the standard World Values

Survey questionnaire because of political sensitivity (World Values Survey Staffs 2002). Market forces are driving a growing survey field by creating an increasing number of private and semiprivate survey companies. The desire to create a professionalized government further encourages the use of survey research to collect public opinion on a broader range of topics. An upside-down funnel (see chap. 1) seems to apply to collecting public opinion, with a few untouchable, sensitive questions regarding the top-level leadership and direct challenges to the regime but a broad range of "nonsensitive" questions, including such topics as work, family, marriage, religion, life satisfaction, and even political participation and governance.

PART TWO

The Formation of Public Opinion

CHAPTER THREE

Support for Reform and Regime Legitimacy

In this chapter I examine popular attitudes in urban China toward market reform and political systems and compare the changes in public opinion between the Deng and post-Deng eras. It will further depict the general political and social trends in urban China and the likely forces of change. Empirical evidence will be drawn from the 1999 Six-City Survey and other ESRIC surveys (see text box in chapter 2 on surveys).

Consequences of Reform

China's economic growth is constantly in the news. Few stories fail to mention the country's rapid marketization and shift toward capitalism. But market reform has brought negative results as well. Just as Chinese politicians like to boast about China's growth to foreign visitors, they are also keen on identifying potential problems associated with the downside of economic

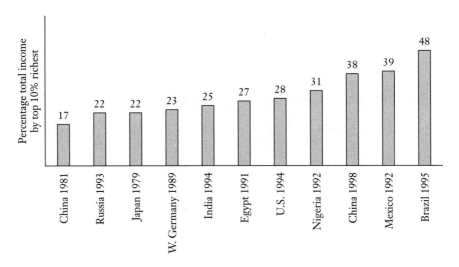

Figure 3.1   Income inequality in selected countries
SOURCES: World Bank 1999, 198–99; China 1981: Riskin 1987, 249; China 1998: Ketizu 2001, 74.

growth. For example, the party's organization department issued an investigative report in 2001 identifying the main sources of conflict in the reform era (Ketizu 2001). According to this report, one alarming problem was the growing income discrepancy, including the gaps between rural and urban Chinese and interoccupational and interregional inequality. An international comparison of income distribution further reveals the problem in China (fig. 3.1). Before reform, China had the least income discrepancy among ten countries representing different geographic regions in the world. Yet by 1995, China's disparities were approaching those of Latin American countries, and China itself became one of the most unequal societies in the world in terms of income. In Xinjiang the growing economic inequality between the affluent local Han Chinese and the Muslim population was one reason behind intensified ethnic conflict in this western region (Ketizu 2001, chap. 7). Chinese authorities are particularly keen to ensure that economic disparities do not fuel ethnic separatism, but the concern also extends to other parts of the country where ethnic identity is not an issue.

The party's 2001 investigative report identified the second source of conflict as that between efficiency and employment. Market reform required state-owned enterprises to improve efficiency, an imperative that immediately challenged overemployment. The egalitarian socialist policy under central planning required full employment and job security, which predictably led to overstaffing, little incentive to work, and low efficiency. The streamlining policy in the post-Deng reform programs resulted in massive layoffs (Muo 2000), which further contributed to a growing income gap between the beneficiaries of reform and those hurt by it. Social welfare was reduced at the workplace, forcing people to rely increasingly on market forces and family self-support (Croll 1999). This resulted in a decline in living standards, particularly among disadvantaged groups and regions (Solinger 1996; Khan and Riskin 1998; Gustafsson and Zhong 2000; Wang and Hu 2000).

The third conflict was between state cadres and the public. The investigative report cited three reasons: an increased tax burden, the authoritarian work style of some cadres, and corruption among state officials. For example, the number of state officials convicted of corruption, from the county level on up, increased from 3,004 in 1993 to 4,436 in 1999, reflecting an 8% annual increase during this period. Among those, high-profile cases involving officials at the provincial and ministerial level and above increased from six cases in 1993 to seventeen cases in 1999 (Ketizu 2001, 86). As a result, resentment against state officials intensified. Angry protesters cut off one party official's ear in one incident and killed two other cadres in another incident in Hunan province (Ketizu 2001, 83; also see Cao 2000).

The final problem facing the party was challenges to state ideology. The investigative report identified three challenges to the party's Marxist pragmatism: a shaken belief in Marxism owing to the collapse of the Soviet Empire, ultra-leftists who opposed market reform, and post–cold war efforts by the West to penetrate China by introducing market values such as individualism and a money culture. These values, authorities feared, challenged the socialist ideal of sacrificing individual interest for the collective good and poisoned social morality (Ketizu 2001, 69–91).

The investigative report also showed a sense of crisis within the party itself, a conclusion that drew public attention in China and abroad. Alarmed by the seriousness of these problems and their destabilizing impact, the Chinese leaders, after originally supporting the study, ordered the report taken off bookstore shelves within a couple of months of its publication.

Some Western scholars joined in this pessimistic assessment of reform. One example is China's growth in gross domestic product. Although the officially claimed annual growth was about 7% in 1998 and 1999, Rawski (2001) challenged the Chinese government's statistics and estimated the actual growth to be between −2% and 2% for 1998 and −2.5% and 2% for 1999. Rawski supported his estimate with several facts, such as the import-export slowdown during the 1997 Asian financial crisis, the losses during the 1998 floods, and the slow growth of some key factors for the overall economic growth, including energy consumption and air transportation (Rawski 2002).

However inflated official fears may have been, without a doubt popular discontent was on the rise. Politically, the post-Deng regime suffered some setbacks in confidence. Most remarkable was a protest in the spring of 1999 by the Falun Gong sect (see text box in chapter 1 on Falun Gong). It was the largest antigovernment action since the student-led urban protests of a decade earlier, and it brought home the point that the perceived failures of China's reform policy can result in public disobedience (Schechter 2000). Unemployment and the rising income gap added to growing labor protests nationwide (Pomfret 2000) and constituted the economic hallmarks of the post-Deng era. These examples led observers to believe that the post-Deng leadership suffered from a crisis of confidence in the legitimacy of the regime (Chang 2001).

On the stability side, the post-Deng leaders seemed to have successfully consolidated political power at the Sixteenth Party Congress in 2002 and the Tenth National Peoples' Congress in 2003. In addition to resuming a high growth rate in the late 1990s and the first few years of the new century, it was the post-Deng leaders' political fortune to benefit from a particular array of international and domestic events.[1] China regained both Hong Kong and Macau from their former colonial rulers—a rare victory of territorial consolidation in an era of other communist powers falling apart. In 1999, Jiang Zemin led China's celebration of the fiftieth anniversary of the People's Republic of China, an event that placed him on the international stage and underlined his holding power for skeptics who had thought he would only be a transitional leader after taking the reins of China's Communist Party in 1989. On the domestic front, the 1999 U.S. bombing of the Chinese embassy in Belgrade and the 2001 U.S. spy plane standoff in Hainan put the post-Deng leaders on the crest of a wave of anti-Western patriotism, allowing them to justify their harsh handling of pro-Western political dissidents.

But in China's complex mix of concurrent social and economic tendencies, more freedoms emerged in some areas just as repression existed in others. Although the post-Deng leaders kept a tight watch over certain key political issues (i.e., alternative political parties and autonomous labor unions) and allowed the economy considerably more leeway, political development was seen in some other areas. These included expanding village and township elections (Carter Center 1999; Manion 2000; O'Brien and Li 2000), increasing intellectual freedom (Goldman 1996), improving the rule of law and reducing bureaucratic inefficiency (Burns 1999), reducing the significance of personal ties in firms that do business with foreign companies (Guthrie 1998), affording more autonomy to social organizations (Saich 2000), increasing the supervisory role of the provincial legislature (MacFarquhar 1998), and reducing interference in residents' lives by urban residential committees (Read 2000).

In the remaining pages of this chapter I will examine the urban survey data and test the crisis and legitimacy hypotheses, respectively. Specifically, I will look at two directly related issues: satisfaction with economic reform and support for China's political system and ideology.

In his interesting study of popular political support in Beijing, Chen (2004) posited two categories of support: regime support and support for specific reform policies, or "diffuse support" and "specific support." Overall, he found a high level of regime support and a low level of specific support (Chen 2004; tables 2.1 and 2.5). In this chapter I will extend Chen's study in several directions. First, I will expand the list of satisfaction categories from Chen's nine items to sixteen items. Second, I will compare Chinese citizens' evaluation of not only China's own system, but also of the political systems in other countries. Third, I define both regime support and reform satisfaction in broader terms, also including support for official ideologies and for the speed of reform. Finally, Chen's study of the period between 1995 and 1999 showed little significant change. In this chapter I will look at both regime support and reform satisfaction over a longer period of time, from 1987 to 1999.

Reform Satisfaction

Reform satisfaction as an assessment of how popular reform policy in fact is in China reveals a conceptual irony: not all reform is perceived as good, and there may be public resistance to policies that result in economic insecurity. According to the crisis argument, therefore, growing economic and social problems would lead to increasing dissatisfaction and decreasing support for reform. The legitimacy hypothesis, however, would turn this around and instead focus on the increasing public satisfaction with and support for the post-Deng leaders' effort to carry on Deng's programs and to further improve living standards. In this section, reform satisfaction and support are examined from several angles. The first is the respondents' direct answers to different aspects of satisfaction, such as economic well-being, political rights and freedom, social services, and the overall level of satisfaction. Second, to avoid the problem, to which surveys are sometimes prone, of being sensitive to particular external events rather than showing the general popular trends (Mayer 1992), it is necessary to examine the trends of change over time. The third way to understand reform satisfaction is by identifying the winners and losers. Particularly, the losers in the new system form a politically unstable group that may hinder further reform. Finally, perceived reform speed is another measure of satisfaction, whether it is too fast, too slow, or just right. An answer of "too fast" indicates people want the government to slow down and reform less, such as by delaying mass layoffs at key industries. "Too slow" means the inverse—a public desire for the government to speed up reform. "Just right" shows satisfaction with and support for the status quo.

Reform satisfaction was measured by sixteen items in the 1999 Six-City Survey (fig. 3.2). Among the top seven most satisfying areas of life (fig. 3.2A), family life and social life were the highest. This is likely a result of improved living standards and more disposable income, a cultural tradition of emphasizing family and inner circle of friends, or a more relaxed social environment under reform even if the political framework stayed the same. I will further discuss the role of family and friends in the chapter on interpersonal trust.

Satisfaction with personal health, housing, economic freedom, and China's image in the world reflected the combined effect of rapid economic development, improvement of living standards, and marketization. Somewhat unexpected was the two-thirds of the 1999 respondents who were satisfied with freedom of speech. Perhaps the respondents did not understand the concept as the freedom to openly challenge the regime. In any case, as long as they stayed within the officially sanctioned framework, people

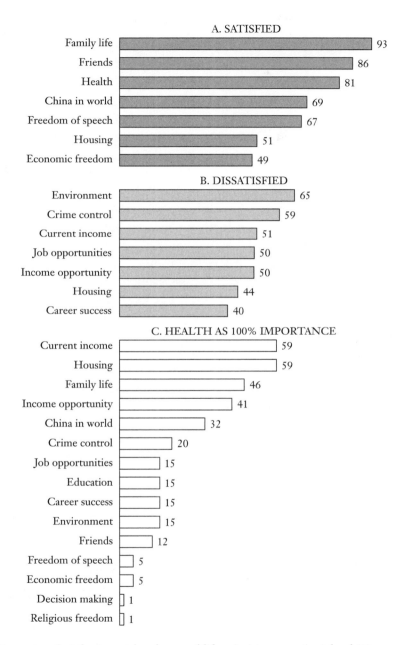

A. SATISFIED

Family life	93
Friends	86
Health	81
China in world	69
Freedom of speech	67
Housing	51
Economic freedom	49

B. DISSATISFIED

Environment	65
Crime control	59
Current income	51
Job opportunities	50
Income opportunity	50
Housing	44
Career success	40

C. HEALTH AS 100% IMPORTANCE

Current income	59
Housing	59
Family life	46
Income opportunity	41
China in world	32
Crime control	20
Job opportunities	15
Education	15
Career success	15
Environment	15
Friends	12
Freedom of speech	5
Economic freedom	5
Decision making	1
Religious freedom	1

Figure 3.2 Satisfaction with reform and life priorities, 1999 (weighted %)
SOURCE: 1999 Six-City Survey.

thought they had plenty of freedom. What the 1999 survey measures is the feeling of being free in China's political environment. It does not measure the freedom of the political system per se.

Among the top seven areas of life with which respondents were most dissatisfied (fig. 3.2B), environmental protection and crime control registered the most concern. Pollution and crime were the results of rapid industrialization and economic freedom. The regime's failure to ameliorate these problems also showed the government's lack of understanding, resources, and knowledge in dealing with these issues in a market environment. Worsening individual economic conditions and the lack of economic opportunities were additional sources of dissatisfaction. Half the respondents in 1999 were dissatisfied with their current income and with income and job opportunities. Many of the 40% who were dissatisfied with their career perhaps had already lost their career when central planning ended. Finally, people seemed split between satisfaction and dissatisfaction with housing, indicating a polarization of the quality of housing people of disparate means can afford. The losers of reform were still living in dilapidated housing left over from the central planning days, while the winners were moving into modern apartments that the losers could never dream of affording. Overall, the 1999 results depicted nicely the predicted reaction to the benefits and costs of reform. Yet satisfaction does not fully describe to what extent people value certain things. For example, knowing that people are satisfied with family life and freedom of speech does not necessarily mean that people think these are important. Only by comparing satisfaction with need can one further assess the success and failure of reform policy.

When asked about the relative importance of the above sixteen items, Chinese respondents were very practical (fig. 3.2C). The most important was personal health. After the guarantee of their basic survival, the next concern was wealth with which one could satisfy the next need—getting married and having a family. When survival, wealth, and family were guaranteed, the next concerns were income and job opportunities, personal safety, a clean environment, education, and career success. The demand for political, economic, or religious freedom was surprisingly low. This list of priorities roughly coincides with the hierarchy of human needs. One way to increase the demand for freedom is to meet basic and intermediate needs first. Finally, somewhat unexpected was the relatively high ranking of China's image, perhaps indicating a rise in nationalism.

It is also necessary to examine the shifts over time with satisfaction. In addition to the advantage of better understanding future trends, comparing urban China in 1999 with earlier surveys can also confirm the 1999 findings. If those results nicely follow a pattern from the past, we are more certain about the consistency of the 1999 survey with earlier surveys. The ESRIC surveys in 1987, 1988, 1989, and 1991 contain some of the same satisfaction items as the 1999 survey. Generally, the enthusiasm for reform in the initial years quickly bottomed out around 1989, when market forces hit hard and reduced the quality of life for many. Enthusiasm has been cautiously rising since then (fig. 3.3). The exceptions were the environment and job opportunities. As shown by the available data, satisfaction with these two items fell.

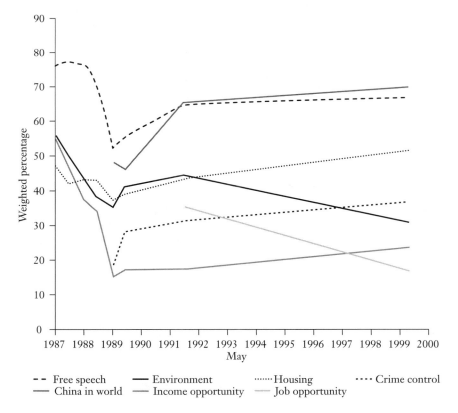

Figure 3.3   Satisfaction with reform, 1987–99 (weighted %)
SOURCES: ESRIC surveys; 1999 Six-City Survey.

These findings are consistent with the common negative impression about rising pollution and unemployment.

As mentioned previously, satisfaction with freedom of speech has stayed high. Even during the most stressful months of inflation, unemployment, and corruption in 1988 and 1989, more than half of the respondents in urban China were still satisfied with their freedom of speech. Since then, the number has been rising, but it still remains below the 1987 level of three-quarters of respondents. This is an indication that political liberalism in the post-Tiananmen decade did not resume the momentum enjoyed during the Hu Yaobang and Zhao Ziyang years (see fig. 1.3). Another item that followed a similar pattern, but at a much lower level, was income opportunity. After peaking in the initial years of urban reform, it dropped to its lowest level in May 1989 and increased slowly over the next ten years, yet it still registered well below the level generated by people's initial excitement. One possibility is that reform has brought fewer income opportunities since 1989. But given the continued improvement of living standards in the 1990s, the more feasible explanation of the slow change in income opportunity is that economic growth, although rapid, did not keep up with the even faster increase in public expectations.

The remaining three items that displayed a positive change were China's image, housing, and crime control. Even though in 1999 crime control was the area in which respondents expressed the second most dissatisfaction (fig. 3.2B), the level of satisfaction was nonetheless a lot higher than in 1989. The government's crime control programs seemed to be working, while, by contrast, it was unsuccessful in environmental protection and creating more job opportunities. Housing had a similar story. It was on the most-unsatisfactory list in 1999, but the level of satisfaction was still the highest since 1987. With the current trend toward massive housing construction in China, satisfaction with housing will likely increase further, and perhaps it will be taken off the most-unsatisfactory list in the future. The increased satisfaction with China's international image was a reflection of China's growing economic influence in the world. It could also be a result of growing nationalism as a competing ideology with socialism and Western democracy.

These comparisons provide some historical perspective on the current situation in urban China. Within the timeframe of the urban data, one knows more about whether the best and the worst scenarios are over or still to come.

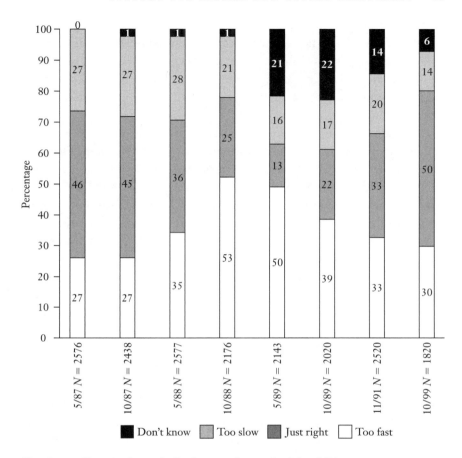

Figure 3.4   Perceived speed of reform, 1987–99 (weighted %)
SOURCES: ESRIC surveys; 1999 Six-City Survey.

People's reaction to the speed of reform is another measure of support for reform. In 1999, overall support for reform seemed to be lower than before (fig. 3.4). With 80% of the urban residents who either wanted to keep the status quo ("just right") or go back to the old system (e.g., the current reform is "too fast"), any radical reform policy would likely meet with strong resistance. Anti-reform sentiment ("too fast") was strongest between 1988 and 1989. Although the percentage of anti-reformers shrank since 1989, it was not significantly smaller in 1999 than before and after the 1989 Tiananmen incident. Another indication of weak support for reform in 1999 was the decreasing number of those who supported radical reform ("too slow"). In fact, the percentage of radical reformers reached a historically low point in 1999. Some of the supporters of radical reform were absorbed into the status quo group ("just right"). This group, though it supports reform on the surface, is less likely to support any change that entails a loss. They are therefore likely to be conservative by instinct.

However, knowing the overall satisfaction with and support for reform does not fully describe the social and economic profiles of the winners and losers. So far, the sources of satisfaction and support have been mentioned only in passing. A more detailed analysis is necessary to associate a more complete list of social and economic characteristics with satisfaction and support. This list includes party membership, income, gender, education, age, occupation, and geographic location. In the 1999 survey, income was measured by the respondent's reported family income level on a scale of 0 to 10. Age was divided into five groups based on the year the respondent turned twenty: pre-1949 (the pre-PRC generation), 1949–65 (the socialist generation), 1966–76 (the Cultural Revolution generation), 1977–84 (the reform generation), and post-1984 (the post-reform generation). These categories corresponded to the difference in political socialization between different generations. Occupations included professional, administrator and manager, clerk, sales and service, private sector,[2] manual laborers, the unemployed, the retired, and none or other. Finally, cities were included in the analysis to examine the impact of the central government's preferential policies and other differential factors in each city. For example, for Wuhan's slow development due to the lack of preferential policy from the center, see Solinger 1996.

In order to provide a more accurate discussion, satisfaction will be examined in several categories in the 1999 survey, including economic opportunity (current income, income opportunity, job opportunity, and economic freedom), political freedom (freedom of speech, participation in decision making, and religious freedom), and overall satisfaction. Each category is based on a factor index of the items under that category. The factor index of overall satisfaction includes all the satisfaction items (see fig. 3.2C). In addition, we will also look at the social and economic profiles of reform support. For reform support, we use the reverse measure—intolerance for reform. "Too fast" is a measure of intolerance and potential opposition to reform and was coded 1; and "just right" and "too slow" were coded 0.

Overall, income, gender, and level of education played a predictable role in promoting satisfaction and support. High earners were understandably more satisfied with the overall reform owing to their improved economic opportunities. They were also more certain than party members that further reform would bring more economic benefits. Male respondents in 1999 were more negative than females about the overall effect of reform and were dissatisfied with both their economic opportunity and their political freedom. This was a reflection of higher male expectations seen in other societies. The more educated showed more awareness of the need for public services and knew that they would receive further benefits with further reform (see table 3.1 and appendix B).

Those who already had means and resources in society tended to be happier with reform. This applied to party members in particular, partly because of their satisfaction with economic opportunities and political freedom. Somewhat unexpected was party members' ambivalence about whether reform was going too fast. This ambivalence probably reflected their uncertainty about how further reform might affect their current economic and political benefits.

Older and middle-aged groups were the winners, with more economic and political benefits than the younger generations. This is also common in other societies where older generations are economically and politically better off than the younger generations, given the difference between income and experience. One other reason for discontent among the younger generations was their rising expectations; the older groups were simply easier to please.

Two interesting points are related to occupation. Professionals showed less satisfaction with freedom and public services. Their dissatisfaction could reflect demands for government responsiveness and political system reform. I will further discuss the role of professionals and intellectuals in voicing public opinion and political reform in the following chapters. The second point related to occupation is the high level of dissatisfaction among the unemployed and manual laborers, because of their reduced economic opportunities. Massive unemployment and rising income inequality were part of the cause. If there was anything surprising, it was the intensity of their desire to slow down reform. To extrapolate from this finding, the end result indicates that in times of economic difficulty, the unemployed and manual laborers

TABLE 3.1
Satisfaction and speed of reform in 1999: a multivariate analysis

	Overall satisfaction	Economic opportunity	Political freedom	Public affairs	Reform too fast
Party member	0.039	0.043	0.023	−0.001	0.036
Family inc. 0–10	0.018	0.028	0.002	−0.003	−0.035
Male	−0.021	−0.017	−0.024	−0.003	0.015
Yrs. of education (0–19)	0.000	0.001	−0.001	−0.006	−0.021
Age groups:					
Age 20 before 1949	0.067	0.099	0.023	0.026	0.068
Age 20 in 1949–65	0.042	0.056	0.030	−0.021	−0.245
Age 20 in 1966–76 (comparison)					
Age 20 in 1977–84	0.003	−0.004	0.002	−0.014	0.042
Age 20 after 1984	−0.001	0.006	−0.016	−0.026	−0.154
Occupation:					
Professional	−0.023	−0.004	−0.042	−0.059	−0.062
Admin./manager	−0.002	0.017	0.009	−0.041	−0.195
Clerical	−0.020	−0.001	−0.038	−0.033	−0.049
Sales/service	−0.014	−0.004	−0.016	0.018	0.147
Private	−0.012	−0.005	0.024	0.039	0.062
Manual laborer	−0.030	−0.033	−0.016	0.015	0.291
Unemployed	−0.082	−0.112	−0.022	−0.015	0.475
Retired	0.009	0.017	−0.013	0.017	0.188
No occupation (comparison)					
City:					
Guangzhou	−0.042	−0.026	−0.047	−0.156	0.041
Xian	0.005	0.034	−0.006	−0.129	−0.144
Wuhan	−0.054	−0.037	−0.020	−0.119	0.160
Chongqing	−0.011	−0.013	0.019	−0.133	0.013
Shenyang	0.054	0.048	0.041	0.070	0.021
Shanghai (comparison)					
_cons	0.382	0.312	0.606	0.551	−0.290
R-sqrd	0.168	0.200	0.046	0.131	0.035
N = 1820					

SOURCE: 1999 Six-City Survey.

Underlined: $p \leq 1$.

NOTE: Since all dependent variables are on a 0–1 scale, the effect of each independent variable can be interpreted as a percentage change. For example, the richest group was 18% more satisfied than the poorest group. The most educated were about 40% less likely to say reform was too fast than the illiterate group. Compared with the Cultural Revolution generation (age 20 in 1966–76), the pre-1949 (age 20 before 49) and the socialist generations (age 20 in 1949–65) were about 7% and 4% more satisfied, and the post-Cultural Revolution generations (age 20 in 1977–84 and after 1984) did not show a significant difference from the Cultural Revolution generation. Similarly, all occupation groups should be compared with the "no occupation" group. For example, the unemployed were 8% less satisfied than the "no occupation" group. All cities should be compared with Shanghai. For example, Wuhan residents were 5% less satisfied and Shenyang residents 5% more satisfied than Shanghai residents. The same methods of interpretation also apply to "reform is too fast." The percentage for satisfaction with reform was converted from a factor index of the sixteen items in fig. 3.2C. The original factor indices for the satisfaction variables were standardized with a minimum value of 0 and a maximum value of 1 (see appendix B). "Reform too fast" values ranged from 0 (disagree) to 1 (agree). Similarly, the probit regression coefficient for each independent variable with "reform too fast" could be interpreted as percentage of change. For example, the unemployed were 47% more likely to say reform was going too fast than the "no occupation" group.

could easily be joined in their protests by service workers and retirees and hence coalesce into a factor of instability.

Geographic location also made a difference in satisfaction and support. Residents in Guangzhou and Wuhan were less satisfied with reform than those in other cities. One reason was their lack of economic opportunities. Another may have been their dissatisfaction with not receiving preferential treatment from the central government (Solinger 1996). For Guangzhou, across-the-board dissatisfaction could also have been caused by residents' comparison of their situation with that of Guangzhou's affluent neighbor Hong Kong. Shanghai seemed to be more capable of delivering public services than other cities, a likely result of a more effective municipal government.

One puzzle is the high level of satisfaction in Shenyang—a city in the rust belt of socialist industrialization that had suffered from economic dislocation and unemployment since reform, and which normally would register greater dissatisfaction. Yet in the multivariate analysis including the respondents' income, occupational status, age, and other factors, Shenyang residents still showed a higher level of satisfaction than the other five cities in the 1999 survey (see table 3.1). In other words, there were reasons other than economic dislocation and unemployment that made Shenyang residents happier. One possibility is that Shenyang suffered less during marketization than the rest of the northeastern rust-belt regions. For example, household consumption in Liaoning province, where Shenyang is the capital city, was consistently higher than the neighboring Jilin and Helongjiang provinces from 1997 to 2002 (see table 3-16 in State Statistical Bureau 1999; State Statistical Bureau 2003). Liaoning's housing consumption was also more favorable comparing with other regions in the 1999 survey. For example, according to the 2000 population census, only 10% of the urban population in Liaoning had less than eight square meters of living space, but this figure was as high as 18% in Shanghai, 15% in Guangdong (capital: Guangzhou) and Shaanxi (capital: Xian), 13% in Hubei (capital: Wuhan), and 12% in Chongqing (table 8-2a in Population Census Office 2002, 1:781). Further research is required to provide a full explanation of Shenyang's difference in satisfaction.

In short, the findings in this section show that although dissatisfaction with economic conditions and public services remained high among Chinese urban residents in 1999, it was probably not alarming. With continued economic growth in the 1990s, conditions in some key areas such as income, housing, and crime control improved and overall satisfaction increased. As a result, urban Chinese became more conservative. To preserve their gains, many of them were cautious about further reform and wanted to keep the status quo.

One area of concern that may support the crisis hypothesis was the intensified dissatisfaction related to the worsening conditions of public service, such as creating jobs and protecting the environment. The other area of concern that may also support the crisis hypothesis was the strong discontent among the hardest-hit social groups such as the unemployed and blue-collar workers. Chapter 6 will discuss how these groups voiced their dissatisfaction.

Regime Legitimacy and Support

In this section, I will discuss whether there is a political crisis in Chinese public opinion. Specifically, I will examine regime legitimacy, political conservatism, and ideology.

REGIME LEGITIMACY

One question in the 1999 survey regarding regime legitimacy was about people's attitude toward China's political structure, which, according to the Constitution of the Chinese Communist Party (http://www.china.org.cn/english/features/49109.htm [accessed March 22, 2005]), is a system of "multiparty cooperation" under the Communist Party. Support of such a system showed support for China's single-party rule. In the 1999 Six-City Survey, when asked whether the Communist-led multiparty system should be changed, 18% of the respondents thought it should be changed, 6% wanted only minor change, 31% did not care so long as their lives could be improved, and 44% did not want any change (question E6). Thus, the majority of people either did not care or did not want any change.

Regime legitimacy can also be measured by public opinion about criteria for evaluating the government. For example, when asked what constituted the criteria for good government, concerns focused on economic growth

(48%), efficiency (35%), clean government (34%), and rule of law (21%). Political transparency (15%), democratic elections (11%), individual freedom (7%), and a coherent ideology (4%) were less important. Thus, the public's needs seemed to grant further legitimacy to an increasingly pragmatic government.

POLITICAL CONSERVATISM

Results were mixed as to how politically conservative urban residents were. The 1999 survey has seven other questions related to urban residents' political views (table 3.2). On the conservative side, the majority of respondents showed political obedience and opposed democratization. On the liberal side, the majority of the respondents supported selecting government through elections, disapproved of government efforts to control political dissidents, and disagreed with the statement that only the government could fully represent the country. The respondents were split on whether the government should promote freedom of speech and social diversity.

The overall level of political conservatism seems higher in China than in democratic societies. For example, about one-third of urban Chinese still believed that dissidents should be constrained and that elections were not

TABLE 3.2
Political conservatism, 1999 (weighted %)

	Agree	Disagree	Don't know
1. People should obey government decisions regarding state affairs.	70	26	4
2. The most important condition for our country's progress is political stability. Democratization under the current conditions would only lead to chaos.	59	27	14
3. Government should decide whether an idea or a theory can be publicized.	48	43	9
4. Society would become chaotic if people's ideas are not unified.	45	48	7
5. Not supporting the government is not patriotic.	41	54	5
6. Government should constrain political dissidents.	37	51	12
7. Elections are not important as long as government policy reflects public opinion.	34	58	8

SOURCE: 1999 Six-City Survey.

N = 1820

NOTE: The 1992 results for questions 1, 3, 4, and 5 were very similar to those of 1999 (not shown).

important as a means of reflecting public opinion. In addition, political conservatism stayed at almost the same level as that found in the 1992 urban survey.

The questions in table 3.2 were combined with a factor analysis to form an index of political conservatism. In a multivariate regression analysis, political conservatism was examined against the respondent's socioeconomic and demographic background. Respondents who were high earners, male, and better educated were less conservative. The reform and post-reform generations were significantly less conservative than the older generations. Those in sales and service, manual laborers, the unemployed, and retirees were more conservative than professionals, administrators, managers, white-collar workers, and the private sector. Residents in the rust-belt city of Shenyang seemed more conservative than residents in other cities (see Tang 2001 for further details).

Among other things, these findings seem to indicate that political conservatism was related to one's socioeconomic status. Those who were low on the income, education, and occupational scales were more conservative.

Best Political and Economic Models

The attitude toward supporting China's political system was further examined by questions related to perceptions of other countries. In the 1999 survey, respondents were asked to rank the three greatest threats and the three best political and economic models for China from a list of countries and areas including China itself. For each country, a value of 3 was assigned if the respondent picked it as the greatest threat (or the best political or economic model), 2 if the second greatest threat (or second-best political or economic model), 1 if the third greatest threat (or third-best political or economic model), and 0 if that country was not picked as a threat or a model. A measure of the respondent's feeling of threat with respect to a given country was created by dividing the respondent's 0–3 score by 3 and multiplying the result by 100. For example, if a respondent picked the United States as China's greatest threat (3), he or she had a maximum feeling of threat of 100 ([3/3] × 100). The average score for each country in the 1999 survey was calculated for each of the three questions. This measure can also be used as a percentage on a scale of feeling with a minimum value of 0, a maximum value of 100, and any value in between. A high score of China as the best model for political or economic development indicated more support for the current system and policy.

When asked which country provided the best model for China's political reform, the highest percentage chose China's own system (fig. 3.5). In parallel to a growing number of Americans who saw China as a threat,[3] the United States was seen as the greatest threat to China's international status, although the American economic system was ranked as the best model for China to learn from.

The respondent's background, including party membership, family income, gender, education, age, occupation, and city were further examined against one's preference of political and economic systems in a probit regression analysis. Party members with more education and those from the pre-reform generations showed significantly more support for China's political system than nonparty members, the less educated, and the reform and post-reform generations. In evaluating the U.S. economic system, the better educated and those in the private sector and in sales and services expressed greater favor than others.[4]

In short, China's own political system was slightly more favored than other political systems, and suspicions about the United States were high. The political and social elite formed the core of this trend, which coincided with the rise of nationalism in the 1990s among Chinese intellectuals (see, e.g., Song et al. 1996).

IDEOLOGY

Attitudes toward the current system were further examined by questions related to ideology. Each respondent was given a list of ideologies (Marxism-Leninism, Maoism, Dengism, Chinese culture, and Western culture), and asked to evaluate the importance of each one for China's future social stability. Support for Dengism indicated the respondent backed the current government, which was based on Deng Xiaoping's pragmatic policy. Support for Western culture probably contrasted with opinions of Maoism, Marxism-Leninism, and Chinese culture. The respondent could choose all or none of the five ideologies as important. Among those who thought each ideology

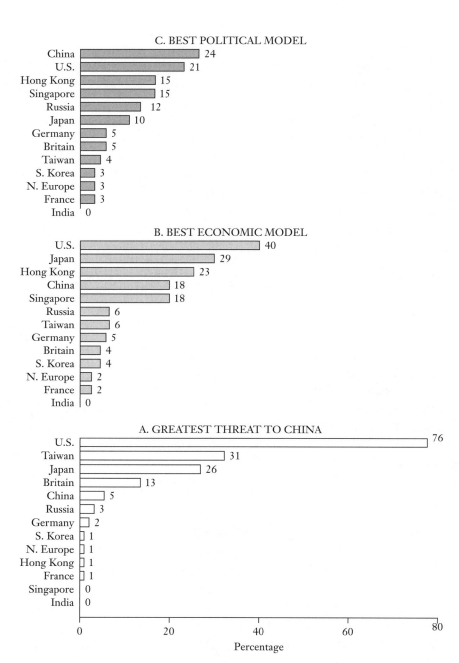

Figure 3.5 The greatest threat to China's development and the best economic and political models for China, 1999 (% who agreed with statement, weighted)

SOURCE: 1999 Six-City Survey.

was "very important," 58% chose the pragmatic Dengism, 55% mentioned Maoism, 42% selected Marxism-Leninism, and 37% chose Chinese culture. Only 8% thought Western culture would be very important.

Once again, the respondent's background characteristics were checked against his or her attitude toward ideologies in a multiple regression analysis.[5] There was an apparent link between educational and socioeconomic status and one's willingness to accept nontraditional and non-Chinese value systems. Party members were firm in upholding Marxism-Leninism and Maoism, though they also liked Chinese culture. To a lesser degree, they also supported Dengism, but they had little interest in Western culture. Those with high incomes seemed to particularly like Dengism, which made them rich during reform, and discounted all other ideologies. Female respondents were more ideological than male respondents in each category. Understandably, the better educated were more pro-Western and less likely to identify with Marxism-Leninism and Maoism. The pre–Cultural Revolution generations still favored Marxism-Leninism and Maoism and showed strong support of Dengism. The youngest generation also showed support for Dengism but was noticeably more pro-Western and anti-traditional than the older generations. The Cultural Revolution generation showed less interest in Dengism than the older generations and the youngest generation, indicating that this group could be a direct victim of Deng's market reform policies.[6]

Overall, Marxism-Leninism and Maoism were still class-oriented ideologies that seemed to attract attention among party members, low-income groups, females, less educated people, and older generations, and in regions with a longer history of revolutionary and socialist influence. Dengism was more readily accepted by both regime supporters (together with Marxism-Leninism and Maoism) and the current or future beneficiaries of market reform (high earners and the young). Western culture had narrow appeal and was accepted only by residents in coastal cities and by young and better educated people who were often anti–traditional Chinese culture.

On one hand, the findings in this section do not suggest a political crisis in urban China. The government enjoys a considerable amount of legitimacy and support, and urban residents seemed to have become more politically conservative and anti-change. The lower social classes were more anti-Western than others and still adhered to revolutionary ideologies.

On the other hand, the picture is not bright all around. The government does not have absolute support and legitimacy. One-quarter of urban Chinese want to change the single-party system and launch democratization, and more than half of them demand more democratic rights and government accountability.

Conclusion

This chapter does not provide a definitive answer to the question of crisis versus stability. In any case, neither extreme fully explains the situation in China. Instead, the data reveal elements of both scenarios and raise the somewhat provocative possibility that the leadership is succeeding in deepening economic reforms while silencing public dissatisfaction, at least in the urban areas where and when the survey was conducted.

In terms of what the survey data show, the results tell a complex story. Economic satisfaction is mixed, with respondents showing more optimism in some areas than in others. In one key area, job opportunities, people felt worse off in 1999 than they did more than a decade earlier, reflecting the deepening of market reform in the post-Deng era.

Negative consequences also appeared in the area of dissatisfaction toward social polarization by manual laborers, retirees, and the unemployed. Moreover, this trend toward polarization will likely continue as China's entry into the World Trade Organization further polarizes the new "haves" and the losers in the state sector. With these potential social stresses in mind, certainly a good argument could be made for the crisis view of post-Deng China.

And yet it isn't that simple. Political dissatisfaction did not seem to be growing in parallel with economic dislocation. The findings show that political conservatism stayed at a high level even compared with the period just after the Tiananmen Square crackdown, when political repression was more blunt and obvious. By 1999, support for China's single-party structure was relatively high. Neither Western-style democracy nor indeed any kind of coherent ideology seemed to capture the respondents' aspirations. Most people, especially administrators and managers, seemed to instead want a pragmatic government capable of delivering economic results. The rewards of compliance and patriotism, which came with those bottom-line results, apparently convinced the leadership to stay the course of the reform program begun by Deng, as long as they could keep public dissatisfaction at a minimum.

In a departure from the situation a decade earlier, in 1999 respondents showed they were wary of the West. They recognized American economic achievement but stopped short of applauding its culture. Respondents showed a low level of acceptance of Western culture, and viewed America in particular as a threat. However, the better educated, the youngest generation, and people in more developed regions were still more pro-West.

Therefore, the picture has both a dark side and a bright side. The dark side depicts China in crisis. In this view the crisis had three causes: reform was pushed too fast for people to adapt, the Communist Party firmly clamped down on free political expression, and bottom-up public participation in key areas was discouraged. This heavy-handed control, mixed with negative reactions to economic change, would soon backfire and be transformed into serious political challenges to the current regime.

The study's findings, though, also revealed a positive side of the picture. The post-Deng leaders had shown their ability to selectively deepen reforms in some sectors, appealing to nationalism as they pushed through unprecedentedly harsh market reforms, while putting on the brakes in certain areas in order to limit the threat of social upheaval. Unlike in 1989, when the leaders were split in their approach to political reform, the post-Deng leaders had been for the most part publicly consistent in emphasizing the importance of maintaining political stability in order to realize further economic growth. The politically conservative urban population, with its strong sense of nationalism, may provide a more favorable environment for the current leadership to continue market reforms and authoritarian rule.

In this chapter I also address the broader debate raised in chapter 1 about whether public opinion follows its own course (Page and Shapiro 1992) or is affected by external events and government policy (Mayer 1992). On one hand, the Chinese survey respondents showed a strong sense of rationality in making their choices in life. Their priority was a guarantee of their economic well-being. Yet the findings in this chapter also show a strong effect of external events and government policy in three aspects. First, support for reform and perception of regime legitimacy are linked to the public perception of the government's reform policy. When government-led market reforms become too costly, public support for reform and for the government will decrease. This is an indication that public opinion is sensitive to government policy. Second, the social stratification and the winners and losers created by marketization further contribute to changing public opinion, making it less uniform and more polarized. This is an indication that public opinion responds to institutional change. Third, this chapter also shows the effects of demographics with respect to public opinion. Young, educated professionals show more acceptance of liberalization and democratization. This demographic effect is particularly strong in China, where the change of lifestyle is not only taking place among generations, but also happens within the same generation.

CHAPTER FOUR

Media Control and Public Opinion

The last chapter was a study of how public opinion reacted to the government's market reform policy. In this chapter I will discuss how the government attempts to shape public opinion through media control. It will focus on two issues: media production and media consumption. On the production side, the topics to be discussed include institutional control, media content censorship, and media market development. On the consumption side, the intended and unintended consequences of media consumption will be examined. Empirical evidence will be drawn from aggregate statistics, the ESRIC surveys, and the 1999 Six-City Survey.

Institutional Control

The Communist Party has firm organizational control over the Chinese media network. Commanded by the Political Bureau and its standing commit-

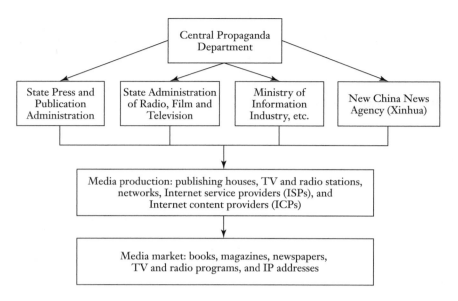

Figure 4.1   State control of media in China, 2003

tee, the party's Central Propaganda Department is the principal coordinator of the media. It does far more than censor material. Its primary function is to mobilize public opinion behind party policy and to promote the party's legitimacy and its official ideologies, including Marxism and nationalism (Dai 1999). It more often tells the media what to do than what not to do in its routine briefings with editorial decision makers (fig. 4.1).

The Central Propaganda Department works closely with the governmental organizations responsible for the three main forms of media. Print media are controlled by the State Press and Publication Administration. Broadcast media fall under the jurisdiction of the State Administration of Radio, Film and Television. The Ministry of Information Industry is the main owner of China's rapidly growing Internet industry. All major media production companies, including publishing houses, television and radio stations, Internet networks, and Internet service providers, are owned by the state but are profit driven at the same time. Media content is sometimes a result of negotiation and bargaining between profit-seeking media companies and the government's effort to maintain control.

China's media market is probably very difficult to control, given its size and the tremendous appetite for information. Foreign media products are easily available to Chinese consumers, such as IP addresses, shortwave radio programs, satellite television programs, and foreign print media. The government often fails to censor sensitive political issues. It has come to the realization that technology has made it impossible to keep foreign media products out of the reach of Chinese consumers. The only way to do it is to satisfy the domestic media market with China's own media products. This strategy requires a rapid increase in China's media production capacity and competitiveness.

The New China News Agency (Xinhua) is the party's principal information supplier. It provides necessary information for future policy making by collecting public opinion and demands and feedback about current party policy. It is also the party's official transmitter of information. Chinese news media are required to use Xinhua as the only news source, thereby creating a monopoly for domestic news service.

By 2004, the flow of Internet information was controlled by the state through its ownership of the eight Internet networks. Of these, CHINA-NET (China Net [Zhongguo Gongyong Jisuanji Hulianwang]), UNINET (China Unicom [Zhongguo Liantong Hulianwang]), and CMNET (China Mobil [Zhongguo Yidong Hulianwang]), all under the Ministry of Information Industry, controlled 77% of the bandwidth of China's international connectivity by June 30, 2004. CNCNET (Zhongguo Wangtong Gongyong Hulianwang) and CHINA169 (China 169 Broadband [Kuandai Zhongguo 169 Wang]), under China Netcom, controlled another 21% of the bandwidth. China Netcom is owned by a cluster of bureaucratic organizations, including the Shanghai municipal government; the Chinese Academy of Sciences; the State Administration of Radio, Films and Television; and the Ministry of Railways. The other three smaller networks—CERNET (China Education and Research Network [Zhongguo Jiaoyu he Keyan Jisuanji-wang]), under the Ministry of Education; CSTNET (China Science and Technology Network [Zhongguo Kejiwang]), under the Chinese Academy of Sciences; and, finally, CIETNET (China International Economy and Trade Net [Zhongguo Guoji Jingji Maoyi Hulianwang]), under the Ministry of Foreign Trade and Economic Cooperation—shared the remaining 2% of

China's international Internet connections as of June 30, 2003. Two other networks, CSNET (China Sat [Zhongguo Weixing Jituan Hulianwang]) and the military-controlled China CGWNET (Great Wall Net [Zhongguo Changcheng Hulianwang]), are under construction (China Internet Network Information Center 2004). By controlling these arteries of information flow between China and the world, the government attempts to screen, filter, and intercept incoming and outgoing materials that are viewed as a threat to national security and other illegal and pornographic content.

Censorship

Although it is becoming increasingly difficult to do so, the party attempts to censor any news or discussion that is considered a threat to regime legitimacy, political stability, or national image. China is currently described by Western human rights groups as having one of the worst records for media freedom. For example, using the legal environment and political and economic controls as measures of media freedom, the 2004 Freedom of Press Report gave 20 points out of 100 to China, 33 to Russia, 59 to India, 77 to Taiwan, and 87 to the United States (Denmark, Iceland, and Sweden were given 92, the highest score; see Karlekar 2004). Using an index of the amount of freedom that journalists and the media have in each country and the efforts governments made to uphold freedom of the press, Reporters without Borders ranked China 161st in its sample of 166 countries. Only Eritrea, Laos, Burma, Cuba, and North Korea were rated worse than China (Reporters without Borders 2003a). The annual U.S. Department of State Country Report on Human Rights Practices discusses China's media censorship in detail. The 2003 report is filled with detailed examples of government censorship, including a temporary ban on foreign and Chinese print and broadcast media. According to the report, in 2002 the Chinese government blocked up to fifty thousand Internet Web sites and detained thirty-six journalists, including fourteen Internet journalists (U.S. Department of State 2003).

Media content censorship is also reflected in the scope within which certain issues can and cannot be discussed. Certain topics are never reported in the current Chinese media, such as urban protests and worker strikes. More often, issues can be covered but only within the officially defined framework. The 1989 Tiananmen Square incident can be mentioned, but no justification for the protests leading to the crackdown is allowed. The Falun Gong religious movement can be only discussed as a harmful cult. Foreign criticism of China is never reported unless such criticism is put in a negative context, such as portraying U.S. human rights criticism as interfering with China's internal affairs. Although ethnic identity is recognized, ethnic independence must be described as separatism. Taiwan's social and economic life is often covered, but Taiwan independence (*taidu*) must also be labeled separatism. Reporting local corruption is allowed, but it can only touch local officials, not central government leaders. Local elections, the rule of law, and economic rights are openly discussed and praised, but no open criticism of the Communist Party's leadership is tolerated. Multiparty competition is considered a taboo topic. The 2003 U.S. invasion of Iraq was widely covered in reports that were implicitly critical of the United States, but no open criticism was allowed in the media because the Chinese government did not want to annoy the United States. The North Korea nuclear conflict in 2003 was rarely mentioned in the Chinese media because China was still officially friends with the North and did not want to create negative publicity about North Korea. The SARS epidemic in 2003 could only be discussed in the framework of national interest, or from the angle of the government's success in detecting the virus. No open criticism of the government's initial effort to hide the extent of SARS was allowed (Reporters without Borders 2003b).[1]

Yet beginning in the late 1970s, a gradual loosening of control has been just as noticeable as censorship (FlorCruz 1999). Now, many previously sensitive topics appear in the media, such as police brutality, human rights, the rule of law (formerly rule of the party), and collective bargaining by trade unions. In the official language, the definition of the 1989 urban protests quietly changed from "riot" to "incident." Religious beliefs, once described as "spiritual opium," are now openly tolerated so long as religious organizations accept the party's leadership. Crimes, police brutality, economic disputes, unethical business practices, petty corruption cases, consumer complaints, legal issues, family, marriage, and divorce have become the most popular media materials. Live coverage of news events is increasing primarily because it symbolizes technological sophistication and implies that Chinese broadcasts are as authoritative as Western ones—but it also makes censorship more difficult.

In recent years, the media have occasionally challenged the party's top-down control. Controversial cases include newspapers and magazines such as the *Southern Weekend* (*Nanfang zhoumo*), published in Guangzhou; *Democracy and Rule of Law* (*Minzhu yufazhi*); *Science and Technology Herald* (*Keji daobao*); *Reader's Digest* (*Dushu*); and *Focal Point* (*Jiaodian fangtan*), a popular CCTV program in the 1990s. Criticism of the government in these media forums ranges from covering high-level corruption cases to questioning the credibility and legitimacy of government policy. Bold editors and reporters keep emerging, even under the government's censorship. Even the officially controlled CCTV is openly discussing its "supervisory" role in government decision making (Zhan and Zhao 2003), as Chinese media grow into a watchdog role.

Media Growth and Marketization

As a result of loosening control while commercial growth is promoted, the Chinese media are going through a revolution. Technological advances and a rapid increase of living standards have created an enormous increase in the media market. Within a period of twenty-three years, from 1979 to 2002, the numbers of magazine titles increased by more than 871%. In the same period of time, the numbers of book titles and newspaper titles increased by 1040% and 1049%, respectively (fig. 4.2). China's media growth during this period almost matched that of societies that had undergone democratization and multiparty elections. Compared to the case of Taiwan, which underwent democratization in the mid-1980s, the growth of newspaper titles in China was almost the same as in Taiwan prior to 1997. The growth in new books and new magazines was much faster in China than in Taiwan (fig. 4.2). It is interesting that this growth took place in China despite single-party rule and its control of the media.

The growth of print media is also easy to see from casual observation on the street. In the late 1970s and early 1980s, one would only find half a dozen newspapers and magazines at a newsstand. Today, one can be easily overwhelmed by fifty or sixty different newspapers and magazines at a newsstand,

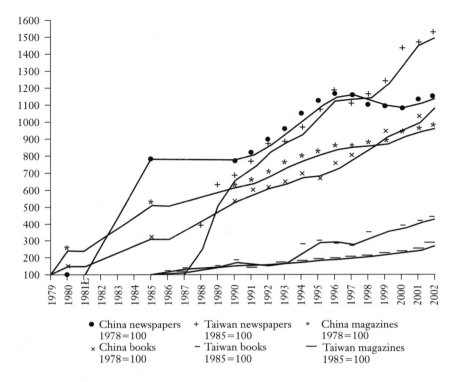

Figure 4.2   Media growth in China, 1979–2002, and Taiwan, 1985–2002 (%)

SOURCES: National Bureau of Statistics of China 2003, *China Statistical Abstract*, Beijing: China Statistics Press, 18; Directorate General of Budget, Accounting and Statistics, Executive Yuan, Republic of China, *Statistical Yearbook of the Republic of China 2003*, table 59, p. 103.

NOTE: Similarly, compared with 1978, the number of radio and TV stations in China increased 229% and 1053% respectively in 2002, while the population only increased 33% (results not shown).

ranging from the official party paper, *People's Daily*, to popular local newspapers and tabloids of movie stars and pop singers.

The low cost of cable subscription and a wide selection of channels make watching television far more enjoyable than before. For example, for an equivalent of $2 a month for a cable subscription, a Beijing household can receive over fifty television channels, with a dozen channels for China Central Television alone, more than ten local Beijing channels, and more than thirty provincial satellite channels. In 2003, a twenty-four-hour news channel, CCTVNews, was launched, indicating the growing demand for news delivered around the clock.

Although the Internet became known to the average Chinese household only in the mid-1990s, it has grown faster than any other media form. From 1997 to 2004, the bandwidth of international connections, a measure of information flow between China and other countries, increased from 25 Mbps in 1997 to 53,941 Mbps in 2004. The number of Internet networks increased from four in 1997 to ten in 2004. World Wide Web addresses grew from about 1500 in 1997 to 626,600 as of June 2004 (China Internet Network Information Center 2004). Private Internet service providers (ISPs) are allowed, although only official news sources can be quoted and no private reports can be linked or published (Harwit and Clark 2001).

Growth in the media sector is also accompanied by privatization and marketization. One of the most important reasons for this growth is the realization that media are an industry and can generate a lot of revenue. The media's profit orientation results in competition among media companies for audience, program diversification, and compromise between political and commercial interests (Donald, Keane, and Hong 2002). In the state-owned media, government subsidies are declining, and production companies are being told to look toward the market for their future survival and growth. In addition to pleasing their bureaucratic supervisors, the media have to actively cultivate their relationship with advertisers (Redl and Simons 2002). The end result is that the need for economic survival increasingly influences news content in the media.

China's entry into the World Trade Organization in 2001 further increased the challenge to traditional methods of control. As a condition of becoming a member of the WTO, China had to open its media market to outside competition (Keane and Donald 2002). China desperately needs to build a technologically sophisticated and economically efficient media sector in order to face foreign competition. These developments suggest further decentralization and marketization will be seen ahead.

Finally, the availability of personal computers and the Internet has essentially privatized Internet content production. In theory, anyone can voice any opinion to the public through the Internet. Even if the government still censors the Internet, this form of privatization has fundamentally shifted content providers' priorities from pleasing their bureaucratic supervisors to pleasing their subscribers.

The current drive in China to modernize the information infrastructure will promote further media growth and create an information explosion. A more informed public will prove more difficult to keep in the dark, and highly responsive media try to meet the consuming public's demands. New technology will create yet more challenges to the government's ability to control the flow of information. The bureaucratic turf war over the control of the Internet (Harwit and Clark 2001; Harrison 2002; Redl and Simons 2002) enhances competition and improves services to attract users, which makes the control from the center more fragmented (Lieberthal and Oksenberg 1988; Lieberthal 1995).

In the near future, both diversification and censorship are likely to continue, with the result that media diversification will put more pressure on censorship. In response to this challenge, the Chinese government has not only intensified censorship, but has also actively attempted to use the media to rally public support by requiring them to carry the official Xinhua news.

Media Consumption

So far I have been describing the institutional environment of the media sector, where growth, marketization, mobilization, and censorship coexist. Now it is time to examine how media consumers react to this environment of conflicting trends.

The first question is media use. If one believes in the negative impact of control and censorship, increased control and censorship should lead to a decrease in media consumption. By contrast, if one believes in the positive consequence of marketization, there should be an increase in media consumption. The available evidence clearly supports the positive influence of market reform on media consumption. The number of Internet users jumped dramatically, increasing more than a hundredfold times from 620,000 in October 1997, to 87 million in June 2004 (China Internet Network Information Center 2004), surpassing Japan (66 million) and ranking second in the world after the United States (201 million, http://www.internetworldstats.com/top20.htm [accessed March 22, 2005]). In urban China, use of other media forms was also on the rise. For example, in the ESRIC surveys and in the 1999 Six-City Survey, daily use of newspapers, television, radio, and magazines were shown to be on the rise. When asked if the respondent used any of the media forms (television, radio, newspapers, or magazines) almost every day, 68% said yes in May 1987, compared with 72% in October 1988, 76% in the 1992 Urban Survey, and 93% in the 1999 Six-City Survey. In that survey, 83% of the 1820 respondents watched television, 57% read newspapers, 29% listened to radio broadcasts, and 10% read magazines almost every day (weighted raw data). In short, intensified state media censorship did not seem to stop public media access from approaching near universality in urban China.

Yet media consumption per se does not mean people grant credibility to the media. In 1999 only 11% of those respondents who would choose to voice their opinion would do so through the media. The majority of respondents preferred instead to go through workplace supervisors, government offices, and other channels (see chap. 6). The low level of media efficacy seems to support the censorship argument. Chinese urban residents did not give much credibility to the media. Admittedly, this is an extreme measure of media efficacy, since the respondents were forced to pick from a list of channels for voicing opinions.

In the seven ESRIC surveys conducted in forty cities between May 1987 and November 1991, respondents were asked about their satisfaction with the objectivity of news reports. Satisfaction began at a high of 53% in May 1987, fell slightly to 49% in October 1987 and 47% in May 1988, dropped significantly to 38% in October 1988, and hit bottom at 20% in May 1989 during the Tiananmen protests. In October of the same year it gradually climbed back to 29%, reaching 37% in November 1991 (weighted raw data, ESRIC surveys). Unfortunately, the 1999 survey did not include questions related to media satisfaction. In the 1990s and into the first few years of the twenty-first century, preliminary evidence indicated that media satisfaction further increased, thanks to expansion of the scope of news coverage and the improved quality of broadcast programming.[2] Once again, the gradual rise of public confidence in the Chinese media suggests that the positive impact of market reform outweighs the negative consequence of government censorship.

Another measure of media consumption is content preference. A Beijing taxi driver once told me that the reason people in China were more interested in international news than in domestic news was that the former was more objective. The growing popularity of foreign media icons seems to

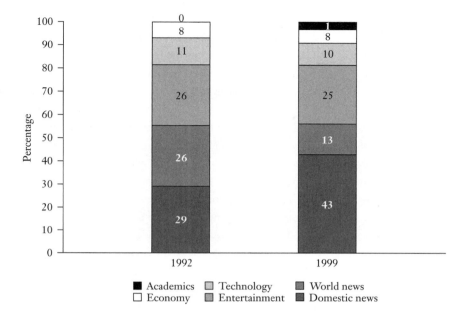

Figure 4.3 Media content preference, 1992–99 (%)
SOURCES: 1992 Urban Social Survey; 1999 Six-City Survey.
NOTE: Percentages are weighted. For 1999, "entertainment" includes lifestyle and "technology" includes special reports.

confirm this view. However, survey results show a reverse shift from the early 1990s to the late 1990s. Interest in domestic news increased, and interest in international news decreased. When asked what was the most interesting content among domestic news, world news, entertainment, technology, the economy, and academics, 29% of the respondents in 1992 and 43% of the respondents in 1999 preferred domestic news, although 26% in 1992 and only 13% in 1999 preferred international news (fig. 4.3). Overall, public interest in domestic news was higher than commonly expected in 1999.

More reporting about real problems is attracting audiences. Expanded domestic coverage of growing social and economic conflict during market reform, including unemployment, domestic violence and other crimes, and economic and legal disputes, is responsible for increased interest in domestic news. One problem with the increased domestic interest is the timing of the 1999 survey, which was conducted around the October 1 celebration of the fiftieth anniversary of the People's Republic. It could be a snapshot of momentary focus on media during a time when Chinese typically watch much more eagerly for clues about the nation's future direction and politics. Yet this domestic focus has not lost its momentum since then, and there have been plenty of domestic events that have caught the public attention, such as China's successful bid for the 2008 Olympics, China's WTO membership, the construction of the Three Gorges Dam, and the successful launch of China's first manned space capsule. Expanded coverage of these events and improved programming are probably responsible for the increased interest in domestic news.

The final aspect of media consumption I will discuss here is accessibility by different social and economic groups. In a market environment, media consumption is affected by one's socioeconomic status. Higher status means more resources and therefore access to the media market. In the state-controlled media sector in China, the need for political control and mobilization creates a gap based on political rather than on socioeconomic status.

With the 1992 and 1999 surveys, we can examine the impact that political and social factors have on media consumption. Specifically, we will look at the impact of party membership, income, gender, education, occupation, age, and geographic location. In 1992 media consumption was measured by the respondent's use of any form of media during the previous week, including television, radio, newspapers, and magazines. None is coded 0, 1–2 times as 1, 3–4 times as 2, and almost every day as 3. This 0–3 scale is divided by 3 in order to convert it into a 0–1 scale. In the 1999 survey, there was information about each of the four types of media. The four 0–3 variables are combined with a minimum value of 0 (did not use any media form) to a maximum of 12 (used all four types of media daily). The 0–12 scale is divided by 12, and the resulting 0–1 scale can be used to compare 1999 with 1992 media consumption.

Party member and female are coded as 1 and non-member and male are coded as 0. In both the 1992 and the 1999 surveys, per capita family income is coded on a scale of 0 to 10 based on income categories. This scale is divided by 10 in order to create a 0–1 income variable for both years. Education is measured by years in school, ranging from 0 to 18 in 1992 and 0 to 19 in 1999. Administrators and managers are compared with other occupations. Any difference between this elite occupational group and non-elite groups will indicate an occupation-based bias in media consumption. Age groups are divided according to the year the respondent turned twenty, resulting in five groups: the pre-socialist generation (pre-1949), the socialist generation (1949–65), the Cultural Revolution generation (1967–76), the reform generation (1977–84), and the post-1984 post-reform generation (post-1984). Finally, the same cities are compared in both years, including Shanghai, Shenyang, Guangzhou (1999 only), Wuhan, Chongqing (1999 only), Chengdu (1992 only), and Xian. Shanghai and Guangzhou are more developed coastal cities. Shenyang is a rust-belt city whose economy has traditionally been based on heavy industry. Wuhan, Chongqing, Chengdu, and Xian are inland cities and are less developed than Shanghai and Guangzhou.

The above factors are included in a multivariate Ordinary Least Square (OLS) regression analysis. In 1999 political status had a statistically significant effect on media consumption, as party members were more likely to be daily media consumers than non-members. Socioeconomic status also played a role in media consumption: higher earners, males, and more educated respondents, as well as the elite occupation groups of administrators and managers, all had more potential to be daily users of media than did low earners, females, the less educated, and the other occupation groups.

The gap was bigger in 1999 than in 1992. For example, every ten years of education would increase media consumption by 10% in 1992, but that increase doubled to 20% by 1999. If minimum education was none and maximum education was eighteen years, media consumption among the best-educated group was 18% higher than the least-educated group in 1992 but 38% higher in 1999. In other words, the impact of education in media consumption doubled from 1992 to 1999. The regional gap was also growing. In 1992 there were no statistically significant differences among the surveyed cities. In 1999, by contrast, the more developed coastal cities of Shanghai and Guangzhou, together with the industrial city of Shenyang, showed higher media consumption rates than the inland cities. In 1992 the youngest age group (post-1984) was the least likely to use media daily. In 1999 this age group showed no significant difference from the other groups, an indication that more youths consumed media in 1999 than in 1992. These findings show that in addition to the traditional political stratification in media consumption, market forces have widened the socioeconomic gap in media consumption and increased its attractiveness for young people. In this respect, Chinese media consumption shows similarities with other market societies (fig. 4.4).

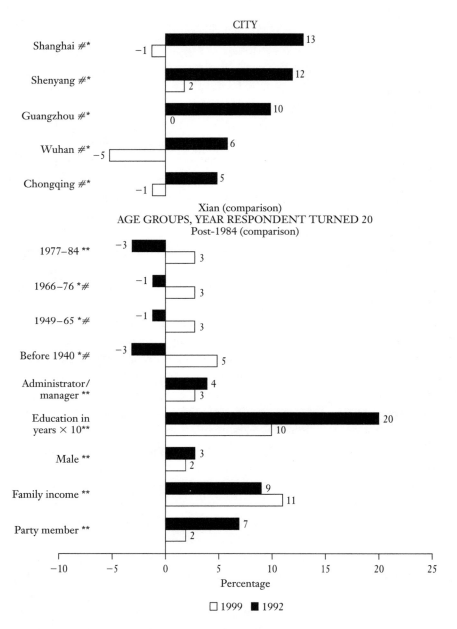

Figure 4.4 Media consumption by social status and geographic location, 1992 and 1999 (OLS)

SOURCES: 1992 Urban Social Survey; 1999 Urban Social Survey.

NOTE: For 1992, all 40 cities were included in the OLS analysis, but only the comparable ones are shown. All variables in the equation are transformed into a 0–1 scale except for education in years.

**: Both 1992 and 1999 coefficients are statistically significant at $p \leq .05$.

#*: Only the 1999 coefficient is statistically significant at $p \leq .05$.

*#: Only the 1992 coefficient is statistically significant at $p \leq .05$.

In sum, market reform brought both benefits and deficits to media consumption, the benefits being increased competition, improved quality, and diversity, while at the same time, increasing gaps in media consumption were based on political and social status.

Intended and Unintended Consequences of Media Consumption

In this final section, I will show how media consumption shapes public opinion in China. Depending on whether one believes in control and censorship or diversification, media can have either negative (brainwashing) or positive (diversification) effects on public opinion. Although in general media control will lead to alienation and apathy, media diversification will generate liberal values.

The dominant view among Western governments, journalists, and scholars on the Chinese media focuses on control. According to this view, by controlling the media, the Chinese government systematically shapes, manipulates, and censors public opinion (Zhu 1990; Chen and Shi 2001; Karlekar 2003; U.S. Department of State 2003). Using a 1993–94 national survey, Chen and Shi (2001) found a negative effect of media consumption on regime support. In their study, regime support is an index (1–4) of trust in government officials, in government decisions, in China's political system, and in the government itself. Media consumption is an index (0–9) of the frequency of weekly media use, including television, newspapers, and radio. In a multivariate analysis controlling for the effects of getting information through the grapevine, life satisfaction, government responsiveness, education, income, gender, age, and party membership, Chen and Shi found that in 1993 and 1994 China's most frequent media users (media index = 9, regression coefficient = $-.08$) expressed about 18% ($9 \times .08/4 \times 100$) less support for the government than someone who never used any media (media index = 0). Chen and Shi concluded that unlike previous studies that showed successful mobilization of the media, this time political control of the media led to alienation and distrust of the government. Given the rapid change of the media market in the late 1990s, therefore, it is necessary to revisit whether the media's role in political mobilization has changed over time.

An increasing number of studies have noted that media growth and marketization significantly softened media control and censorship. The explosion in the volume of information and the increased attention to audience preference have created a more informed and politically savvy public (Donald and Keane 2002; Keane and Donald 2002; Redl and Simons 2002). Media growth and particularly Internet growth promote public debate and facilitate issue-based communities similar to interest groups in Western-style democracies (Yang 2003). According to this view, media consumption should promote political activism, rather than alienation.

Thus, the debate centers on whether media consumption promotes political obedience or political activism. Using the information available in the 1999 survey, I will examine media consumption on a wider range of topics. To examine the consequences of political mobilization, it is necessary to discuss the effect media have on regime support, official ideology, and nationalism as an effort to rally public support. If the mobilization effort is successful, media consumption should promote support for the government, official ideology, and nationalism. As a counterexample, I will examine the media effect on pro-Western tendencies. If the campaign to promote official ideology and nationalism is successful, it follows that media consumption should decrease pro-Western tendencies.

To examine political alienation, it is necessary to look at the effect of media on political activism, political efficacy, and support for civic values. If media consumption creates alienation, one should expect that media consumption leads to less political efficacy and less support for civic values. Alienation itself also measures the degree of political activism, so that if media consumption results in alienation, it should also reduce political activism.

These seven concepts—regime support, official ideology, nationalism, pro-Western tendencies, political activism, political efficacy, and support for civic values—will be measured using information in the 1999 Six-City Survey. *Regime support* is measured by question E6: do you think the current single-party system should be changed? Possible responses were (o) should be changed, (1) is irrelevant if life is good, (2) no alternative so status quo, and (3) is very good and should continue. A high value indicates more support for the single-party political system. *Official ideology* is a factor index of the respondent's evaluation of Marxism-Leninism and Maoism. For both

Marxism-Leninism and Maoism, the respondent was asked to evaluate their importance in China's economic and social development (questions E7a, E7b, E7a_a, and E7a_b). The four variables are highly correlated and are thus combined in a factor analysis. The new factor index measures the respondent's support of the party's official ideology. *Nationalism* is a factor index of the respondent's assessment of China as the best model for its future economic (question B5a) and political development (question B6a). A high value means a more pro-China tendency. Similarly, *pro-Western tendencies* are a factor index of the respondent's assessment of the West as the best model for China's future economic (question B5a) and political development (question B6a). *Political activism* is measured by whether the respondent takes political action if dissatisfied and by whether the respondent makes suggestions at work. "Political action" is based on the respondent's answer to the question about likely action if the respondent is dissatisfied with social life (D6). Possible actions include (1) report to the government, (2) report to the media, (3) protest/petition, (4) other means, (5) complain, and (6) do nothing. Responses 1 through 4 are coded 1, and responses 5 and 6 are coded 0. "Making suggestions at work" is a continuous variable ranging from never (0), talking to co-workers (1), making suggestions only if asked to (2), taking initiative sometimes (3), and taking initiative often (4). For both political action and making suggestions at work, a high value indicates more political activism. *Political efficacy* is a factor index of the level of agreement with two statements: "people like us can affect social development as long as we often voice our opinions" (question C8_a) and "ordinary people can affect government decision making" (question C8_b). A high value of efficacy means more belief in popular influence on politics. Finally, *support for civic values* is a factor index combining the respondent's agreement with the following five statements: (1) "one should participate in public affairs" (question C8_c), (2) "government should not decide whether an opinion can be circulated" (question C8_d), (3) "government should not decide everything for the country" (question C8_e), (4) "social diversity will not lead to chaos" (question C8_g), and (5) "patriotism should not require supporting the current government" (question C8_h). A high value of the index indicates high support for liberal values.

All these variables, if not already on a 0–1 scale, are forced into a 0–1 scale. For example, the 0–3 regime support scale is divided by 3, and the 0–4 scale for making suggestions at work is divided by 4. Variables based on factor scores are also converted into 0–1 scales by adding the minimum value to the factor score and dividing the result by the sum of the minimum and maximum values. For example, if the factor index for pro-Western tendencies has a minimum value of −1.98 and a maximum value of 1.47, the 0–1 scale is created by (pro-West factor score + 1.98)/(1.98 + 1.47). The new variable should vary between 0 and 1. Media consumption is the same factor index converted into a 0–1 scale as that used in figure 4.4. The regression analysis will use each of these eight variables as the dependent variable and media consumption as the independent variable. In order to isolate the media effect, other factors will be controlled for, including life satisfaction, party membership, family income, gender, education, age, city, and occupation.[3] The 1992 Urban Survey has identical questions on political action, making suggestions at work, and political efficacy. These items are also included in the analysis to show any change from 1992 to 1999.

The regression results (fig. 4.5; see also appendices C and D) show interesting parallel trends in mobilization and liberalization. Some results show the media mobilized support for the state. Compared with a non-consumer (media consumption = 0), the most frequent media consumer (media consumption = 1) in China was about 16% more supportive of the single-party system, about 6% more nationalistic, and about 5% more supportive of Marxism-Leninism and Maoism. These findings suggest a mobilization effect.

Yet there is also evidence that media consumption worked the other way and promoted liberalization. Again, compared with a non-consumer, the most frequent media consumer was about 14% more likely to make suggestions at work, was 13% more likely to take action if dissatisfied, had about 5% more efficacy, and expressed 4% more support for civic values. Although media consumption increased support for the official ideology by 5%, it also encouraged pro-Western tendencies by about 7%. Compared with 1992, seven years later, media consumption played an increased role in promoting both political activism and efficacy. In 1992 the impact of media on workplace participation (making suggestions at work) was strongly negative (−56%), while media consumption did not lead to more efficacy (−3%, not significant). On one hand, media impact on taking political action dropped

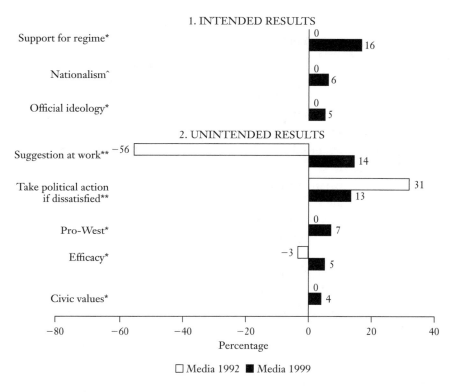

Figure 4.5 Effect of media on mobilization and liberalization, 1992 and 1999 (OLS)

SOURCES: 1999 Six-City Survey; 1992 Urban Social Survey.

NOTE: Additional independent variables (see appendices C and D) include life satisfaction, party membership, family income, gender, education, age, city, and occupation. City and occupation do not show any significant effect and are not included in the equation for official ideology. Life satisfaction for 1992 is a 0–1 index of satisfaction with family, career, and income (v46, v105, and v106). For 1999, life satisfaction is an index of 16 items, including wealth, income opportunity, housing, health, family, friends, education, crime control, job opportunity, economic freedom, environment, religious freedom, career success, and China's reputation in the world (b3_a–b3_m, b3_p).

*: $p \leq .10$ in 1999.
**: Coefficients for both 1992 and 1999 are statistically significant at $p \leq 1$.
^: $p \leq .12$.

from 31% in 1992 to 13% in 1999. On the other hand, media impact on making suggestions at work increased from −56% in 1992 to 14% in 1999. This contrast indicates a possible shift of media emphasis from public political action to workplace co-option. The media served to promote political stability by discouraging open challenge to the regime and encouraging intra-system participation.

The 1992 findings partially confirm what Chen and Shi (2001) found about how media propaganda can alienate the public. In 1999 the role of media became more visible. It became more effective at political mobilization and promoting support for the regime. But in this process, increased media consumption also had the unintended consequence of political liberalization. Thus far, control and liberalization do not seem to be a zero-sum game. The existence of one does not require the elimination of the other. This balance is possible owing to the profit motive: it keeps control and mobilization in check because in excess, these elements may cause a loss of audience and therefore money. Similarly, media's role in liberalization is tolerated because it may increase audience interest. The result is further diversification.

The growth of the Internet further encouraged its users to express different opinions. For example, at the Fourth Plenum of the Sixteenth Party Congress in September 2004, the party passed the Central Committee Decision on the Enhancement of the Party's Governance Capability. Internet chat room reaction to this document ranged from criticism of the party's ideological monopoly and the lack of democracy to diehard support of the party's leadership; opinion ranged widely between these two extremes (table 4.1).

In addition to providing a forum for a wide range of opinions, the significance of Internet chat rooms lies also in their ability to create a direct dialogue between official policy and public opinion. In the past, the state did not have to publicize public opinions collected through state-controlled courts, ombudsman's offices, and government-administered public opinion polls. The open forum in the Internet chat rooms made public opinion available to all 87 million Chinese Internet users and their friends and family members, as well as all the Chinese-speaking Internet users in the world. The state can no longer claim unified public support by denying the existence of different opinions. The Internet has become an important new link between the state and society.

In the future, maintaining the balance between political mobilization and tolerance in the media will continue to encourage the bifurcation between political conservatism and liberalization in public opinion. So long as the government feels secure enough to continue this bifurcation, the current trend toward media reform will result in a healthy diversification of public opinion.

TABLE 4.1

Internet chat room reaction to the Decision on the Enhancement of the Party's Governance Capability, passed at the Fourth Plenum of the Sixteenth Party Congress, September 2004

"What we need more are democracy and the rule of law."

"The key is to separate the People's Congress from the Party, establish an effective system of social supervision. Otherwise, it's empty talk."

"Every one must be equal in front of the law."

"The phrase 'adherence to the leading position of Marxism in the ideological sphere' reminds me of religion in medieval Europe."

"The key to governance is to implement democratic elections in the party."

"The speed of the train depends on the engine car."

"That's train, not cars. Cars run by themselves. Today is no longer the train era. It is the age of cars."

"There are many capable people. Do you dare to hire them?"

"Fighting against corruption can solve all other problems in China."

"It is also important to solve the problems of creating jobs, unemployment, layoffs and social security."

"As long as most people can be the owners of their own houses in 5 years. . . ."

"Deed, not empty words, please."

"I hope in one day, students don't have to worry about tuitions, patients don't have to worry about medical cost, everyone will have the right to work and the working people will feel happy from their heart."

"Why was Mao Zedong able to control corruption?"

"The officials' moral standards were higher in Mao's time than today."

"Because Mao Zedong implemented democracy and mobilized the masses to fight against corruption. . . . Corruption can be completely wiped out in a month if democracy is implemented. It is that simple!"

"Because Mao Zedong said that governing the country was to govern bureaucrats and eliminate the gap between the rich and the poor."

"The Decision thoroughly carried out the party's baseline of resolutely developing the economy, promoting reform and opening and firmly adhering to the 4 cardinal principles for a hundred years. It broke the American imperialist dream of peaceful evolution among China's 4th generation leaders. The key is to purge the corrupt elements from the party and the state, prevent China's Gorbachevs and Yeltsins from gaining political power, prevent pro-American and pro-Japanese forces from entering the key state and military organizations, and prevent those treacherous dogs from gaining influence."

SOURCES: http://www.xinhuanet.com/newscenter/zht0919/index.htm (accessed April 17, 2005); http://comment.news.sohu.com/comment/topic.jsp?id=222247462 (accessed April 17, 2005).

Conclusion

This chapter has shown a funnel-shaped media environment, with a narrow top and a bell-shaped bottom (see chap. 1). Political control and censorship are in the firm hands of the party and the state in China. The party has gone even further than censorship, actively using media to mobilize regime support. As a result, at least in large cities, the level of media accessibility was high, although media efficacy grew at a slower pace in the 1990s. Meanwhile, market competition has been introduced into media production, which has brought both positive and negative consequences. On the positive side, it has promoted diversity, the desire for media credibility, and political liberalization. On the negative side, it has created a social gap, based on status and wealth, between those who can access media and those who cannot.

In the long run, the question is whether media freedom depends on China's transition to democracy. It is easy to link the lack of media freedom with China's undemocratic political environment. As long as single-party media control exists, the media will never be free. In the meantime, the inverse argument is no more convincing, as democracy by itself will not guarantee media freedom. For example, manipulation by the elite of public opinion through the media and the media's self-censorship are well documented in studies based on Western democracies (Margolis and Mauser 1989; Goldberg 2002, 2003; Greenwald 2004). China's political system is undeniably a factor that contributes to a form of media control that is more extreme than in the West. Yet it is evident that if control by elites and self-censorship also exist in democracies, changing the political system will not eliminate the problem entirely. In addition to the institutional barrier, the lack of consistency and diversity is also a result of China's lack of technological means to absorb the modern information explosion and keep pace with the managerial know-how of modern media. Yet Chinese media are rapidly becoming more sophisticated, and in some cases media producers go out of their way to receive training and consultation from their international peers. This is a learning process that will improve media performance even under the current regime.

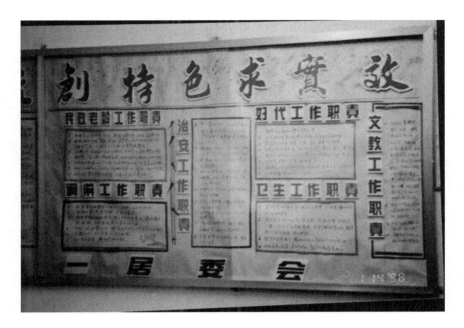

A wall display of its six functions (elder care, marriage counseling, public safety, public health, women's issues, and culture and education) in a Shanghai residential council in 1998. Other functions of the residential council include household registration and the implementation of government policies, such as family planning and the anti–Falun Gong campaign. In recent years, employees of the residential councils have been younger and more educated. Some of them are laid-off workers from state-owned enterprises. The most common place to draw an urban sample begins in residential councils where household registration records are kept. By Wenfang Tang.

Local survey team members checking household registration records with the director of a Muslim residential council in Xian. October 1999. By Wenfang Tang.

Announcement: A training session for the 1999 urban survey will be held at 7:00 P.M. in the Office of the Student Union. Don't miss it!" Northwestern University, Xian, October 1999. By Wenfang Tang.

A project manager (standing) conducting an interviewer training session. Wuhan University, October 1999. By Wenfang Tang.

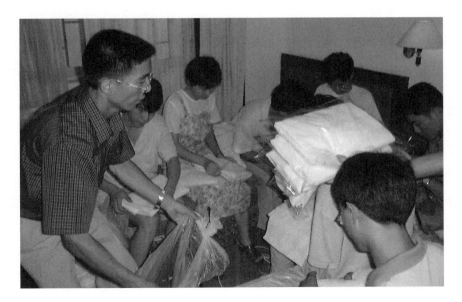

A student leader distributing to the trained student interviewers of Wuhan University the gifts for each interviewee, in this case a tablecloth. August 1999. By Wenfang Tang.

A typical Shanghai residential building where the survey interviews were conducted. August 1999. By Wenfang Tang.

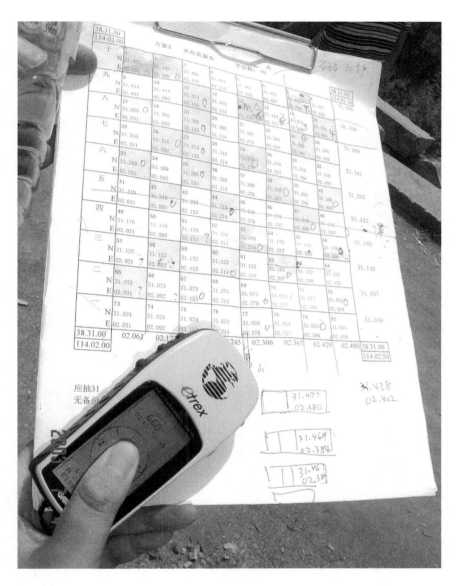

Spatial sampling: (1) Randomly selected townships and city districts are divided into a number of 50 × 50 m squares using GPS. (2) A predetermined number of squares is randomly chosen. (3) A predetermined number of households is randomly selected from each square. (4) Finally, an individual is randomly selected from each household. By Wenfang Tang.

One sample township was hidden in the Taihang Mountains in Lingshou county, Hebei province. A communist base area during the anti-Japanese invasion, Lingshou is one of the poorest counties in the country to receive government subsidies. By Wenfang Tang.

The first household we located in the first randomly selected square, in Lingshou County, Hebei province, 2003. By Wenfang Tang.

All household addresses in each randomly selected spatial square are recorded. Lingshou, 2003. By Wenfang Tang.

We never knew what we would find until we got there. Sometimes the spatial square landed in an open field. Huairou, Beijing, 2003. By Wenfang Tang.

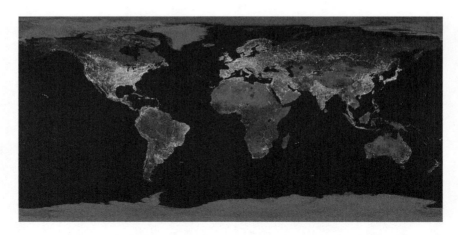

World map with earth lights at http://earthobservatory.nasa.gov/Newsroom/
NewImages/Images/earth_lights_lrg.jpg (accessed March 24, 2005). Data courtesy
Marc Imhoff, the Goddard Space Flight Center (GSFC), National Aeronautics
and Space Administration (NASA), and Christopher Elvidge of the National Geo-
physical Data Center (NGDC), National Oceanic and Atmospheric Administration
(NOAA). Image by Craig Mayhew and Robert Simmon, the Goddard Space Flight
Center, NASA.

CHAPTER FIVE

Interpersonal Trust and Sociopolitical Change

Since the mid-1980s, rapid economic change has fundamentally transformed people's lifestyles and aspirations. In urban China, traditional single-story housing (*pingfang*) used to create closely knit neighborhood communities that were enhanced by the residential councils and neighborhood committees under local governments. Urban residents once knew everything about their neighbors. Now these traditional communities are quickly disappearing, torn down as apartment high-rises shoot up from the rubble of the old neighborhoods. An increasing number of urban Chinese are moving into private apartments, an environment largely out of reach of the neighborhood committees and therefore conducive to more privacy. This and other changes in lifestyle may affect interpersonal relations. This chapter focuses on public opinion about a specific aspect of those relations: interpersonal trust. I will compare interpersonal trust in China and other societies, and in the process look at how interpersonal trust is affected by culture, socialist legacies, and marketization. I will then discuss whether interpersonal trust promotes democracy in general and in China particularly.

The Social Capital Theory and the China Exception

In the 1990s the theory of social capital drew attention to the study of the conditions of democratization. Under this theory, part of the social infrastructure presumed to be necessary for democracy includes interpersonal trust. In their influential study of Italian communities, Putnam, Leonardi, and Nanetti (1993) found over time and in different regions that membership in non-family-based associations led to increased social capital based on interpersonal trust, which promoted viable democratic institutions. The social capital theory has also been applied to other societies in Europe (Perez-Diaz 1994), the United States (Putnam 1995), and Africa (Gyimah-Boadi 1996). Inglehart (1999) revitalized the early studies of civil culture and democracy (i.e., Almond and Verba 1963) by showing the positive effect that interpersonal trust has on the successful functioning of democratic institutions.

One conclusion that comes out of social capital theory is that non-family associational membership—in other words, civil groups—generate interpersonal trust, which promotes democratic institutions. In China, the lack of such independent civil groups in a corporatist state would presumably result in less interpersonal trust, which may be a reason for China's lack of democracy.

Yet empirical studies have generated some counterintuitive findings that challenge these assumptions. For example, in the 2000 World Values Survey, when citizens in different countries were asked whether they thought most people could be trusted, China showed one of the highest levels of trust (fig. 5.1).

One immediately wants to know whether the high level of trust in China is due to a mistranslation of the World Value Survey question. This is nonetheless unlikely because trust is a fairly simple concept (*xinren*) which even an uneducated person would understand. The World Value Survey results are further confirmed by other surveys independently conducted in China. For example, the 1992 ESRIC 40-City Survey and the 1999 Six-City Survey reported 60% and 69% trust rates, respectively, while the 1990 World Value

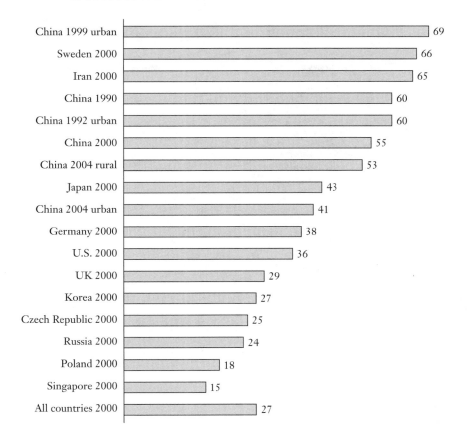

Figure 5.1   Interpersonal trust: an international comparison (%)
sources: 1990 World Values Survey (including China); 2000 World Values Survey (including China); 1992 Urban Social Survey; 1999 Six-City Survey; Research Center for Contemporary China 2004.
note: The percentages are based on the "yes" answer to the question "Do you think most people can be trusted?" All percentages are weighted.

Survey in China reported a similar rate of 60% (fig. 5.1). The 2004 Values and Ethics Survey by the Research Center for Contemporary China at Peking University also reported a high level of trust among its rural respondents, although the urban respondents showed a decline in trust (Research Center for Contemporary China 2004). The consistent findings in different surveys suggest that the high level of trust is at least not accidental, since surveys independently conducted in China yielded similar results.

The results raise the question of whether empirical findings show any link

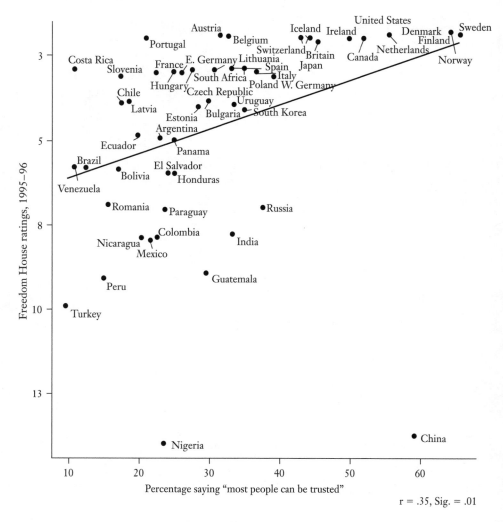

Figure 5.2   Scatterplot of interpersonal trust, 1990–96, and level of democracy, 1996
SOURCE: Seligson 2002, 278.

between trust and democracy in China. When the levels of trust in different countries are examined against the Freedom House ratings of political rights and civil liberties (http://www.freedomhouse.org/research/index
.htm [accessed March 22, 2005]), a seemingly strong and positive relationship is found between trust and freedom. The biggest outlier is China, where
a high level of trust coexists with a low level of freedom (fig. 5.2; Seligson

2002). This finding is both expected and surprising. It is expected in the sense that the freedom ratings are consistent with the popular impression that China lacks democracy. But it is surprising in the sense that trust in China does not behave according to social capital theory, namely, promoting democracy.

The China exception raises two questions to be explored. First, what does trust mean to the Chinese? Identifying the sources of trust makes it easier to understand the difference between China and other societies in how trust is perceived. The second question is what trust leads to in China. Specifically, I will examine the impact of trust on other democratic values. The social capital theory assumes that trust plays an important role in the development of democratic institutions. Yet the link between trust and democratic institutions is spurious unless we can clearly show how trust promotes democracy. For example, Seligson (2002) showed that trust promoted freedom only in a small group of industrial democracies and that there was no clear relationship between trust and democracy in Latin American countries. In China, trust shows no relationship to freedom. But we don't know whether that trust promotes other democratic values and behavior, such as tolerance, autonomy, and political activism. These values and behavior may also be used as measures of democracy and a civil society.

What Does Trust Mean in China?

The first question is the meaning of trust. Trust may mean something different in China than in other societies. Specifically, the scope of trusted people may be more limited in China than in other societies. Chinese people live in a tightly knit network of Confucian social relations where one's inner circle of family and friends is clearly distinguished from strangers (see text box in chapter 1 on Confucianism). Social obligation and trust in turn extend only to one's inner circle. The Chinese media often complain about the lack of public ethics, exemplified by such as behaviors as spitting, littering, or not giving one's seat on the bus to an elderly person or a pregnant woman. Indeed, Chinese visitors to the United States have to observe norms of public behavior not practiced in their own country, including helping a stranger who is having a medical emergency (Lieberthal 1995). This sort of social behavior suggests that Chinese only relate to their own inner circles, and that the concept of trust extends only to trusting one's "own people" and not strangers. This kind of trust is easy to develop, since the inner circle has more built-in certainty and security. That may be the reason trust is high in China.

Before we examine whether in China trust extends only to one's inner circle, we need to know whether group membership has anything to do with trust, as the social capital literature suggests. The 2000 World Value Surveys have information on group membership in the countries in figure 5.1. The respondents in each country were asked whether they belonged to any of fifteen types of welfare service, religious, cultural, labor, political party, community action, human rights, environment, professional, youth, sports, women, peace, public health, and other groups (questions v39–v53). In the combined 2000 World Value Surveys sample, the respondents' answers to the fifteen questions were added up and divided by 15, resulting in a 0–1 scale. A value of 0 represented no participation in any group, and 1 represented participation in all fifteen groups. In each country, each respondent's answers to the fifteen questions were added up and divided by the maximum number of group participation in that country. For example, the highest numbers of group participation were 10 in China and 15 in the United States. The combined group participation for each respondent was divided by 10 in China and by 15 in the United States, resulting in a 0–1 scale in each country. In an OLS regression analysis, trust was examined against group membership and other factors including age, education, gender, and income.

The differences between China and other countries are quite interesting. As predicted by the social capital theory, group membership effectively promoted trust in every country in figure 5.1. The overall impact of group participation is also strong and statistically significant. As group participation increased from 0 to maximum participation, trust increased by 23%. So far, these findings confirm the social capital theory and show a clear impact of group participation on interpersonal trust. The only exception was China, where group membership had no effect on interpersonal trust (fig. 5.3). This is understandable, given the lack of independent social organizations in China. The failure of predicting trust by group membership in China makes one even more curious about the sources of the exceptionally high level of interpersonal trust.

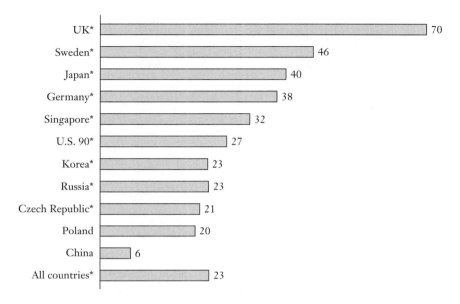

Figure 5.3 Trust by group membership: an international comparison, 2000 (OLS)
SOURCE: 2000 World Values Survey.
*: $p < .10$.

NOTE: Percentages are based on OLS coefficients using trust as the dependent variable, indicating the percentage of increase in trust when group membership changed from 0 (no group membership) to 1 (maximum group membership). For example, in Japan, trust increased by 40% when group membership increased from 0 to 1. In addition to group membership, other independent variables included in each equation but not shown are age, gender, education, and income. The coefficient for the United States was from the 1990 World Values Survey. The OLS regression coefficient was 14 ($p = .13$) for the United States in 2000.

One problem with the 2000 World Value Surveys is that they lack adequate information on informal social interactions outside formal group membership. It seems intuitively that one's closeness to family members, neighbors, friends, co-workers, schoolmates, and so on should also build interpersonal trust. It will therefore be very helpful to know to what extent informal social interaction promotes interpersonal trust and which informal social groups contribute to interpersonal trust more than others.

Fortunately, the 1999 Six-City Survey has questions about whom the respondents feel closest to: neighbors, family, friends, co-workers, relatives, schoolmates, oneself, or lovers. Closeness to each group is measured from 0 (most distant) to 1 (closest).[1] In the 1999 sample, the two closest groups on the 0–1 closeness scale were one's neighbors (.71) and family (.66). Friends and co-workers scored third and fourth highest (.39 and .24). Relatives and loners (those who spend the most time by themselves) scored .21 and .16. The two most distant groups were schoolmates (.07) and lovers (.03). Indeed, although family remains one of the most important sources of social contact, informal social interaction goes beyond one's immediate family. Neighborhood-based social communities, one's circle of friends, and co-workers are also important sources.

The next question is whether these other channels of informal social groups promote interpersonal trust. This is done by performing a regression analysis. The results indicate that interactions with neighbors, friends, schoolmates, family, and co-workers are all statistically significant in promoting interpersonal trust. Another interesting finding is that family ties do not seem to be the most important channel. Instead, ties with neighbors and friends are the top two most important sources of interpersonal trust (fig. 5.4A; see also appendix E). Therefore, in addition to family and formal group membership, it is also important to look at the role played by informal social interactions in building interpersonal trust.

Included in the same equation with informal social interactions are questions about party membership, private business owners (*siying qiyezhu* and *getihu*), family income, gender, college education, and age. The impact of these factors on interpersonal trust and some associated assumptions are also worth mentioning. If the party rules by psychological terror, then presumably party members should have less trust than non-members (Arendt 1951). In a market economy based on legal contracts, more trust is likely to be displayed among private business owners than among others (Friedman 1962). The modernization theory has shown that socioeconomic status is positively related to political activism and democratic values (Inkeles 1974; Verba, Nie, and Kim 1978). Therefore, income and education are likely to promote interpersonal trust. In the Six-City Survey, age is divided into five groups, depending on the year the respondent turned twenty: pre-1949 (the pre-socialist generation), 1949–65 (the socialist generation), 1966–76 (the Cultural Revolution generation), 1977–84 (the post–Cultural Revolution generation), and post-1984 (the reform generation). Finally, it is also necessary to check the importance of gender in interpersonal trust.

Let us begin with the effect of age. The two Cultural Revolution generations (1966–76 and 1977–84) were the least trusting, but both the

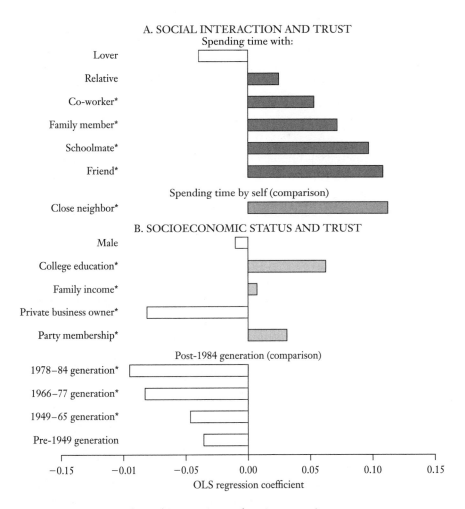

Figure 5.4 Impact of social interaction and socioeconomic status on trust, 1999 (OLS)

SOURCE: 1999 Six-City Survey.

NOTE: The OLS coefficient can be interpreted as percentage change. *: $p \leq .10$. Neighbor ties compares to no neighbor ties. For example, close neighbor ties would increase interpersonal trust by about 10% over no neighbor ties. Spending time with all other groups compares with "spending time by self." For example, compared with loners, those with close friend ties would have about 10.2% more interpersonal trust. The city is included in the analysis (results not shown). All age groups are compared with the post-1984 reform generation. For example, the post–Cultural Revolution generation is almost 10% less trusting than the reform generation. See appendix E for further details on the variables.

pre-socialist and post-reform generations were more trusting. These findings indicate the negative consequences in interpersonal trust under radical socialism. The modernization theory correctly predicted the positive relationship between trust and socioeconomic status, suggesting that those with means and resources tend to trust more. Both income and college education increased trust, but gender did not make any statistically significant difference (fig. 5.4B).

The more interesting findings appear among party members and private business owners. Party members were more trusting than non-members, but private business owners were less trusting than other professions (fig. 5.4B). Both findings seem to contradict our earlier predictions.

One provocative explanation for the more trusting party members is that the Communist Party is functioning as a formal association that promotes interpersonal trust, just as social capital theory would predict. Under this view, modernization is transforming the party into a modern political organization complete with rules to follow and professional staffing by rational technocrats (Tang and Parish 2000). The modernization of the party organization therefore makes its members function similarly to members in any modern association. As a result, more interpersonal trust is developed.

Regarding the second interesting finding, that private business owners were less trusting, the reason is likely to be found in the Chinese economic environment. In a little more than twenty years, the private sector in China grew from being virtually nonexistent in the late 1970s to being half the total industrial output and half the total number of industrial firms in 2001 (see fig. 1.1). In this kind of hybrid market environment, on which the government still exerts significant influence, the rules of the game are far from clear. Legislation and the development of formal market institutions struggle to keep up with the chaotic pace of economic growth. Private businesses have to operate in a rapidly changing, highly uncertain, and severely underregulated economic environment. Government officials may lean on businesses for payoffs in exchange for licenses or other facilitators—the nuts and bolts of corruption. Being overly trusting in such an environment is probably not the best survival skill. This finding on how the market economy negatively affects trust can perhaps further explain why Japan and South Korea had relatively low levels of trust even though they were influenced by the Confucian idea of the social network.

This finding does not contradict the positive relationship between a well-regulated market economy and a civil society in general, and interpersonal trust in particular. Trust is more likely to develop in a well-established market economy in which business behavior is well regulated and predictable, than in an emerging hybrid market such as China. For Chinese private business owners to be more trusting, the institutional environment has to become more predictable.

In short, this section reported some interesting findings. The high level of interpersonal trust in China is not generated by associational group membership, but by a combination of close family ties and lively informal social interactions. Perhaps the former can be described as modern trust and the latter as traditional trust. If there is any formal group in China in which membership has a significant impact, it is the Communist Party, which is undergoing a modernizing process and promoting modern trust. (See chap. 1 for more on the party's modernization efforts.)

Does Trust Lead to Political Reform?

So far I have examined what promotes trust. This section examines what trust promotes. We know that trust helps democratic institution building, but we do not know how it works. For example, trust may promote other democratic values and behavior that are more directly responsible for creating and sustaining democratic institutions. Studying how trust relates to political values and behavior may cast some light on how trust promotes democracy.

Let us begin with whether trust leads to political tolerance, tolerance for ambiguity, independence, and faith in political systems. According to some studies of civil society (Almond and Verba 1963), these values are helpful in sustaining a democratic system. Tolerance for different political opinions and social groups is obviously a basic requirement for democratic coexistence. Tolerance for ambiguity ensures political compromise and prevents political extremism. Independence facilitates diversity and political participation (Norris 1999). Faith in political systems gives legitimacy to democratic institutions. What needs further exploration, however, is whether trust actually strengthens these values. The 2000 World Value Surveys asked questions concerning these values.

Tolerance (questions v68–v77). "On this list are various groups of people. Would you please sort out any that you would not like to have as neighbors? (A) People with a criminal record (v68), (B) people of a different race (v69), (C) heavy drinkers (v70), (D) emotionally unstable people (v71), (E) Muslims (v72), (F) immigrants/foreign workers (v73), (G) people who have AIDS (v74), (H) drug addicts (v75), (I) homosexuals (v76), and (J) Jews (v77)." Each group was coded 1 if mentioned by the respondent and 0 if not. A 0–1 tolerance scale was calculated by dividing the number of mentioned groups by 10 (total number of groups).

Ambiguity (question v183). "Which of the following two statements comes closest to your own point of view? (A) There are absolutely clear guidelines about what is good and evil. These guidelines always apply to everyone, whatever the circumstances. (B) There can never be absolutely clear guidelines about what is good and evil. What is good and evil depends entirely upon the circumstances at the time." Possible responses were (1) Agree with statement A, (2) disagree with both, (3) agree with statement B, (9) don't know (coded as the mean). A 0–1 ambiguity tolerance scale was calculated according to the formula (ambiguity score − 1)/2.

Independence (question v105). "People have different ideas about following instructions at work. Some say that one should follow the instructions of one's superiors even when one does not fully agree with them. Others say that one should follow the instructions of one's superiors only when one is convinced that they are right. With which of the following opinions do you agree? (1) Should follow instructions, (2) depends, (3) must be convinced first, (9) don't know" (coded as the mean). A 0–1 independence scale was calculated according to the formula (independence score − 1)/2.

Faith in the system (questions v147–v162). "Each of the following items represents a system: (A) the church (v147), (B) the armed forces (v148), (C) the press (v149), (D) television (v150), (E) labor unions (v151), (F) police (v152), (G) government (v153), (H) political parties (v154), (I) parliament (v155), (J) the civil service (v156), (K) large corporations (v157), (L) the environmental protection movement (v158), (M) the women's movement (v159), (N) the European Union (v160), (O) NATO (v161), (P) the United Nations (v162). For each item listed, how much confidence do you have in it? A great deal (3), quite a lot (2), not very much (1), or none at all (0)?" Each respondent's faith in each institution was converted into a 0–1 scale using the formula (faith score)/3. The final 0–1 faith-in-system scale was calculated as (sum of faith scores of all items)/(maximum faith score [16]).

The impact of trust on these items was examined in OLS regression analyses while controlling for age, income, education, gender, and country (not shown). Interestingly, the overall pattern seems to establish a negative relationship between trust and political and social tolerance. As trust increased, people actually became less tolerant of different opinions and groups. Similarly, trust also made people less tolerant of ambiguity. It could be that trust was based on conformity and uniformity. It meant less tolerance for suspicion, which led to a greater desire for black-and-white answers (fig. 5.5).

As mentioned before, political independence should create a critical mass that can effectively check government decision making. In reality, however, trust by itself did not seem to encourage independence. In the 2000 World Values Survey, the dominant pattern was a negative impact of trust on political independence. The reason could be that trust led to delegated decision making in which voters let their entrusted representatives make decisions on their behalf. The problem is that interpersonal trust, because it discourages political independence, does not support participatory democracy in which voters are more directly involved in decision making.

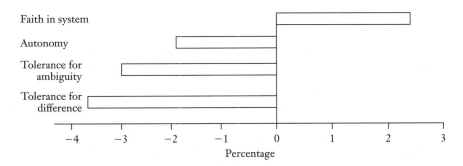

Figure 5.5 System dependence and political tolerance by trust, 2000 (OLS)
SOURCE: 2000 World Values Survey.
NOTE: Each percentage point of change in trust is the OLS coefficient using tolerance (79 countries and N = 98,436), tolerance for ambiguity (71 countries and N = 81,387), autonomy (76 countries and N = 88,567), and faith in system (79 countries and N = 98,436) as dependent variables and trust as an independent variable. Other independent variables included in each equation are age, income, education, gender, and country (results not shown). All regression coefficients are statistically significant at .00.

As predicted, trust did increase support for political systems. The 2000 World Value Surveys showed that interpersonal trust increased people's faith in political and social institutions in all the countries where data were available. This finding suggests that trust is not necessarily related to democracy but is related instead to political and social institutions that perform universal functions, such as national security, welfare, crime control, business practices, and so on. Trust can therefore increase support for the system in democratic as well as non-democratic countries.

It may be too early to conclude that interpersonal trust does not promote democratic values and behavior in China, unless we also examine the role of trust in forming other values related to democracy. Specifically, we will examine the impact of trust on political activism, voluntary voting, economic cooperation, support for civil society, and law-abiding behavior. Political activism reflects demands for bottom-up political participation in decision making. Voluntary voting shows one's feeling of efficacy in the electoral system and also one's desire for political participation. Economic cooperation may have a spillover effect on political cooperation. Support for civil society indicates that the government's sphere of influence is more limited, and that there exists more private space in public life. Law-abiding behavior facilitates political stability, predictability, and transparency. If trust positively affects these values, it stands to reason that trust may also positively affect political change and democratization.

The 1999 Six-City Survey has information on these items. Political activism is based on question (D6), "What would you do if you were dissatisfied with issues in social and public life?" Respondents were asked to select one of the following choices: (1) talk to government officials, (2) contact the media, (3) protest and petition, (4) adopt illegal means, (5) find my own way to change the situation. These options are coded 1. Options (6) complain and (7) take no action are coded 0. Voluntary voting is measured by those who participated in the last local People's Congress elections and voted voluntarily (coded 1) as opposed to those who did not vote, or only voted because other people did (coded 0). Economic cooperation is measured by question (C6_d), in which respondents were asked to what extent they agreed with the statement "It is easier to cooperate with other people than with family members and relatives in doing business" (0 = strongly disagree, 1 = disagree, 2 = agree, 3 = strongly agree). A 0–1 cooperation scale was created by dividing the cooperation score by 3. Support for civil society was judged by the extent of agreement with the following statements: "(1) Public affairs are messy, so it's better not to get involved"; "(2) The government should censor ideas"; "(3) The government should decide state affairs, big or small"; "(4) Diversity creates chaos"; and "(5) Support for the government is patriotic" (o = strongly agree, 1 = agree, 2 = disagree, 3 = strongly disagree). The five items are combined in a factor analysis to create a o–1 civil-society index.[2] Law-abiding behavior is judged based on the extent to which the respondent agreed with the statement (E3) "One should obey the law, even if it is imperfect." The o–1 law-abiding-behavior scale is created using the same method as that used for economic cooperation.

The outcome was that trust had a positive impact on these political values and behavior. When individual background factors such as party membership, income, gender, education, age, and occupation were held constant, trust increased political activism, voluntary voting, economic cooperation, support for civil society, and law-abiding behavior by about 21%, 19%, 18%, 9%, and 8%, respectively (fig. 5.6).

Thus, trust can promote democracy if democracy is defined by these political behaviors. Yet it fails to do so if democracy is measured more narrowly —in other words, by political and social tolerance, tolerance for ambiguity,

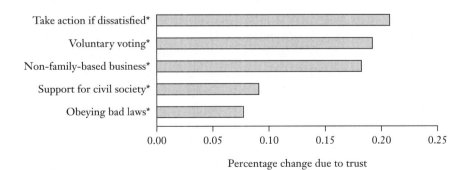

Figure 5.6 Impact of trust on sociopolitical attitudes and behavior in China, 1999 (OLS)

SOURCE: 1999 Six-City Survey.

*$p \leq .10$.

NOTE: Each percentage point of change is the OLS coefficient for trust, using each attitude or behavior item as the dependent variable. Other independent variables included in each OLS equation are party membership, family income, gender, college education, age, private sector (*siying yezhu* and *getihu*) and city.

and political independence. One obvious reason for the inconsistency lies in the different items we examined. Trust increases some democratic values, but not others. This is true in most societies regardless of political system.

Is China Different?

The answer to the question of whether China is different is both yes and no. China is different in several ways. The first is its exceptionally high level of interpersonal trust compared with other countries. This seems counterintuitive to many scholars and often to the Chinese people themselves. Yet independent surveys seem to report similar high levels of trust. The second difference is that China stands out as the most obvious case among the World Value Survey countries whose responses relating to freedom failed to reach a standardized measure of freedom (as expressed by the "freedom ratings"). The third difference is that trust is likely to be based on informal family and social ties in China, but on formal group membership in other countries. This difference probably explains the contradiction of why trust is high in China but failed to reach the minimum level in the freedom ratings. Trust is high in China because it is extended to a smaller and more informal circle around the individual. Therefore, parochial trust as such is less likely to measure up to the freedom ratings, which are based on democratic political institutions. There is one exception in which group membership does promote interpersonal trust—the Chinese Communist Party. This is the fourth and arguably most interesting difference, because increased trust within the party could open more doors for faster political reform and democratization.

China is less unique in what trust can and cannot do. Once trust is established, it tends to promote political participation and support for civil society, as well as political dependency, support for the status quo, laziness in acquiring information through independent sources, and intolerance of ambiguity, whether in China or in other countries. Even the increasing resemblance of the Communist Party to a civil group is not that unique, if it is seen as part of the global convergence of political values and institutions under economic integration.

The ultimate goal of political change in China is, of course, the development not only of democratic values but also of democratic institutions. To a large extent, future political change in China depends on change within the Communist Party itself. If the findings in this chapter are correct, the party is slowly transforming itself into a civil association similar to those in democratic countries. During this transformation, associational trust will replace traditional trust, and the demands for democratic institutional changes from within the system will likely increase as well. Only at such a stage will trust in China better correlate with trust as measured by the freedom ratings. One trade-off in this transformation from tradition to modernity is that when traditional trust is replaced by associational trust, the overall level of interpersonal trust is likely to decline. People will have to learn to rely more on institutions and less on interpersonal trust and mutual support.

This chapter is a case study about how culture and tradition shape public opinion. Family orientation and informal social interaction are the primary factors in the high level of interpersonal trust in China. Second, the findings here also address the impact of institutional change on public opinion. The level of trust in the private sector is low because marketization negatively affects trust. Yet the attempt to promote modern governance in a global market forces the party to behave like a modern organization that promotes interpersonal trust. Third, this chapter shows how idiosyncratic leaders and their policies shape interpersonal trust, as reflected in the low level of trust among "Mao's children," who grew up during the Cultural Revolution. Finally, the case study of interpersonal trust shows little evidence that China's single-party political system discourages interpersonal trust. This leads to the intriguing idea that even the unchallenged Communist Party can promote interpersonal trust. In that analysis, culture—with its inherent trust infrastructure—can override the political system. Similarly, in the same single-party system, interpersonal trust behaves the same way as in democratic systems in that it promotes democratic values and citizen participation.

PART THREE

Mass Political Behavior and Political Change

CHAPTER SIX

Publicizing Private Opinion

The last three chapters mostly discussed how public opinion is formed. The next three chapters will examine mass public behavior and political change. Studies on public opinion surveys have called for further research on the mechanisms through which public opinion can affect political outcomes (see chap. 1). The topic of this chapter is how people in urban China voice their opinions. This process includes the extent to which private opinions are voiced, the channels used to express those opinions, and the responsiveness of the political system to the people's opinions. The results will cast light not only on how the state interacts with society, but also on internal processes of the Chinese political structure.

Research Questions

In this chapter I will focus on three questions about voicing mass opinion.

1. *To what extent can popular opinion be voiced in urban China?* There is reason to believe that without an independent media, legitimate political opposition, and national free elections, mass opinion cannot be
effectively expressed and incorporated in policy making. Nonetheless, recent developments indicate that the "public space" is growing
(J. Zhang 2001) and there is more room for expressing private opinions publicly. I will examine not only whether the system responds to
popular opinion now, but also whether responsiveness to popular opinion has changed over time.

2. *What are the channels of expressing opinions and how effective are they?* I
will examine the effectiveness of the channels for voicing opinions and
how they have changed over time. A variety of these channels are available, beginning with more traditional, institutionally oriented channels originating in work units, and continuing through government
bureaus and mass organizations, mass media appeals, personal networking, and newly emerging elections and elected representatives.[1]

     In China, work units have up until now assumed responsibility for
much of people's lives. The supervisor is a linchpin in the dispersal
of benefits and for many other issues, including settlement of disputes,
permission to marry, permission to divorce, and birth control. Given
the importance of the workplace, one would expect problem solving
at work to be a primary channel for voicing opinions. Second, individuals can also voice their opinions and express their dissatisfaction by
writing to or visiting government ombudsmen (*shangfang*) or through
officially approved mass organizations, such as labor unions, women's
associations, youth leagues, writers' and artists' collectives, and other
professional associations. The third recently invigorated channel for
voicing opinions is the media, including letters to the editor of a newspaper or calling a local television station. In issues related to consumer
affairs, public facilities, and sometimes government corruption, media are in certain cases quite effective (see chap. 4). The fourth chan-

nel for voicing individual complaints is through personal connections (*guanxi*). In a study of political participation in the 1970s, Falkenheim (1978) found that Chinese citizens were more likely to use informal lobbying and personal networks than formal channels in problem solving. It is a common belief in China and among Western scholars that a network of personal ties is the key to the articulation of interests and career success (Bian 1994a; Yang 1994). The final channel is voting and contacting elected deputies. Reforms in electoral laws, such as fixed terms, multicandidacy, and secret ballots, have made voting and contacting people's deputies more meaningful (see text box in chapter 1 on election laws). Such reforms can also be expected to make deputies more responsive to public opinion (see Tang and Parish 2000 for further discussion of these channels).

3.   *Who is more likely to get their opinions heard in urban China?* Another issue that remains unsettled is the role of personal resources in voicing opinions. A large body of literature on market societies emphasizes the vital role of personal resources in increasing political participation and the rewards that individuals reap from that participation. Even with no conspiratorial elite, the tendency of those with more education, higher occupational status, and higher incomes to participate gives a strong upper-class bias to the input and output of most political systems.[2] Evidence is now beginning to emerge that even before their demise in the late 1980s, European socialist states also had an upper-class bias in their patterns of political participation (see Bahry and Silver 1990; Finifter and Mickiewicz 1992). Although his data lack cross-national uniformity, Verba shows that education promotes local political awareness in India and Nigeria (Verba 1978, 10). Unlike participation at higher, more formal levels (i.e., voting), which involves other interested groups that provide information and goad people to action, parochial participation requires considerable personal initiative and individual resources (Verba, Nie, and Kim 1978, 313).

Similarly, one might expect less expression of opinion by lower-status occupational groups than by white-collar workers in China. One reason is that any initiative on the part of manual workers is beaten down by managerial authority. Through the late 1990s, manual workers in the state sector fell behind professionals and technical workers in economic terms (Tang and Parish 2000). With the growing inequality of income and unemployment, manual workers (including workers that have been downsized) have become increasingly angry but are also intimidated by the fear of losing their jobs.

We will also include age and gender as resources for voicing opinions. Around the world, the middle-aged and the elderly typically participate more in routine politics than do the young. The former are economically better off than the latter and have more resources available for political participation. Males typically participate more than females (e.g., Jennings 1983; Shapiro and Mahajan 1986). One might expect the participation gap between the sexes to be narrower in China than in most cities of the developing world. Virtually all adult women in Chinese cities work, and the male-female education gap has narrowed rapidly (e.g., Bauer et al. 1992). Nevertheless, research on other socialist societies shows that the gender gap remains (e.g., Carnaghan and Bahry 1990). Thus, the exact prediction for China is indeterminate.

One might also predict sharp differences depending on one's work unit type. A state-run entity is different from a private firm in terms of its relationship with the government and in its access to financial resources and political information. These differences may formulate very different institutional cultures that affect whether and how people voice their opinions.

This study will rely heavily on three public opinion surveys: first, the 1987 ESRIC Political Participation Survey, based on a random sample of 2415 respondents in Beijing, Shanghai, Tianjin, Guangzhou, Shenyang, Wuhan, Chongqing, and Harbin; second, the 1992 ESRIC Urban Survey, including 2495 respondents in forty cities; and finally, the 1999 Six-City Survey of 1820 respondents in Shanghai, Guangzhou, Shenyang, Wuhan, Chongqing, and Xian (see text box in chapter 2 on urban surveys). These surveys provide information on the voicing of complaints and on voting.

Political Efficacy

It is helpful, before discussing whether individual opinions can be expressed, to examine the sense of political efficacy among Chinese urban residents. Individual opinions are less likely to be voiced if political efficacy is weak. By contrast, a strong sense of efficacy among individuals may lead to constant challenges to the government.

The sense of political efficacy was measured by several questions in the 1999 Six-City Survey. Agreement with the statements "The public can affect government decision making," "Individuals can affect social development," and "One should complain to the government about dissatisfaction with one's life" suggests more efficacy. Overall, political efficacy declined significantly from 1992 to 1999. In 1999, far fewer urban residents thought they could affect government decision making (37%) or social development (44%) than in 1992 (61% and 56%). In 1999, only 15% of respondents said they would complain to the government if they were dissatisfied with their lives, as compared with 24% in 1992.

The decline of efficacy was further shown by another question regarding one's likely action when facing an unsatisfactory supervisor at work. One could either (a) "tell the supervisor or other leaders," (b) "say nothing but disobey the supervisor," or (c) "say nothing but obey the supervisor." Answer (a) indicated more efficacy than (b) and (c). This question indicates people's willingness to engage in political participation through institutional channels. Thirty-one percent of respondents in 1999 said they would obey the supervisor anyway, though only 12% said so in 1992. Fifty-seven percent in 1992 said they would confront their supervisor or other leaders about a wrong decision, but only 48% would do so in 1999. Thirty-one percent in 1999 said they would not say anything but neither would they obey the supervisor, though only 21% said so in 1999.[3]

If the declining efficacy is due to a lack of responsiveness by the government, one would expect low levels of both mass expression and government responsiveness. In the next section I will discuss to what degree this is true by looking at how urban Chinese residents voiced their opinions and how the political system responded.

Voicing Complaints

In the 1987 Political Participation Survey and the 1999 Six-City Survey, respondents were asked about dissatisfaction with problems at work and outside of work, whether the dissatisfaction was voiced, and the official response
to reported dissatisfaction:

1. In regard to raises, promotions, housing assignments, work assign-
   ments, leadership styles, etc.:
   A. Have you had any opinions, dissatisfaction, complaints?
   B. If yes, have you ever expressed them?
   C. If you have not expressed them, what was the reason? Please
      choose one.
      1. did not know to whom
      2. no use even if I did
      3. feared revenge
      4. too many opinions, wouldn't make a splash if I did
      5. unrelated to my interest
      6. other
   D. Did you ever get any response?
   E. Was your problem solved?
2. In regard to price policies, public transportation, living environ-
   ment, management of public affairs, etc.
   [A thru E same as above]

The results are shown in figure 6.1. In 1987, understandably, most people
were dissatisfied with some issue either at work (75%) or outside of work
(82%). It was more common to voice complaints at work (54%) than outside
the workplace (34%). Once the complaint was voiced, the two types of complaints got broadly similar response rates and similar rates of favorable solutions to those complaints. Thirty-seven percent of those who voiced a non-
work-related complaint got a response. Of these, 41% solved the original
non-work problem. Forty-five percent of those who voiced a work-related
complaint got a response and 39% of these had their problems solved. Or,

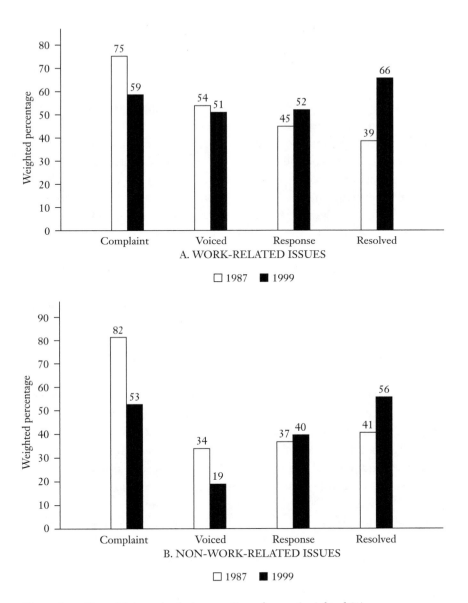

Figure 6.1　Complaints and solutions, 1987 and 1999 (weighted %)

SOURCES: 1987 Political Participation Survey; 1999 Six-City Survey.

NOTE: Each percentage point is relative to the prior action—e.g., "response" is a percentage of those who voiced a complaint.

to state the results somewhat differently, among those who voiced non-work-related complaints, the problem was solved for 15% (.37 × .41) of all complainers. For work-related complaints, the problem-solving rate was a similar 17% (.45 × .39).

From 1987 to 1999, work-related complaints dropped 16%, from 75% to 59%, and non-work-related complaints dropped almost 30%, from 82% to 53%, reflecting an improvement in working and living conditions in urban China during this period. The gap between work-related and non-work-related complaints in 1987 further widened in 1999. In 1987, 54% voiced their work-related complaints and 34% voiced their non-work-related complaints. In 1999, a similar 51% of those who had work complaints voiced them, but only one-fifth voiced their non-work-related complaints (19%), perhaps a result of declining efficacy. The response rates in 1999 for work complaints (52%) and non-work complaints (40%) were similar to those in 1987. From 1987 to 1999, problem-solving rates had increased 27% for work complaints and 15% for non-work issues. In other words, among those who voiced non-work-related complaints, the problem was solved for 22% (.40 × .56) of all complainers. For work-related complaints, the problem-solving rate was 34% (.52 × .66).

The U-shape, with high levels of complaints and high problem-solving rates but low rates of voicing complaints in 1999, replaced the linear decrease from having complaints to problem solving in 1987. The U-shape is particularly clear for non-work-related complaints (figure 6.1B). This pattern indicates two conflicting tendencies. Political apathy was on the rise as living conditions and political responsiveness both improved in urban China.

These results can be compared with Verba's (1978) six-nation study of parochial participation on issues related to job, income, housing, education, and health care. In his study, an average of 61% of the respondents had a complaint, with respondents from Nigeria (74%) and the United States (71%) being the most dissatisfied and respondents from Japan (34%) and the Netherlands (39%) being the least dissatisfied. All these responses suggest that China moved from a highly discontented urban population in 1987 to a population approaching the international average in 1999.

In China, the reluctance to voice complaints was largely unrelated to fear of authority (fig. 6.2). When asked why some complaints went unvoiced, respondents most commonly cited the lack of feeling of efficacy for both work

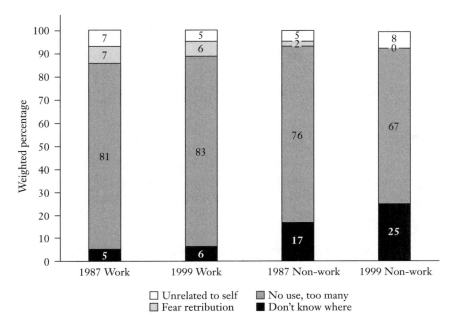

Figure 6.2   Reasons for not voicing complaints, 1987 and 1999 (weighted %)
SOURCES: 1987 Political Participation Survey; 1999 Six-City Survey.
NOTE: The total number of observations is 603 for work issues and 877 for non-work-related issues in 1987, and 305 for work issues and 817 for non-work-related issues in 1999.

and non-work issues ("no use" or "too much dissatisfaction").[4] Though fear of retribution was more of a concern at work than outside of work, it was a very minor factor for both locations. As one would expect, not knowing where to voice one's complaint was more of a problem for issues outside of work. The increased percentage of people not knowing where to voice non-work complaints in 1999 was a result of growing confusion and loopholes created by the shift from bureaucratic control to market forces. Thus, when it came to parochial concerns, even when the number of people not knowing where to voice complaints increased to 25%, the remaining majority seemed to know where to voice complaints and not to fear retribution in this highly bureaucratized system. Indeed, the most important reason for not voicing complaints was popular apathy, not direct political control.

To summarize the findings in this section, once complaints were voiced, the Chinese political system did seem to respond to popular opinions on parochial issues, and this responsiveness improved between 1987 and 1999. The problem-solving rate for non-work complaints doubled from 1987 to 1999. However, the voicing of complaints did not increase, partially because of the confusion in the transition from planning to market and partially because of rising apathy among urban residents.

In both 1987 and 1999, people were also asked which channel for voicing complaints would be most effective, and which channel they actually used to voice their complaints.

B.

    a. If yes, through which of the following channels did you express your complaint? Please choose one.

       1. work unit leaders

       2. mass organizations, such as labor unions

       3. government bureau

       4. newspaper, television station, etc.

       5. personal connection

       6. people's deputy

       7. other

    b. Comparatively speaking, which of the above channels do you think is the most effective?

There were significant differences between the channels perceived to be the most effective channels and the channels people actually used (fig. 6.3). Some reputedly effective channels were in fact rarely used. There was a pervasive belief in China that personal connections, in other words circumventing normal channels, were the most effective way to get things done. But although in 1987 one-tenth of respondents said this would be the most effective way, very few actually used personal connections either in 1987 or in 1999. In 1999, fewer people even believed that connections were an effective method of problem solving.[5]

In the 1980s and 1990s there were many high-profile cases in which let-

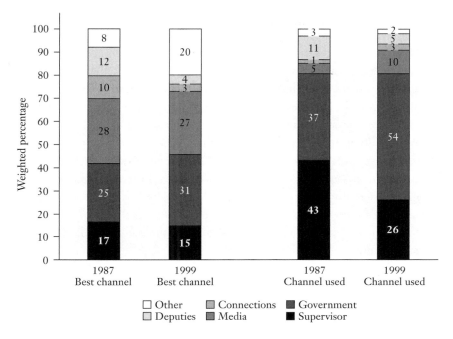

Figure 6.3   Expected channels and channels actually used in voicing non-work-related complaints, 1987 and 1999 (weighted %)

SOURCES: 1987 Political Participation Survey; 1999 Six-City Survey.

NOTES: Number of observations (left to right): 475, 209, 659, and 209.

ters to the editor or calls to television stations led to the exposure of bureaucratic malfeasance and the solving of personal problems. It is not surprising that many in both the 1987 and the 1999 samples said media contacts would be effective. However, though 28% in 1987 and 27% in 1999 said just that, only 5% in 1987 and a slightly higher 10% in 1999 actually used this channel to try to solve their own non-work-related issues.

In reality, for non-work-related issues the dominant mode of trying to solve problems through one's work unit declined from 1987 to 1999, reflecting the decreasing role of the work unit, which had once been the center of life. Contact with the government (government bureaus and mass organizations combined) increased from 1987 (37%) and became the dominant mode of problem solving by 1999 (54%). Contact with a people's deputy accounted for 11% of all contacts in 1987, but this figure had dropped to 5% by 1999.

Thus, in non-work-related issues, there was a gradual movement away from the traditional institutional channels of interests articulation. The apparent "movement" was slight, however, with government remaining as the dominant model of problem solving. The relatively new channels, such as people's representatives and media, were still actually used only about 15% of the time in attempts to solve non-work-related issues in both years. Although most actual articulation of interests remained within older, established channels—namely, work units, government bureaus, and mass organizations, including labor unions, youth leagues, and women's associations —the reduced role of work units in Chinese urban life shows an interesting shift away from the traditional function of work units in controlling and arbitrating almost every aspect of workers' lives.[6]

For all channels, overall responsiveness increased from 15% in 1987 to 22% in 1999 (table 6.1). Both traditional channels (such as the workplace, government agencies, and mass organizations), and newly emerging channels (such as elected local People's Congress representatives) were all more responsive in 1999 than in 1987. One exception was the media, the responsiveness of which was at more or less the same level in 1987 and 1999.

TABLE 6.1
Problem solving by channel, 1987 and 1999 (weighted %)

Non-work disat channels	1987 replied	1987 resolved	1987 success rate (replied × resolved)	1987 N	1999 replied	1999 resolved	1999 success rate (replied × resolved)	1999 N
Supervisor	39	40	16%	262	51	49	25	53
Government/ mass organ	37	33	12	232	38	59	22	111
Media	36	34	12	45	32	31	10	25
Connections	16	60	10	17	*	*	*	5
Deputes	45	67	30	63	50	84	42	11
Other	18	59	11	28	0	0	0	2
Total	37	41	15	652	39	56	22	210

SOURCES: 1987 Political Participation Survey; 1999 Six-City Survey.

NOTE: In 1999, only five respondents gave the "personal connections" response and one had the problem solved. Results were omitted because there were not enough cases to show a meaningful difference.

Finally, the 1987 and 1999 surveys had parallel questions on voting and knowledge of candidates:

3. Did you participate in the last local People's Congress election?
   A. If yes:
      1. I participated because it was required by my work unit leaders.
      2. I participated because everyone else did.
      3. I participated voluntarily.
   B. If no:
      1. It was a formality—not interested.
      2. Wanted to, but had other obligations.
4. Did you know about the candidates in your district?
   1. Basically yes
   2. Some
   3. No

Although elected officials themselves were more responsive as a channel for voicing complaints, the Communist Party–dominated noncompetitive electoral process failed to attract urban residents' attention in 1999. The overall voter turnout dropped more than 30%, from 88% in 1987 to 57% in 1999. Those who did vote felt more coercion (required voting) in 1999 (54%) than in 1987 (43%), and fewer people followed others to vote (18%) or voted voluntarily (28%) than in 1987 (23% and 34%). This lack of interest in elections was further reflected in the decline of knowledge about candidates. In 1987, half of the respondents (54%) had knowledge or some knowledge about the candidates, but only one-third did in 1999 (34%).

The findings in this section can be summarized into three points. First, although traditional channels in voicing opinions remained dominant over time, the emphasis within traditional channels shifted from the work unit to government bureaus. Second, the overall responsiveness by all channels increased over time, particularly in government bureaus and mass organizations, at the workplace, and through elected local officials. Third, unlike in village elections, urban district elections as a process in 1999 failed to serve as a channel for voicing popular opinion even though the product of that process had become more responsive. The lack of meaningful competition in these urban elections was perhaps the reason urban residents seemed uninterested.

Personal and Organizational Resources and Voicing Opinions

The 1987 and 1999 surveys divided respondents into various types to see how people of different ages, education levels, income, and occupations approached voicing their opinions. In both surveys, occupations were grouped as follows: (a) administrator and manager, (b) government clerk, (c) enterprise clerk, (d) technical and professional, (e) sales and services, (f) manual laborer, (g) private vendor, and (h) other or none. Income was the logarithm of 1986 per capita family income to base 10 for 1987, and an eleven-point scale in the 1999 survey (in yuan): (1) <1000, (2) 1000–3000, (3) 3001–5000, (4) 5001–8000, (5) 8001–10,000, (6) 10,001–20,000, (7) 20,001–30,000, (8) 30,001–50,000, (9) 50,001–100,000, (10) 100,001–200,000, and (11) >200,000. The two different income scales are converted into a 0–1 scale so their effects on the dependent variable will be more comparable. Age is measured by the year the respondent turned eighteen and expressed as generations: pre-socialist (pre-1949), socialist (1949–65), Cultural Revolution (1966–76), reform (1977–84), and post-reform (post-1984). Education ranged from zero to sixteen years.

The 1999 survey also included the respondent's work unit type: (1) party and government organizations, (2) government-affiliated nonprofit organizations (*shiye*), (3) state-owned enterprises, (4) collectively owned enterprises, (5) private enterprises, (6) foreign joint venture firms, and (7) no work unit. Traditionally, party, government, and government-affiliated organizations enjoyed higher political and social status than enterprises. Access to privileged or controlled information is one measure of this discrepancy. For example, certain classified official documents were circulated in government organizations but not in enterprises. Yet in recent years, private and firms with foreign investors have grown rapidly and are in some ways catching up. The much higher salaries that these firms can offer have lured some of the best talent in the private work force. In the meantime, many state and collectively owned enterprises have undergone a decline in economic importance and social status. The different types of organization affect problem solving and voting behavior as a measure of the relative importance of the private sector.

For variables related to voicing complaints, work- and non-work-related issues were combined, resulting in a scale from 0 to 2. For example, the respondent was coded as 2 if the answer was yes to voicing both work- and non-work-related complaints, 1 if the answer was yes to only work- or only non-work-related complaints, and 0 if the answer was no to both.

PROBLEM SOLVING AND VOTING

There was an interesting shift of generational effect from 1987 to 1999 on problem solving. The revolutionary generation had enjoyed the highest problem-solving ability in 1987 but had finally lost its influence by 1999, by which time the socialist generation had replaced the revolutionary generation as one of the most influential groups (see fig. 6.4).

By 1999, the overall importance of occupation in problem solving had declined compared with the 1987 survey. Instead, in 1999, income and education, regardless of the type of work unit, were stronger predictors of problem solving. In 1987, both the administrative elite (administrators and managers) and the private sector were more capable of problem solving than other occupational groups. This bimodal pattern suggests the importance of both administrative and market resources (fig. 6.4).

When work unit type was included in the 1999 multivariate analysis, the bimodal pattern seemed to continue (fig. 6.5). Although employees in the party and government organizations still enjoyed the highest rate of problem solving, employees in joint venture firms and the private sector outperformed those in state nonprofits, state-owned enterprises, and collectively owned companies.

The above individual characteristics were also checked against the respondent's participation in elections (fig. 6.6). The revolutionary generation paid little attention to voluntary voting in 1987, but this age group became the one most engaged in electoral politics in 1999. The bimodal pattern be-

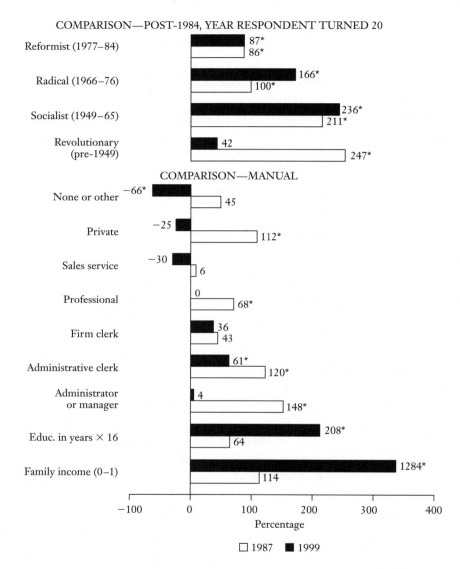

COMPARISON—POST-1984, YEAR RESPONDENT TURNED 20

Reformist (1977–84) 87* 86*

Radical (1966–76) 166* 100*

Socialist (1949–65) 236* 211*

Revolutionary (pre-1949) 42 247*

COMPARISON—MANUAL

None or other −66* 45

Private −25 112*

Sales service −30 6

Professional 0 68*

Firm clerk 36 43

Administrative clerk 61* 120*

Administrator or manager 4 148*

Educ. in years × 16 208* 64

Family income (0–1) 1284* 114

Percentage

□ 1987 ■ 1999

Figure 6.4 Problem solving by socioeconomic status, 1987 and 1999 (logistic regression)

SOURCES: 1987 Political Participation Survey; 1999 Six-City Survey.

NOTE: Percentages are converted from odds ratios. Gender and city are included in the logistic regression but not shown.

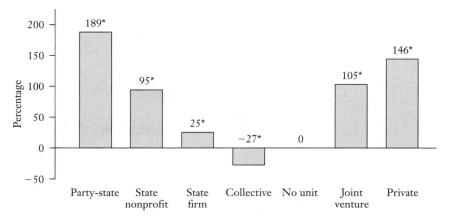

Figure 6.5   Problem solving by work unit type, 1999 (logistic regression)
SOURCE: 1999 Six-City Survey.
*: $p \leq .10$.
NOTE: All work unit types compare with self-employed or unemployed. For example, those working in government were almost 189% more likely to solve their problems than the self-employed or unemployed. All percentages are based on odds ratios from logistic regression. Occupation, age, family income, education, gender, and city are controlled for but not shown. Frequency weight is used in the logistic regression to produce more robust results for the small private sector.

tween the political elite and the private sector was also reflected in voluntary voting in 1987, in which both groups were more involved than other occupational groups. Again, the occupational effect was weak in 1999. Income and education as factors shifted from discouraging voluntary voting in 1987 to promoting it in 1999. The shift from occupation-based voting to voting based on income and education seems to further suggest the change from mobilization to participation based on market resources.

The findings in this section show that (1) the senior revolutionary generation is losing its influence in problem solving but focusing more on electoral participation, (2) standard variables such as income and education have become stronger predictors of political participation than administratively defined occupational groups, and (3) the private and semiprivate sectors are gaining momentum in politically asserting themselves. These findings suggest that, at least for non–politically sensitive issues, political participation and interest articulation have shifted significantly from state-sponsored to market-driven channels. This shift in turn provides concrete evidence of the broader social and economic changes that define urban life in contemporary China.

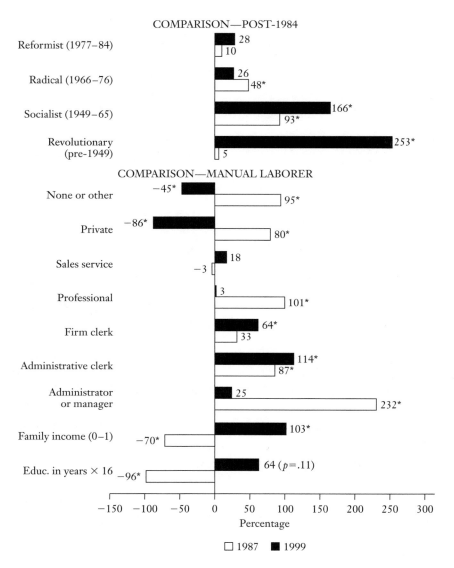

Figure 6.6 Voluntary voting in local elections and socioeconomic status (logistic regression)

NOTE: Percentages are based on odds ratios from logistic regression. Gender is included but not statistically significant.

Conclusion

The encouraging news is that popular opinion can be publicly expressed in urban China, and most channels for voicing opinions became more responsive over time. Personal connections, by contrast, are not as dominant a channel for problem solving as many in China believe. Work units, once the all-encompassing universe of one's life, became less important in one's political world. Economic development and modernization, as reflected in more personal and organizational resources, did seem to promote more political participation.

The not-so-encouraging news is that most of the issues about which people could voice their opinions and hope to see some resolution involved parochial or lower-level political issues (Bialer 1980), ranging from personal welfare to public policy issues such as inflation, the environment, and public services. There was no evidence that the highest levels of the Chinese political system were responsive to broader political issues and challenges. Political apathy was on the rise even as the system became more responsive at more parochial levels. The effectiveness of urban People's Congress was limited, as it fell short of truly expressing voters' choices. The state sector was still the dominant sector in China's urban political world, although the private sector was catching up.

There are several interesting findings here. The first is the coexistence of political apathy and increased responsiveness by the political system. In industrial democratic countries, citizens typically become more critical of the government (Norris 1999). In post-Communist Russia and the Czech Republic, voter turnout decreased after democratization due to disillusion with the government (Kluegel and Mason 2000, 229). One possibility is that Chinese urban residents reacted in the same way as voters in Russia and the Czech Republic did under greater freedom when they did not see any fundamental change as a result of greater voter participation. This finding suggests that democracy cannot run on autopilot once electoral and other democratic institutions are created. Political efficacy, it appears, does not necessarily go hand in hand with democratic institutions. Even in industrial democracies, democratic institutions do not promise citizen participation, as indicated by the notoriously low voter turnout in U.S. presidential elections.

Ironically, the declining sense of political efficacy reassures political stability for post-Deng leaders. Chinese urban residents showed not only relatively strong support for the current political system and a rising sense of nationalism (see chap. 4), but also a reduced desire to challenge the authorities. Admittedly, unwillingness to challenge the authorities does not necessarily equate public satisfaction. Public distrust and dissatisfaction with parochial issues such as overtaxation, evictions, or even layoffs can and do erupt into sometimes violent protests. Public anger with the negative consequences of accelerated market reform can be temporarily diverted by tragedies such as the NATO bombing of the Chinese embassy in Belgrade and by celebrations such as the fiftieth anniversary of the republic. Another possible explanation for the decline in citizen efficacy is that people are frustrated and disillusioned with the narrow channels of interest articulation. One solution is to widen the existing channels and create truly democratic institutions. Again, though, democratic institutions alone do not guarantee citizen participation.

The second interesting finding is the bimodal pattern of political participation between the state elite and the private sector. The bureaucratic elite's lasting importance is still highly visible, but no longer exclusive. The private sector is increasingly showing its potential. China's political environment seems to be shifting from a sort of monolithic state corporatism to a bureaucratic market society.

Regarding the channels for voicing opinion, the reduced role of work units in problem solving is interesting to note. In addition to their economic functions, work units have also been one of the main vehicles for social and political control in Chinese urban life. However, non-economic tasks overburdened Chinese work units and made them inefficient. The declining importance of work units in problem solving seen today could be a result of their effort to strengthen market efficiency: state-run work units are being released from performing non-economic tasks so they can keep up and focus on economic issues. In the meantime, the declining role of problem solving by the traditional work unit means that it exercises far less control, and employees enjoy greater freedom outside of work. This is a significant shift away from traditional workplace socialism, with a profound effect on lifestyle and public expectations of privacy. The next chapter will continue the discussion of workplace politics.

CHAPTER SEVEN

Work and Politics

Since most people of working age spend many of their waking hours each day at work, it is also important to study how public opinion and mass political behavior develop at the workplace level. The shifting role of public opinion in turn offers insights into the possibility that Chinese labor may become more autonomous over time. The workplace in China has experienced important changes since Andrew Walder published his seminal book on work and authority in Chinese industry in the mid-1980s. In that study, the Chinese party-state exercised total control of workers' social, economic, and political lives. In return for their political loyalty and obedience, workers received job security, subsidies, and welfare benefits. Walder described this patron-client relationship as "communist neo-traditionalism" (Walder 1986). Since the mid-1980s, however, the traditional patron-clientelism has gradually begun to be replaced by market contracts. Tang and Parish (2000) found that in the early 1990s, state domination of the Chinese workplace was partially replaced by a market-driven managerial authority. The authors predicted an increase in tensions between labor and management owing to the extended authority as well as the continuing manipulation of in-kind benefits by their firms. They called for further regulation to limit the arbitrary power of management and for an autonomous union structure that would handle labor disputes (2000, chap. 6).

In this chapter I examine the changes in the Chinese work environment since Premier Zhu Rongji announced deepened enterprise reform in 1997, which resulted in massive economic restructuring. Specifically, I will report the impact of market reforms on the Chinese workplace, including job opportunity and preference. Next I will examine labor disputes and solutions together with institutionalized participation, that is, making suggestions at work. In the final section I will describe the role of labor unions in promoting employee interests.

The primary data source is the 1997 Employee Survey conducted by the All-China Federation of Trade Unions. This survey consists of 107 questions covering work conditions, income and welfare, labor disputes, the role of labor unions, and the respondent's background information. The survey is based on a three-step proportional sampling, a random sample of cities and counties in fifteen predetermined provinces, a random sample of work units in each city or county, and, finally, a random sample of employees in each work unit. The resulting total sample consists of 54,000 employees in 15 sectors and 2,335 work units under different types of ownership (state, collective, stock, private, overseas Chinese, foreign, and jointly owned). The final sample also includes not only employees in economic enterprises, but also those in public organizations and government agencies, representing all salary-earning employees, who make up 50% of the total Chinese working population of 700 million. A random subsample of 12,165 will be used for this study. Further details of the survey are attached in appendix F.

One potential problem of the 1997 survey is sampling error and response bias. For example, a survey conducted by labor unions may show a higher percentage of union members than is actually the case. Or it may induce the respondents to support labor unions more than they really want to. One way to solve this problem is to refer to aggregate statistics and rely more on the latter. Another is to pay more attention to multivariate analysis than the univariate results (chap. 2). That is, instead of looking at how many people are union members or how many people support labor unions, we are more interested in who is more likely to be a union member or to support labor unions.

In addition to the 1997 Employee Survey, this study will also rely on aggregate data found in Chinese official statistics, such as *China Statistical Yearbooks* and *Trade Unions Statistical Yearbooks*. The problem with relying on official statistics is possible misreporting, a problem highlighted by recent challenges to the official economic growth rates in the late 1990s (Rawski 2001, 2002). For example, unemployment may be underreported in the official statistics. One solution is to look at the rate of change in unemployment rather than the total number of the unemployed.

Job Opportunity and Preference

One needs to examine the Chinese work environment in order to understand mass opinion and behavior at the workplace level. One measure of work environment is the degree of marketization in employment opportunities. Tang and Parish (fig. 3.5 in Tang and Parish 2000) found a significant increase in market-based competitive hiring and a decrease in administrative job assignments from the 1980s to the 1990s in Chinese enterprises. With new information from the 1997 Employee Survey about the type of work unit, including enterprise (*qiye*), public (*shiye*), and government (*jiguan*) organizations, we can examine the channels through which employees were recruited by different types of work units (fig. 7.1).

The labor market is more controlled in government (*jiguan*) and state nonprofit (*shiye*) organizations. Eighty percent of the people in government and 75% of those in nonprofit units were recruited through government-arranged job assignment or transfer, as compared with only 54% in enterprises. The latter recruited more through the free labor market (30%) than through public (15%) and government units (13%). Among all the working respondents (total), 31% were recruited through administrative assignment, 29% through transfer, 8% through internal hiring (i.e., replacing a parent who is taking early retirement), 26% through market competition, and 7% through other channels. Among the three types of work units, internal hir-

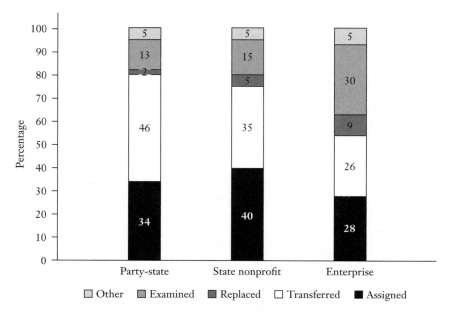

Figure 7.1 Job channel by work unit type, 1997 (%)
SOURCE: 1997 Employee Survey.
NOTE: The total number of observations for each bar is 692 (party-state), 2133 (state nonprofit), and 7987 (enterprise).

ing (*dingti*) continued to be a more important channel for children to replace their retiring parents in enterprises (9%) than in nonprofit (5%) and government units (2%).

A logistic regression analysis including size of firm, job rank, education, party membership, gender, urban registration, and job seniority indicates that market hiring was more common in the private sector and at a lower socioeconomic status. Non-party members at lower ranks; all workers in private, overseas Chinese, and foreign firms; and those with less education, a rural household registration, and less seniority were more likely to go through market hiring channels than others (details not shown).

LABOR MOBILITY

Labor mobility is another indicator of labor market development. Among the 33% of respondents who reported having changed jobs at least once in the 1997 survey, employees in private, overseas Chinese, and foreign firms; those in smaller firms; and those working in economic enterprises (*qiye*), and having a rural origin were more mobile than workers in larger public firms, noneconomic units (*shiye* and *jiguan*), and urban residents. This is similar to the finding about market hiring. However, unlike the case with free-market hiring, employees with a higher socioeconomic status (rank, education, and seniority) were more mobile and had more frequent job changes than others.[1]

UNEMPLOYMENT

Unemployment is yet another indicator of marketization. Like other post-socialist societies, China witnessed massive unemployment in the 1990s. Official statistics show that from 1991 to 1997 unemployment increased by 64%, compared with a rise of 108% in Russia and 22% in the United States (Editorial Office 2000, p. 256). The 1997 Employee Survey also included a sub-survey of 1013 laid-off and unemployed workers. Among these respondents, 68% tried to find a new job, 74% of these tried but failed, and only 26% of those who tried to find new jobs were successful. To state it differently, only 18% (.68 × .26) of laid-off and unemployed workers could eventually find another job. Eighty-seven percent of those who were unsuccessful in finding new jobs failed because they were rejected; only 13% turned down a job offer. Among all those laid off and unemployed in the sub-sample, only 10% received retraining, and 25% were lucky enough to receive assistance by their work units for reemployment. For the most part, in 1997 anyone who was laid off or lost his or her job stood very little chance of getting help.

DESIRED UNIT

Walder (1986) described work unit preferences according to the administrative hierarchy under central planning (principled particularism). Workers preferred to work in higher-level state units in order to receive better benefits. The private sector, which emerged during market reform, offered higher incomes, but also more risk. The question now is whether these new economic opportunities can lure more qualified employees.

The 1997 Employee Survey asked the respondents to rank their first and second choices if they could choose their work unit again. The choices were government agency (gmt), public organization (npf), state-owned enterprise (soe), foreign direct investment firm (fdi), private household business (geti), domestic private firm (pe), township-village enterprise (tve), and urban collective enterprise (uce). Each type was coded 2 if it was picked as the first choice and 1 if it was picked as the second choice. The preference score for each respondent was calculated using the formula ([1st choice + 2nd choice]/3) × 100. Each respondent's score can be interpreted as the feeling thermometer from 0 (minimum) to 100 (maximum) for a unit type. For example, the feeling thermometer is 100% for government agencies if the respondent picked this unit type as both first and second choices, 66% if the respondent made it his or her first choice, and 33% if it was the second choice.

In 1997, Chinese employees showed a continued preference for the state sector. The top three choices were government agency, nonprofit organization, and state-owned enterprise. Private firms (foreign and domestic) were more desired than collective firms. The least-desired type was collective firms, which probably could offer neither sufficient income nor benefits (fig. 7.2). In an OLS regression analysis including rank, education, party membership, gender, urban residency, and age, there was an anti-market bias among the potential losers of reform. Party members, female workers, urban residents, and older employees all preferred to work in the public sector (gmt, npf, soe) and were less likely to work in private firms. By contrast,

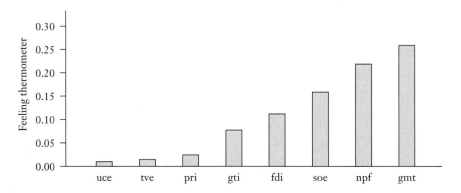

Figure 7.2   Work unit preference, 1997 (%)
SOURCE: 1997 Employee Survey.

the educated were interestingly bifurcated, desiring both government agencies and private firms (results not shown). The psychological change from socialism to a market economy seems to be coming more slowly than expected. Most employees still favored the party-state and the security of state-run nonprofit sectors, even though the incomes these offered were lower than in the private sector. With the further deepening of market reform since the 1997 survey, the private sector and foreign investment have grown rapidly. Private and foreign firms are offering more benefits and attracting more talent. It is possible that preference for private-sector jobs has increased since 1997.

JOB GOALS

The 1997 Employee Survey had a question about the respondent's primary and secondary considerations for a new job if he or she could choose one. The choices were income (income), opportunity to use talent (talent), job security (security), welfare benefits (welfare), maintaining a family (family), job status (status), and workload (workload). As with figure 7.2, each goal was transformed into a 0–1 scale and was interpreted as the feeling thermometer for that item with a minimum value of 0 and a maximum value of 1. The top three choices (income, talent, and security) were by no means uniform and represented opposing preferences such as materialism, self-fulfillment, and dependency. Indeed, the top three choices are negatively related to each other in the data set (results not shown). They suggest a diverse range of work values including both new market values and the socialist legacy (fig. 7.3).

In a logistic regression analysis of each of the top three job goals, the impact that ownership, firm size, rank, education, party membership, gender, urban residency, and seniority have on how goals are determined was further examined (details not shown). In general, employees in private overseas Chinese firms were more willing to give up security in exchange for having their talent recognized. Stock firms encouraged sacrificing income for talent. Employees with high expectations (those of high rank, and/or education, males, and junior workers) took the meaning of work (talent) more seriously and seemed to be less concerned with security. The risk-adverse included party members, women, rural people, and more senior employees. The more cash-conscious and materialistic and more risk-taking group included young,

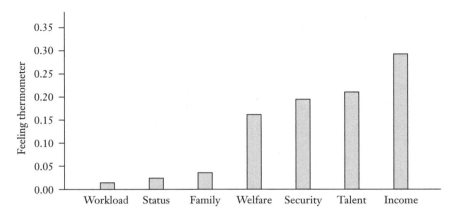

Figure 7.3 Job priority, 1997 (%)
SOURCE: 1997 Employee Survey.
NOTE: The feeling thermometer is measured as I = most desired and o = least desired.

male, and urban workers. This contrast between the risk taking and the risk adverse is often reflected in Chinese families. The child may be taking a risky job but potentially make more money while the parents hold secure but less profitable jobs. The husband may work without fringe benefits in a highly paid private firm while the wife brings home a stable paycheck with benefits such as health care and housing for the family. One family, two systems.

In conclusion, diversification is a better description of the Chinese work environment than marketization because both public and private firms are important in shaping popular preferences. The educated choose jobs in both the private and government sectors, indicating that the latter still attracts workers who have broader choices open to them. Diversification is further reflected in job goals, such as materialism, self-fulfillment, and risk taking. None of these goals was significantly more valued than the other two.

Administrative stratification between the state and collective units still existed regardless of market reform. Collective firms remained at the bottom of the food chain, reflecting low income, harder working conditions, and low social status in this type of firm. Predictably, these firms mostly employed less educated rural workers.

Private firms played a positive role in invigorating the economy. They created a lively labor market by using testing to select the most qualified workers and increasing labor mobility. However, the public sector still retained the more experienced and better educated party members. On average the private sector attracted less educated, rural, and low-ranking non-party members than did government organizations, although, with deepened marketization and globalization, the balance is tilting in favor of the former.

Joint stock ownership played a positive role in labor market hiring and in promoting a sense of community and work as a means of self-fulfillment.

Employee Participation in Labor Disputes and Decision Making

The next question is about how employees participate in workplace politics. Several factors may increase employee participation in labor disputes and decision making. One factor is the effect of the market. When the security-based traditional social contract between the state and employees is replaced by autonomous and profit-driven managers, labor turmoil will inevitably rise (Edwards 1979). As a result, labor disputes will increase, and an authoritative manager will further suppress employees' opportunities to participate in work unit decision making. On the other hand, it may be argued (Friedman 1962) that the market economy may strengthen people's awareness of individual rights and have a spillover effect on the demand for bottom-up political participation. The second factor in workplace participation is the economic modernization effect, which is commonly believed to lead to democratization (Huntington 1991). This school of thought argues that the world would eventually converge under modernization, regardless of whether the system is driven by the market or by socialism (Inkeles 1974). As living standards and education improve, people will develop the need to insert their influence from the bottom up. Among different social groups, employees with higher socioeconomic status are more likely to be involved in challenging the management, according to this argument. The third factor is the deprivation effect. In his book *Why Men Rebel*, Ted R. Gurr (1971) maintained that people would challenge the government not because of the market effect or modernization, but because the government failed to deliver promised benefits and services. In other words, it is the widening gap between popular expectations and the actual delivery of services that creates a bottom-up challenge for political authorities. This argument leads one to expect more hostility among those whose economic interest is more threatened by reform.

This section focuses on two dimensions of labor-management relations, labor disputes and making suggestions at work. The former is a spontaneous act; the latter is an institutional channel through which employees can make their voices heard.

A quick look at the official statistics reveals a rapid increase in labor disputes in the late 1990s and early 2000s. Between 1996 and 2001, the total number of officially reported labor disputes more than tripled, and the number of workers involved in these disputes more than doubled (fig. 7.4).

In the 1997 Employee Survey, 8.4% of the employees had at least one labor dispute with their work units in the previous five years. The respondents were asked to pick the top three reasons for getting involved in a labor dispute. The most common reasons were pay (61%), welfare benefits (58%), job contracts (18%), and job exit (6%).

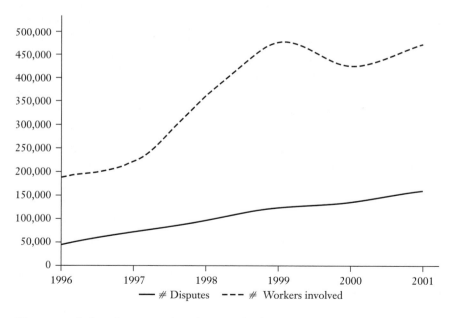

Figure 7.4 Labor disputes and workers involved, 1996–2001 (#)
SOURCES: *Statistical Yearbook of China*, various years.

Another dimension of bottom-up participation is making suggestions at work. Rather than openly challenging the authorities, making suggestions at work is an institutional mechanism left over from the days of central planning. This channel was intended to boost labor incentive, and it continued to function even under more authoritative management. In the 1997 survey, nearly half (48%) of the total respondents made suggestions at work during the last year, and 34% of those who made suggestions actually had their suggestions adopted. This type of participation seemed to be more effective than the success rate of labor dispute resolutions (11%)

In an OLS regression analysis of the likelihood of getting involved in labor disputes, low-ranking, male, non-party, and rural employees working in private firms showed a higher probability of doing so (see appendix G). As will be discussed later in this chapter, once an employee was involved in a labor dispute, labor unions were more important than individual resources (education, rank, etc.) in solving the problem.

In contrast to the low probability of employees in higher socioeconomic groups participating in labor disputes, the OLS regression analysis of making suggestions indicates that employees with higher rank and education and who had party membership and seniority working in large or stock firms (part market driven, part state owned) were all more likely to make suggestions and to have their suggestions adopted than those of lower socioeconomic status (see appendix G).

In short, everyone is involved in labor disputes to one degree or another. Involvement in labor disputes seems to support the deprivation theory. The socioeconomically more disadvantaged groups tend to be more active in this area. Yet the market effect on participation in labor disputes is also seen, because more workers in private firms participated in labor disputes than in other type of firms, owing either to more repressive management or to workers' increased awareness of their rights under market contracts.

Although modernization alone did not lead people to take part in labor disputes as much as predicted, it did seem to play an important role in getting workers involved in workplace decision making. In particular, a higher socioeconomic status increased the likelihood that an employee would make suggestions and the chances of getting one's voice heard at work. Interestingly, the market was competing with the administrative hierarchy in promoting workplace participation, as both the market-driven firms and the state sector increased institutional participation. Stock firms, as a compromised form of ownership between the market and the state, were therefore more effective in promoting employee participation in management decision making than either fully private or public firms.

Can Labor Unions Protect Employees' Interests in China?

Chinese labor unions are officially organized under a single umbrella, the All-China Federation of Trade Unions (ACFTU). The ACFTU, which is firmly under the leadership of the Communist Party, is usually chaired by a member of the party's Politburo or even its standing committee. According to the revised 2001 Trade Union Law, every wage earner has the right to be a union member. Though not mandatory, union membership in China is among the highest in the world. For example, 55% of the non-agricultural labor force in China was made up of union members in the mid-1990s. This rate is higher than in any other country except Russia (75%), according to the International Labor Office's 1997–98 *International Labor Report* (International Labor Office 1999). The high rate of union membership guarantees a steady income for labor unions owing to the required union dues (2% of wages). Sixty percent of union dues is kept by the grassroots union, 35% by the local ACFTUs, and the remaining 5% by the central ACFTU in Beijing.[2]

Despite high membership rates, the question ultimately is whether Chinese labor unions represent employees' interests. The rubber-stamp argument says that unions are a policy instrument of the party. As such, since the current priority of the party is market efficiency and growth, labor unions are supposed to help repressive management increase profits and keep workers in check. In this sense, unions are caught between promoting the interests of workers and those of management. Prominent Chinese labor union scholars call for the separation of labor unions from the party-state and for labor unions to become an autonomous political organization. They argue that without this autonomy, labor unions' representation of workers' interests is an empty slogan (Feng 2002, 130).

The socialist legacy view sees the positive side and focuses on what it calls the internalization of political mobilization under socialism (Huntington 1968). Chan (1993) argues that labor unions were in fact playing a greater role in protecting workers' interests from the time that market reforms began, thanks in part to the lessons they learned from observing other postsocialist societies and in part to the increasing necessity of protecting workers under intensified market competition. According to this view, Chinese labor unions are indeed playing a real role and are far from being mere rubber stamps.

Still others see Chinese labor unions as a double-edged sword. In the Chinese corporatist state, labor unions must function within the officially defined framework of party domination. Within this framework, however, unions are also allowed to promote workers' economic and political rights (Wilson 1986; Zhang 1998).

What do Chinese workers think? The 1997 Employee Survey showed the respondents' evaluation of labor unions' role. Regarding the different roles listed in the questionnaire, 34% of respondents said unions were best at protecting employees' interests, 19% said promoting worker participation in democratic decision making, 13% said promoting labor incentives, and finally, 16% said worker training. The remaining 18% thought unions were not playing any role. Thus, the majority of the respondents believed one way or another that labor unions served the functions of protecting workers' interests and promoting democratic participation.

Another question is whether employees go through labor unions to solve work-related problems. In the 1997 Employee Survey, 32% of the respondents said they would go to friends and family to solve a work-related problem, 30% to the labor union, 14% to a manager, 13% to the party, and 2% to government, although 9% said they would go through other channels. Together with relying on friends and family, labor unions seemed to be one of the most popular channels for problem solving.

One potential problem with the above findings is that the 1997 survey was conducted by labor unions themselves. It is possible that the respondent, knowing the union was behind the survey, overstated the positive role and importance of labor unions. This is a common problem in survey research in general, and in China in particular. As mentioned earlier, one way to solve this problem is to rely less on the univariate percentages and more on multivariate analysis. For example, instead of focusing on *how many* people believe labor unions play a positive role, we are more interested in *who* feels more positive about the labor union.

DETERMINING LABOR UNION'S ROLE

The main interest of this study is whether union effectiveness has an impact on labor relations and employee welfare. The question is how union effectiveness, labor relations, and employee welfare should be measured.

The respondent's overall evaluation of union effectiveness is measured by a factor index of several questions in the 1997 survey:

86. Does the labor union help employees with their daily life difficulties?
87. What is your labor union's overall performance?
89. Can the labor union protect your interest when your rights specified in the Labor Law are violated?
91. How do you evaluate your labor union's role in promoting equal consultation and collective bargaining?
92. How do you evaluate your labor union's role in mediating labor disputes?
94. Have labor unions' social status and importance increased in the past two years?

Each of the above questions will be recoded (if necessary) so that a higher value means more effectiveness. The index based on a factor analysis had a mean of 0 (standard deviation = 1), a minimum value of −3, and a maximum value of 2.3. The factor index score of each respondent was transformed according to the formula (factor score + 3)/5.3. This transformation created a new variable of overall union effectiveness with a minimum value of 0 and a maximum value of 1, making the interpretation of the regression results more intuitive.

Next, how effective unions are in labor relations and employee welfare will be examined, together with other background factors. There are many questions in the 1997 survey relating to labor relations and employee welfare. Ten will be taken from among these: involvement in labor disputes, group dispute involvement, dispute resolution, making suggestions at work, adopting suggestions, firm-employee relations (high value = better), party-employee relations (high value = better), pay delays, job security, and job satisfaction. These ten indicators will be transformed using methods similar to those used for calculating the union effectiveness score, resulting in ten

0–1 scales. These ten indices will serve as ten dependent variables, thereby examining how these dependent variables are affected by the unions and other background characteristics.

In order to isolate the impact of union effectiveness on work politics and welfare, it is necessary to conduct multivariate analyses including the factors of the firm and the individual's background. The multivariate analyses included the following variables in the 1997 survey and from the *1999 China Statistical Yearbook*: ownership type (collectively owned, privately owned, jointly owned, stock ownership, Taiwan–Hong Kong–Macau owned, other foreign owned); firm size (logged); work unit classification (company, nonprofit, government); annual economic growth in each respondent's province (1995–97); 1998 per capita income in each respondent's province (in 10,000 yuan, *1999 China Statistical Yearbook*); and the respondent's rank (1 = worker, 2 = technician, 3 = group head, 4 = office head, 5 = bureau chief, 6 = organization leader), education (years), party membership (0 = nonmember, 1 = member), gender (male = 0, female = 1), urban residency (0 = rural household registration, 1 = urban household registration), seniority (year respondent began working: 1 = after 1977, 2 = 1966–77, 3 = 1959–66), and job classification (0 = white collar, 1 = blue collar). The statistical details of the above variables are presented in appendix F.

LABOR UNION EFFECTIVENESS AND WORKPLACE POLITICS

First, labor unions' effectiveness is analyzed in an OLS regression. Figure 7.5 shows the effect of labor unions on mobilization and control, employee participation in decision making through organized channels, and employee welfare.[3] The control effect is best shown by the unions' discouragement of labor disputes. The most effective labor union could block the chance of an employee's involvement in individual labor disputes by 20% and in group disputes by 13%. The mobilization effect includes improved firm-employee relations (63%), improved party-mass relations (58%), and improved labor incentives (job satisfaction, 44%). The participation effect has a nuanced twist. Although labor unions did not seem to promote participation in labor disputes or making suggestions at work, they did facilitate adopting workers' suggestions (40%) and solving labor disputes (55%) once the suggestions were made and the disputes had begun. The welfare effect is shown in pro-

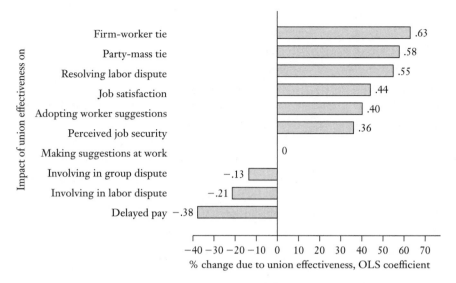

Figure 7.5 Impact of union effectiveness on work politics and welfare, 1997 (OLS)
    NOTE: All coefficients are statistically significant at .10 except for "making suggestions at work." The value of each bar can be interpreted as the probability of change on each issue when union effectiveness changes from 0 to 1. For example, although union effectiveness does not seem to encourage or discourage making suggestions at work, it does increase by 40% the chance of one's suggestion being adopted. Each issue is treated as a dependent variable, with union effectiveness as an independent variable. Other variables included in each equation (but not shown) are ownership type, unit type (firm, nonprofit, jiguan), rank, education, party membership, gender, urban origin, and seniority. See appendix G for the complete table.

moting job security and guaranteed income. Union presence increased one's sense of job security by 36% and prevented pay delays by 38%. Thus, labor unions helped facilitate a corporatist work environment. In this environment, spontaneous political participation was indeed controlled, but at the same time the bottom-up influence of decision making occurred within the officially proved framework.

With the union effect controlled, the OLS regression analysis also examined the influence of individual and work unit background characteristics on workplace control, mobilization, participation, and welfare (see appendix G). As mentioned in the last section, as one's socioeconomic status increased, the probability of getting involved in labor disputes decreased, and the probability of making suggestions and having them adopted increased. Socioeconomic status also seemed to improve job satisfaction and, to a limited extent, labor relations. Pay delays were more common among younger rural migrant workers and those in nonprofit organizations. Fear of losing one's job was mostly felt among less-educated blue-collar urban employees in nonprofit or government units.

Second, it is also necessary to look at who was more likely to evaluate labor unions favorably. Union effectiveness was examined in a multiple regression analysis against work unit (ownership, logged work unit size, enterprise vs. nonprofit and government unit, 1995–97 provincial economic growth rate, and 1998 provincial per capita income in 10,000 yuan) and individual characteristics (rank, education, party membership, gender, urban-rural residency, seniority, blue-collar vs. white-collar, and laid off vs. working).

In the same regression analysis, labor unions were viewed as less effective in small work units, in overseas Chinese-owned firms, and in provinces with low per capita income or high growth rates. Union lovers carried a class label, including lower-ranking employees or party members.

It is no surprise that labor unions were more effective in larger and higher-level organizations, given the fact that the state-controlled All-China Federation of Trade Unions has been unable to keep up with China's rapid economic restructuring. More developed regions generate high levels of union dues, allowing unions to become more active. The unions' role in protecting workers was compromised in high-growth regions because that role could not keep up with the party's priorities in economic development. In the same multivariate regression analysis, laid-off and unemployed workers were less likely to view unions favorably than those who were working. However, in a separate analysis of the laid-off or unemployed workers sub-sample, unions did seem to play a positive role in creating job opportunities and job retraining for laid-off workers.

Chinese labor unions are facing a challenge as foreign investment comes into the country. During a visit to Motorola (China) Electronics in Tianjin (July 7, 2004), I was told that this fully foreign-owned company with 8000 Chinese employees did not have a party committee nor a labor union. Employees were encouraged to engage in individual "direct dealing" with the management, effectively eliminating workers' collective bargaining power. The Tianjin government resisted the All-China Federation of Trade Unions' request to set up a labor union in the company so that this big fish could be kept in the local economy.

In sum, the findings in this section confirm the dual role of labor unions in China. They serve as an instrument of the party in political control and mobilization, but also facilitate bottom-up participation and promote employee welfare. They have to support the party's development priorities even at the cost of their own protective role, yet on balance their orientation tilts toward benefiting the disadvantaged.

Conclusion

Market reform has profoundly transformed the Chinese workplace. The social contract between the firm and the employee is more based on specific legal obligations than on broad political patron-clientelism. China today is a corporatist workplace that operates under managerial arbitration in the context of a growing labor market. This corporatist workplace seems to tolerate institutional interest articulation but discourages direct challenges from outside. It thus uses labor unions to fulfill the role of control and interest articulation.

Economic diversification has led to a diversified work environment in which the state sector best resembles the corporatist workplace. Most people feel more comfortable working in such an environment, as evidenced by the fact that the corporatist workplace manages to recruit the most qualified workers. The fast-growing private sector, on the other hand, seems to resemble primitive market capitalism. It provides competitive employment and income opportunities and operates under less legal and union control, but it also creates more conflict and hostility between workers and management. The small number of joint stock firms (with elements of both state-run firms and private enterprise) appeared able to avoid the problems in both the state and private sectors. Joint stock firms can generate more market efficiency than the state sector and a more benign labor-management relationship than the private sector. Further growth of stock firms will likely meet with resistance from middle managers in state-owned firms because they would have to give up their authority and bureaucratic perks.

Labor disputes did not seem to be an inherent problem of the corporatist workplace. They are, rather, a temporary result of economic restructuring. Indeed, under further economic development and with increased revenue, the government and firms will be better able to deliver services, and employees will be more likely to channel their political energy into participating in the institution rather than challenging it.

In the bigger picture, the status of labor unions is important not only for the articulation of employees' interests in the workplace, but also for China's future political system. It is true that labor unions are limited in how fully they can represent employees' interests, and this limitation can be lifted only by allowing unions to be politically independent. Such independence of labor rests on a country's level of affluence and the adaptability of a given political system. Large-scale strikes and work stoppages organized by independent labor unions can be tolerated only if a country is willing and able to accept the resulting economic losses and political turmoil.

CHAPTER EIGHT

Intellectuals and Political Change

One hope often expressed by Western leaders is that China will democratize and so come to fit more smoothly into the world order.[1] Yet seeing how few and disunited the Chinese dissidents today calling for democratization actually are, observers are at a loss to specify any viable Chinese political force pressing for democratization (Nathan 1998, 62). In fact, there is significant evidence that a politically vigorous Chinese stratum with an increasingly strong interest in reform, if not democratization, does exist. Broadly speaking, this interest is represented by party intellectuals. The chapter begins with a definition of "intellectuals" and a quantitative outline of their place in Chinese society today. I then discuss competing hypotheses about their relationship with the party-state. Survey data are used to test these hypotheses. The data are taken from several sources: the 2000 Population Census; the 1999 Six-City Survey conducted by this author; the eight surveys conducted by the Economic System Institute of China, including the 1992

China Urban Survey; and the seven semiannual surveys on social reaction to reform from 1987 to 1991 (see appendix A).

Intellectuals in Contemporary China

The modern term "intellectual" (*zhishi fenzi*) has been used to denote those who in imperial times passed the official examination. *Xiucai* were those who passed the examination at the prefectural level, *juren*, at the provincial level, and *jinshi*, at the national level. Other labels have also been used, such as *xuezhe* (scholars). Under socialism, "intellectuals" were similar to the intelligentsia in the Soviet Union: people with higher educational degrees holding non-manual jobs. These included not only professionals and government officials with higher education but also enterprise managers and directors (see Lane 1985, chap. 5; Hamrin 1991).

Intellectuals are obviously an extremely important part of Chinese society, but they are also a tiny part. In the 1990 population census, there were only 12 million persons with higher-education degrees, just 1.9% of the total employed population. Ten years later, in 2000, the number of college-educated Chinese had rapidly increased to 44 million, but they still made up only 4.6% of the total employed population.

This 4.6% is in turn made up of two groups that are rather different in status: holders of regular four-year college degrees, who now get into universities through national competitions, and graduates of two-year junior colleges, with degrees from technical colleges or local night schools and continuing education programs. Most intellectuals belong to the latter, less-educated group. Only 15 million (34%) of the 44 million had regular college degrees, and the remaining 29 million (66%) had junior college degrees (Population Census Office 2002, table 4-1).

This chapter, however, focuses on differences between establishment intellectuals and non-establishment intellectuals, or within-system and outside-of-system intellectuals (Moody 1977; Goldman 1981; Hamrin and Cheek 1986; Schopflin 1993, 30; Cheek 1994; Ding 1994a; Hua 1995; Walder 1995a). True, given the nature of the communist state, this boundary is somewhat blurred. Virtually all intellectuals are involved in the system to some degree.[2] Nevertheless, some intellectuals are more involved than others. Thus, one can distinguish government and party officials (*guojia jiguan, dangqun zuzhi fuze ren*) with higher education from other professionals not working directly for the state and the party. The latter group includes (1) teachers at primary, middle school, and university levels, (2) health care workers, (3) engineers and technicians, (4) accountants, statisticians, and economic planning staff, (5) cultural professionals (reporters, editors, writers, actors, athletes), (6) legal workers, (7) priests and monks, (8) science management professionals, (9) researchers, and (10) enterprise directors and managers. Most "establishment" or "in" intellectuals are party members ("party intellectuals"), but most "out" intellectuals are not. For the purposes of this study, however, "party intellectuals" is synonymous with "establishment intellectuals," and "non-party intellectuals" is synonymous with "non-establishment intellectuals."

This bifurcation, one must remember, is a highly institutionalized one. It begins early in the education system. In elementary and high school, everyone is encouraged to join the organizations of Young Pioneers (*Shaoxiandui*) and the Communist Youth League (*Gongqingtuan*). Those who will follow the path into the establishment are appointed class leaders and given various political and administrative responsibilities. In his study of Tianjin elites, Walder (1995a) found that recruitment into administrative positions was based on both political and educational credentials. Party membership contributed much more than education to gaining administrative positions. In contrast, political credentials were not important for obtaining professional positions; only education mattered.

Before 1978, Mao limited the number of party intellectuals and their role in the decision-making processes of the state. After 1978, however, intellectuals came to play an important although not dominant role in middle- and high-level administration and management. According to the 2000 population census, they filled 35% of the positions in the government administrative and managerial apparatus (junior college–educated and above, Population Census Office 2002, table 4-6).

Various statistics can be used to describe the relative importance of party intellectuals. According to the 1992 Urban Social Survey, for example, although 32% of the middle- and high-level positions in the government administrative apparatus were filled by intellectuals, 87% of these intellectuals were party intellectuals, and only 13% were non-party intellectuals. As for the 21% of the factory administrative positions filled by intellectuals, 86% of these were party intellectuals, and only 14% were non-party officials.

Overall, nearly half of the 44 million intellectuals were professionals (49%, mostly teachers, health care workers, and technical personnel), followed by clerical workers (21%), state and party administrators and directors of public firms (12%), sales and service workers (8%), blue-collar workers (8%), and others (2%). Seventy percent of the 44 million had junior college degrees. The percentage of those who held four-year degrees was higher among administrators and managers (11%), professionals (13%), and clerks (9%) than among sales and services workers (1%). Less than 1% of either blue-collar workers or agricultural workers held four-year degrees (Population Census Office 2002, table 4-6). The high percentage of workers with two-year degrees is partially a result of the on-the-job retraining (*huilu*, "returned to the oven") for people who did not have a chance to go to college prior to 1978.

The 1999 Six-City Survey asked the respondents whether they thought of themselves as intellectuals. Most of the 18% of respondents who said yes were non–party members (67%), though only a third were party members. Overall, the self-identified intellectuals were clearly in a higher social stratum than non-intellectuals. Most intellectuals worked in professional, administrative, managerial, and government white-collar jobs, but most non-intellectuals worked in service, sales, and blue-collar jobs. Intellectuals were more likely to work in government and government nonprofit units, but most non-intellectuals worked in lower-level units. Two-thirds of the intellectuals were junior college and college educated, but only 6% of non-intellectuals were. Compared with non-intellectuals, intellectuals in general tended to be older and were likely from the socialist (1949–65) and the reform and post-reform (post-1976) generations (table 8.1).

This socioeconomic gap was also found between party and non-party intellectuals. For example, party intellectuals were more concentrated than non-party intellectuals in a few upper-level occupational groups such as professionals, administrators, and government clerks. Similarly, many more party intellectuals worked in the more prestigious state and public organizations than non-party intellectuals did. Four-fifths of the self-identified party intellectuals were college educated, but only half of the non-party intellectuals were. The percentage of party intellectuals educated at a regular four-

TABLE 8.1
Socioeconomic characteristics of intellectuals and non-intellectuals, 1999 (weighted %)

	Intellectual	Public non-intellectual	INTELLECTUAL TYPE Party	INTELLECTUAL TYPE Non-party	Entire sample $N = 1820$
1. Occupation					
Professional	22	4	26	21	7
Administrative	8	1	23	1	2
Managerial	8	3	9	8	4
Govt. clerical	22	7	34	16	10
Company clerical	5	4	2	7	4
Sales service	4	11	1	5	10
Manual labor	15	58	3	21	51
Private household	1	3	1	1	3
Other	15	9	1	20	9
Total %	100	100	100	100	100
2. Work unit type					
Government	7	2	14	3	3
State nonprofit	26	10	33	23	12
State firm	41	52	47	38	50
Collective firm	6	18	3	8	16
Joint venture firm	4	2	0	6	3
Private firm	2	8	1	3	7
Other	14	8	2	19	9
Total %	100	100	100	100	100
3. College education					
Below college	40	94	20	49	85
Junior colledge	29	5	34	27	9
4-year college	31	1	46	24	6
Total %	100	100	100	100	100
4. Year respondent reached age 20					
Post-1976	33	22	16	42	24
1966–76	30	44	29	30	42
1949–65	30	23	49	20	24
Pre-1949	7	11	6	8	10
Total %	100	100	100	100	100

SOURCE: 1999 Six-City Survey.

NOTE: "Intellectual" refers to self-described intellectual ($N = 327$: 218 non-party, 109 party). All percentages are weighted.

year college was nearly twice as high as for the non-party intellectuals. Most party intellectuals belonged to the socialist generation, but non-party intellectuals mostly belonged to the reform generation (table 8.1). A multivariate analysis (results not shown) including age, education, income, party membership, work unit, and occupation confirmed the bivariate results in table 8.1. These are certainly evidence that, in general, party intellectuals enjoyed a higher socioeconomic status and were in a better bargaining position than non-party intellectuals (Djilas 1957; Konrad and Szelenyi 1979; Kennedy 1991).

All in all, it is clear that non-party intellectuals were more numerous, were often excluded from the political center, and suffered from a lower socioeconomic status. These facts by themselves seem to indicate that a large stratum of non-party intellectuals would resent the privileged minority of party intellectuals. The former furthermore might demand reforms in order to gain equal access. In fact, however, the true extent of any such resentment is in doubt, and the demand for reform seems to come as much from this minority of party intellectuals as it does from the bulk of the intellectual stratum.

Finally, one should distinguish between the handful of most influential intellectuals and a much larger number who are not so well known. The study of a few of the most prominent intellectual leaders is a powerful tool for understanding the intellectual climate in China,[3] since they have considerable influence on other members of their group and on Chinese society. Just how much influence, however, is a different question. Moreover, full analysis of the vast number of views, many published, making up the Chinese intellectual climate is outside the scope of this chapter.

Particularly worth studying would be the extent to which the Western ideology of liberalism has now become part of the political culture shared by party and non-party intellectuals.

History of Intellectuals and the Party-State

To assess the extent to which intellectuals tend to demand reform, it is necessary to remember the traditional normative role of Confucian scholars, each of whom was "resolutely to take responsibility for the well-being of the world" (*yi tian xia wei ji ren*). This traditional concept became intertwined with the implicit Marxist belief that society's true physical, psychological, and social needs can be "discovered" by those who are wise and informed, who then go on to guide society. This otherwise foreign Marxist approach further convinced many Chinese intellectuals that they indeed had a mission to rule. As Charles Lindblom (1977, chap. 19) so adroitly reminds us, this Marxist role for intellectuals is diametrically opposed to the way "good" decisions are made in liberal democratic societies. Liberal democratic societies emphasize that society is very complex and humans very fallible. No elite can discover universal truths by mastering this complexity and overcoming this fallibility. The preferences of the mass of individuals are the best indicators of society's true needs and wants. This alternative model, which downplays the role of intellectuals, has had little appeal in China. Chinese intellectuals in the twentieth century typically believed that they were capable of understanding the "laws of history," and that they have a "moral mission" to lead China's modernization (Metzger 1992, 1998).

This elitist attitude in turn led to an uneasy relationship between intellectuals and the party. After all, intellectuals had traditionally oscillated between co-optation and protest. On the one hand, the "vanguard" party needed intellectuals both to articulate its claim to leadership in Chinese society and to provide technical expertise in economic construction. On the other hand, the Communist Party was always worried that intellectuals would challenge its authority (Link 1992, 29). Thanks to this ambivalence, the relationship between the state and the intellectuals has gone through two stages since the 1949 Revolution.

The first stage subordinated intellectuals to the will of the state more than the second. Initially, intellectuals were considered petty bourgeoisie (Mao 1967a). Many had been educated in the old system that the Communists sought to overthrow. Mao suspected that they were ""fellow-travelers," not fully committed to the Revolution. Unlike peasants, workers, and soldiers, intellectuals were never elevated in status by being designated a main force of the revolution. True, Mao Zedong stressed the importance of intellectuals in winning the Chinese Revolution and the need to recruit large numbers of them into the party, the military, and government organs. Yet he felt secure enough to do so only when the party's organization and leadership were sufficiently consolidated and immune to potential intellectual erosion. As he saw it, the party should use bourgeois intellectuals to produce its own revolutionary intellectuals while reeducating the former to serve the Revolution (Mao 1967c).

Under Mao, one of the most frequently attacked characteristics of Chinese intellectuals was not their political outlook but their anti-empirical and elitist academic style. Mao criticized many intellectuals for being "antique collectors" (only accumulating knowledge and not knowing how to use it) and for "shooting the wrong target with their arrows" (trying to apply their knowledge to China without any understanding of Chinese society). He ordered intellectuals to associate themselves with manual laborers. He argued that if they did not, intellectuals would accomplish nothing (Mao 1967b, 1967d, 1967e).

These policies established a social contract between the party and intellectuals after 1949. The party-state would provide opportunities for intellectuals to use their talent and would reward their efforts with social prestige and material benefits if they (1) obeyed the leadership of the Communist Party, (2) accepted Marxism-Leninism and Maoism as China's guiding ideology, (3) derived their knowledge from and applied it to concrete conditions in China, (4) performed adequately, and (5) gave up their political autonomy as a social group and their elitist values.[4] Repeatedly, however, Mao felt the intellectuals were failing to honor this contract.

After the Communists took power, the first major test of this relationship was in 1956, when the party invited intellectuals to give their advice on how to improve its leadership. The intellectuals responded by not only giving their advice on how to improve it but also by challenging the very bases of the regime, such as socialist economic planning, the idea of "the people's democratic dictatorship," and the monopoly of political power by the Communist Party. The party, feeling that the contract had been broken, struck back. As a result, intellectuals suffered tremendously during the anti-rightist movement in 1957.

Although the anti-rightist movement was a political campaign against intellectuals, the Cultural Revolution (1966–76) went even further. It was a social and academic campaign often punctuated with violence and sadism and aimed at forcing intellectuals to change their elitist attitudes, at lowering their social status, and at making their lives more closely related to those of peasants and workers. Educated urban youths (both high school and college graduates) were sent to the countryside. Professionals and administrators were sent to reeducation schools, where they had to learn to be self-sufficient by doing manual labor to meet their own material needs. Education was to serve production directly. For example, physics was about the mechanics of tractors, chemistry concerned the nature of chemical fertilizers. Theoretical research was suspended. For many intellectuals, the Cultural Revolution was the darkest decade of their lives.

In the post-Mao era, the party developed a basically new contract with the intellectuals, seeking to elicit their support by allowing them a kind of quali-fied autonomy. In the third plenum of its Eleventh Congress in 1978, the party decided to abandon its longtime policy of keeping China on the so-cialist road of class struggle and political correctness. Instead, the most im-portant task became economic modernization. Deng Xiaoping realized that the party could not modernize China by means of political campaigns and that it had to rely on intellectuals to achieve this goal. Thus he was less con-cerned with ideological resistance and the arrogance of intellectuals. Reedu-cating them was not his main concern. His pragmatism was epitomized by a well-known saying of his: "Whether the cat is black or white, it's a good cat if it catches mice." The party should concentrate on how to keep power, and the intellectuals, on contributing to economic modernization. Thus a new, ma-jor differentiation between intellectual and political life was institutionalized.

The party's new relationship with the intellectuals is reflected in several facets. Those who where victimized during the anti-rightist campaign in the 1950s and during the Cultural Revolution in the 1960s and the 1970s were rehabilitated, and their material benefits were improved (Ministry of La-bor 1985). Intellectuals were openly praised as the driving force in economic modernization (Zhang et al. 1992), surpassing workers, peasants, and sol-diers for the first time since the Cultural Revolution. They were encouraged to show their political loyalty to the party by promoting economic and tech-nological modernization, rather than spending their time at political study meetings (Deng 1983). During reform, intellectuals were recruited into the party and given high-level positions or hired as policy advisors (Rosen 1991). Studies openly praising J. S. Mill, F. A. Hayek, and Western liberalism were published (see Li 1998). The leaders after the 2002 Sixteenth Party Congress openly consulted China's top intellectuals on such important issues as the rise and fall of nations, economic globalization, constitutional reform, how to manage crisis, world and regional security, and military technology (*New York Times*, June 2, 2004). All these new changes significantly improved the social status of intellectuals.

Although the conditions in the old social contract have been adjusted and professional performance is much more important now than during the Cultural Revolution, the bottom-line political requirement remained firmly in place. The state seeks a qualified intellectual autonomy, balancing the in-tellectuals' desire for freedom with the state's demand for loyalty. It is true that intellectuals are not required to be actively involved in party politics, but neither are they supposed to challenge its power. The message seems to be that they should mind their own business. There have been a few times since their rehabilitation when intellectuals crossed the line and challenged the political monopoly of the party, as they did in 1957, triggering the anti-rightist campaign. In 1987, the party responded with an anti-bourgeois spiritual pollution campaign, and in 1989, following the government's violent crackdown on anti-government protests, many intellectuals were purged or arrested.

Scholarly Debate about the Role of Intellectuals in Communist Societies

It was with the emergence of this new contract between the state and intellectuals that the distinction between establishment and non-establishment scholars became so important. After all, under Mao's contract, if the idea of an establishment intellectual was not an oxymoron, at the very least party members with higher education (i.e., establishment intellectuals) were rare. The new contract thus created new questions: how do establishment and non-establishment intellectuals differ in their political attitudes? More specifically, how do they differ in terms of general satisfaction with the status quo, pro-market values, and activism? From existing studies we know that intellectuals in communist states can develop liberal ideas and be more critical of the state than non-intellectuals (Silver 1987; Tang and Parish 2000; Chen 2004). Yet the distinction between establishment and non-establishment intellectuals needs to be further examined.

As already mentioned, one can reason that intellectuals outside the establishment enjoy fewer centrally allocated benefits, see themselves as educationally superior to the party intellectuals, and so exhibit the bitterness syndrome (*xiao ren dang dao*) described above. Thus they would be more likely to support a faster transition away from central planning and the party's monopoly of power. Such a transition would provide non-establishment intellectuals with those increases in authority and material benefits that they feel they deserve (Walder 1995a). Conversely, establishment intellectuals should be more satisfied with their lifestyle and with the party-state. They should also be likely to support the status quo, since any rapid change would weaken their privileged position. In Russia, for example, state subsidies for literary journals, writers, artists, filmmakers, and researchers were dramatically reduced during reform, which led to increasing frustration among the Russian intelligentsia (Zaslavsky 1995, 127).

One would think that this theory is correct and could be applied to China.[5] After all, those with vested interests in the status quo and who resist reform should be the ones who are in the political center. It is striking, therefore, that in China today this logic runs into difficulties. This is especially surprising because the advantages enjoyed in post-Mao China by establishment intellectuals are small in comparison with most of non-establishment intellectuals, and this small gap is likely to disappear altogether. Economic reform has provided more opportunities for improving one's livelihood outside the planning system and has reduced the ability of the center to maintain its relative advantage and keep up with the pace of income growth in society (see Walder 1995a; Walder 1995b, chap. 1). If this is true, the "in" intellectuals should be more dissatisfied with the status quo than the "out" intellectuals.

Yet gray areas remain. There is doubt about which group of intellectuals exhibits less general satisfaction with the status quo, and it is not clear that non-establishment intellectuals favor the rise of the market economy more than establishment intellectuals do. The latter may favor it as much, or almost as much. Direct and indirect evidence suggests both kinds of intellectuals favor a market economy more than non-intellectual members of the establishment do. For instance, according to a 1991 survey carried out in post-socialist societies such as Bulgaria, East Germany, Hungary, Poland, Russia, Slovenia, Czechoslovakia, and Estonia, education reduced support for socialist principles such as egalitarianism, the distribution of wealth based on need, and a belief in the state as the prime vehicle of welfare benefits for everyone. This negative impact was stronger among post-socialist societies than among advanced capitalist states (Mason 1995, table 3.4). Another reason is that intellectuals, whether inside the establishment or out, are more likely to be ideologically committed to market reform.

If in post-socialist societies intellectuals in general favor the market more than non-intellectuals, there are still differences between establishment and non-establishment intellectuals in the degree to which each group supports market reforms. The latter are more likely to be the beneficiaries of free-market reform. They are more competitive in the labor market, more likely to earn higher incomes, and have more job mobility under free competition. Therefore, they are expected to favor equality of opportunity and market competition. By contrast, whether establishment intellectuals favor pro-market reform is less clear. On the one hand, they may share an understanding of the problems with central planning. They may also have a competitive edge once put under the control of the "invisible hand." On the other hand, if they depend on the old system both politically and economically, any change will hurt their vested interests. In this case, party intellectuals, many of whom are also party bureaucrats, are likely to hold a critical view of the market.

At the same time, however, the pro-market values of both groups of intellectuals may be attenuated by a shift to post-materialism (Inglehart 1990). In the long run, with more education and (in most cases) better jobs and incomes, intellectuals may develop new, post-materialist concerns that focus on individual development and freedom of expression and, in the process, become less interested in material advantages compared with non-intellectuals.

Apart from the questions of general satisfaction with the status quo and attitudes toward the market, there is the issue of political activism. According to the modernization school, intellectuals in general throughout the developing world are expected to be politically more active than others. Education leads to a stronger sense of political efficacy and a stronger desire to participate politically (Lipset 1961). They also have more contact with the West and thus more understanding of the basic elements of a democratic system, such as free elections and checks and balances. Thus they are more likely to challenge the monopoly of power by the Communist Party.

Others, however, have described Chinese intellectuals as generally elitist and anti-democratic. Indications of such elitism includes Chinese students' feelings of superiority and their refusal to associate themselves with workers and peasants in political movements despite ideological ideals of doing just that (Perry 1991, 1994). Another aspect of elitism is the desire of many Chinese intellectuals to be advisers or consultants for the establishment. Whether in imperial times in centuries past or during the 1989 urban protests, they eagerly sought patrons among top leaders (Cheek 1994; Esherick and Wasserstrom 1994). Moreover, virtuocratic standards in recruitment into the bureaucracy are designed to promote political loyalty and obedience among party intellectuals. This tendency ensures the continuity of the "incestuous relationship" (Perry 1994, 78) between the state and intellectuals.

A third view also rejects any thesis that intellectuals as a whole seek democratization and agrees that Chinese intellectuals are in general unenthusiastic about democratization. According to this third view, however, a small minority of Chinese party intellectuals are pro-democratic. Ding Xueliang (1994a, 1994b, 1994c), for instance, argues that the majority of Chinese intellectuals are not a driving force for democracy. This is because most of them trained under the old socialist system, a process that has led to the current spread of neo-authoritarianism in intellectual circles, especially among intellectuals seeking to advise the establishment.[6] The real hope for democracy, Ding holds, lies instead with "independent-minded official intellectuals." They alone have the institutional resources and quasi-autonomy needed to exert their influence and challenge the authority of the state.[7] According to this view, then, one should expect some establishment intellectuals to be more likely than their non-establishment counterparts to challenge the power and authority of the state and the party. Ding implies that this tiny minority of insiders can be extremely influential.

Three hypotheses can be derived from this discussion regarding intellectual attitudes inside and outside the political center with regard to the status quo in general, the market, and political activism. Hypothesis I is that during the current second stage in relations between the state and intellectuals, establishment intellectuals have become increasingly similar to non-establishment intellectuals. With more educational credentials, a technocratic orientation, and rising expectations that resemble those of non-establishment intellectuals, establishment intellectuals are also likely to be more dissatisfied with the status quo, to be more supportive of rapid reform, and to have more pro-market and pro-democratic values than non-intellectuals. This first hypothesis emphasizes the convergence of different intellectual groups under modernization, regardless of the institutional impact (Inkeles and Bauer 1959; Inkeles 1950, 1960, 1968, 1974, 1976). The remaining two hypotheses focus on the institutional impact on intellectual attitudes. Hypothesis II is about the negative consequences of the socialist institutions: that establishment intellectuals, having been "bought off" or co-opted by more benefits, feel threatened by the prospect of decreasing status under reform (Zaslavsky 1995) and thus will remain more satisfied with the old system and the status quo. These people would be less supportive of rapid reform and of pro-market and pro-democratic values than would non-establishment intellectuals. Conversely, non-establishment intellectuals will be more critical of the status quo and hence committed to reform, especially because their superior education and inferior compensation provoke in them a traditional complaint that "mediocrities are blocking the road" and keeping the higher positions out of the hands of the more talented and qualified. Hypothesis III is about the unintended positive impact of socialist institutions on establishment intellectuals. With an elitist outlook, control of resources, and experience in participation in decision making, establishment intellectuals are expected to show more political activism than non-establishment intellectuals.

Which hypothesis best reflects reality? To answer the question, in this chapter I will discuss differences between intellectuals and non-intellectuals, as well as those between establishment intellectuals and non-establishment intellectuals. I will examine three areas: reform satisfaction and support, socioeconomic attitudes, and political activism. As already indicated, the following statistical analysis is based on survey data from the 1992 China Urban Survey and the 1987–91 Semiannual Surveys on Social Reaction to Urban Reform by the Economic System Reform Institute of China (see appendix A for further details about these surveys).

Findings I: Satisfaction and Support for Reform

One question is whether intellectuals are more satisfied with the post-Mao reforms than non-intellectuals. In the 1980s, as shown earlier, intellectuals benefited from reform in many ways. With all the favorable changes, one should expect intellectuals to be more satisfied and supportive of the current regime than they were before. Yet the educated consistently showed dissatisfaction with various aspects of reform even if their material conditions were improving (see Tang and Parish 2000). There is thus a gap between objective benefits and subjective attitudes. One problem in the previous studies is that education and party membership were examined separately; it is also necessary to examine their combined effect. For example, education may lead to more dissatisfaction and alienation if one is outside of the establishment, but it may lead to more activism if one is inside the party-state. Being inside the system, in other words, may provide more opportunities to voice one's opinion and increase one's sense of political efficacy.

In the 1987–91 ESRIC survey data, four dimensions of the respondent's dissatisfaction with reform were examined: economic opportunity, political freedom, government credibility, and welfare and security. Each item was an index (factor score) of several questions. The first dimension, *economic opportunity*, included the opportunity for more income, the freedom to choose an occupation, the opportunity to use talents at work, and the extent to which one was interested in one's work. The second dimension, *political freedom*, included the respondent's satisfaction with the extent to which he or she enjoyed individual political rights and freedom of speech under reform. The third dimension, *government credibility*, referred to the respondent's opinion about morale under reform (including corruption), the rule of law and legal reforms, the reputation of the Communist Party, and government efficiency. The fourth dimension, *welfare and stability*, included the respondent's feelings about consumer price stability, availability of medical care, housing conditions, income level, and the supply of consumer goods. Urban residents enjoyed several decades of security and stability with regard to these items under central planning. During reform, however, these benefits were likely to decrease. Finally, the degree of approval of the pace of reform was examined: people who said the pace of reform was just right or too slow were coded as approving of reform. Altogether, then, opinions of establishment intellectuals versus those of non-establishment intellectuals were examined with regard to these five dimensions, as were the opinions of non-intellectuals.

Other things being equal, such as age, gender, income, and survey period, all intellectuals were more critical of government performance than non-intellectuals (fig. 8.1). A college degree, whether from a junior college or a four-year college, and whether it was earned early or late in life, was positively correlated with opinions more critical than those of the average citizen. Both types of intellectuals were equally critical of social welfare conditions and of the pace of reform. Both groups wanted a quicker pace of reform, although there were some distinctions by type of intellectual. In two domains, economic opportunity and political freedom, non-establishment intellectuals were more critical. When it came to government credibility, it was the establishment intellectuals who were the most critical, per-

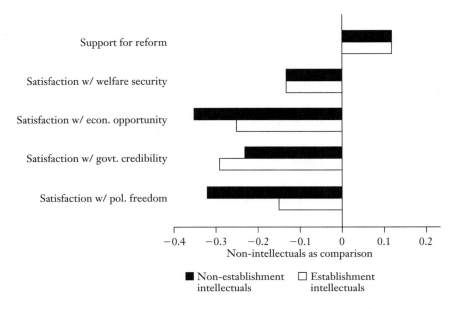

Figure 8.1 Support for and satisfaction with reform by intellectual group (OLS)
SOURCES: 1987–91 ESRIC surveys.

haps because they were more knowledgeable about how government actually functioned.

In more recent years of economic reforms, intellectuals' ambivalence toward its fast pace appeared to fade. Comparisons between the 1987–91 results and the 1999 data indicate that there was less anti-reform sentiment (reform was too fast) in 1999 than in the combined sample of the seven ESRIC surveys (fig. 8.2). Although both groups of intellectuals continued to show more support for market reform than the general public, anti-reform attitudes weakened from the late 1980s and early 1990s to late 1999. This trend was more noticeable among party intellectuals than among non-party intellectuals.

These findings are interestingly ambiguous, at least relative to the hypothesis. There is some support for the traditional hypothesis II (docility of party intellectuals). Throughout the late 1980s, objective conditions for non-establishment elites often lagged behind those of administrative and managerial elites, among whom party membership is concentrated. Greater

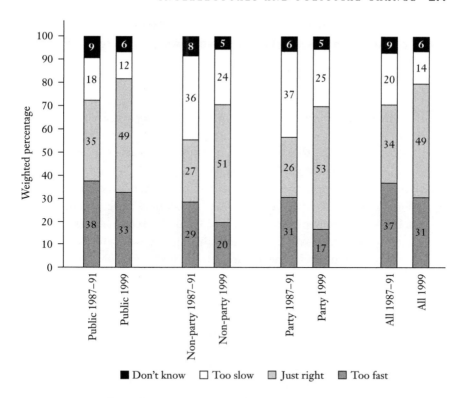

Figure 8.2 Intellectuals and support for reform, 1987–91 and 1999 (weighted %)
SOURCES: Figures for 1987–91 are based on a combined sample of the 7 ESRIC surveys; figures for 1999 are from the 1999 Six-City Survey.

dissatisfaction with economic conditions among non-establishment intellectuals is therefore understandable. Moreover, it is also understandable that although non-establishment elites, being excluded from the political center, craved political freedom so that they could have more of a voice, establishment elites were concerned about other issues. Other evidence, however, tends to support hypotheses I and III. It is striking that, while they were not so eager for greater political freedom, establishment intellectuals nonetheless were more critical of the government apparatus of which they were a core part and were more supportive of reform than non-establishment intellectuals in 1999. As early as the late 1980s and early 1990s, they were far from blind to the problems of their own bureaucratic apparatus. Even if they often did not see political freedom as a way to solve those problems, they gave the government a somewhat lower rating with regard to "credibility" than did intellectuals outside the political center.

Findings II: Socioeconomic Attitudes and Perceived Opportunities

This section continues to explore the question of whether establishment party intellectuals remain very different from non-establishment intellectuals. Hypothesis I suggests that, thanks to recruiters' increasing emphasis on educational credentials, the establishment intellectuals have become more like the non-establishment, non-party intellectuals. Hypothesis II, by contrast, suggests that there remains an inevitable gulf between the two groups. Three sets of attitudes relevant to these two hypotheses will be examined.

INCOME FAIRNESS

The first issue is perceived fairness. One question in the 1992 Chinese Urban Social Survey is about the respondent's sense of income fairness: "Compared with your ability, is your income reasonable?" The respondent could answer (a) very reasonable, (b) reasonable, (c) unreasonable, (d) very unreasonable, and (e) don't know. Among the three comparison groups, 68% in each of the two intellectual groups answered either "unreasonable" or "very unreasonable," but only 45% in the non-intellectual group said so.

This is in contrast to the real income differences in the same survey. The weighted 1991 per capita family income for establishment and non-establishment intellectuals and for non-intellectuals, respectively, were 518 yuan, 512 yuan, and 427 yuan. Together, the two intellectual groups made about 20% more money than the non-intellectual group. This gap is small compared with that in Taiwan and other market societies and may be one reason intellectuals thought they deserved more.

When asked about the reasons for their low income, the three groups responded quite differently. When asked whether incompetence or lack of ability was a factor, the answer was 3%, 9%, and 14% for establishment and non-establishment intellectuals and non-intellectuals, respectively. When asked whether social injustice was the main reason, the answer was 38%, 33%, and 17% for the same three groups.

These data also show that establishment and non-establishment intellectuals had a lot in common. The vast majority in both groups felt their compensation was unreasonably low. To some extent, however, establishment intellectuals were even more dissatisfied: fewer blamed themselves for their low incomes, and more felt unjustly treated. Again, the distribution of intellectual dissatisfaction with the regime tilts a bit more toward the intellectual group in the political center.

CAREER SUCCESS

There are other lines along which party and non-party intellectuals seem to have converged. One of these is a set of 1992 survey items on the determinants of career success. What is particularly significant is the convergence in responses regarding the determinants of success after reform. The 1992 urban survey asks the respondent to pick the most important key to success before and after reform. The longer list of potential responses about success was divided into five categories: (1) chance or luck (willing to take risks, good at grasping opportunities, luck), (2) merit and ability (have knowledge, capable), (3) good family background, (4) connections or *guanxi* (networking, good ties with leaders) and (5) other (cruelty, other).

In the pre-reform period, the perceptions of party and non-party intellectuals were considerably different (fig. 8.3). Although a large percentage in each group thought merit was more important than any other reason for success, fewer non-party intellectuals (37%) than party intellectuals (62%) saw merit before 1978 as the most important factor. More non-party intellectuals (20% and 29%) saw family background and connections as most important than did party intellectuals (only 10% and 17%). Understandably, those who got into high positions thought their success was due to merit, but those who did not get in thought something other than merit played a role, such as personal connections and parental help.

In the post-reform period, however, party and non-party intellectuals were much more similar in their responses. After 1978, each group thought merit was the most important reason for success (47% for party intellectuals and 43% for non-party intellectuals). This convergence meant party intel-

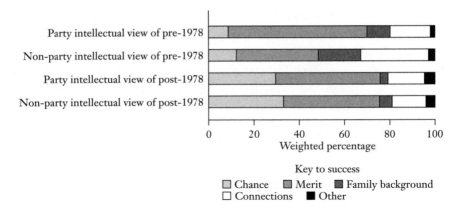

Figure 8.3   Reasons for success as perceived by 2 intellectual groups (weighted %)
SOURCE: 1992 Urban Social Survey.

lectuals recognized merit less and non-party intellectuals recognized merit slightly more. For both groups, family background and connections became less important compared with the pre-reform era, and, for both, chance became much more important, such as the willingness to take risks and grasp opportunities. In the eyes of both sets of intellectuals, then, the basis of career mobility changed dramatically with reform, and both groups came to view the conditions of success in increasingly similar terms.

MATERIALISM

Finally, the 1992 Urban Survey and the 1999 Six-City Survey contain questions regarding the respondents' attitudes toward materialism and the market. One such question in the 1992 survey is, "What is the most important purpose of education?" Respondents were asked to choose among the following reasons: (a) get a better job, (b) improve social status, (c) improve personal character, (d) individual development, (e) obtain knowledge, (f) learn to think, (g) learn to get along with people, (h) get an ideal mate, and (i) make more money. Items (a), (b), (h), and (i) are related to immediate material gains and are coded 1; the others are coded 0. The second question in the same survey is related to the purpose of one's work: "When you look for a job, what is the most important consideration?" The choices included (a) income, (b) light workload, (c) security, (d) interest, (e) feeling of accomplishment, (f) career advancement, (g) more leisure time, (h) other. Items (a), (b), and (c) are related to materialistic concerns and are coded 1; the others are coded 0. The third question in 1992 is related to one's preference for equal opportunity versus equal results: "One view sees more equality in income and welfare benefits as a reflection of fairness in society. Another view sees fairness not in terms of equality of income and benefits, but rather in equal opportunity to compete. The third view holds that the government should set a pay scale according to one's contribution to society. Which view do you prefer?" View 2 is coded 1, and views 1 and 3 are coded 0. The 1999 survey has questions about the respondent's tolerance of income gaps and unemployment, reflecting the respondent's attitude toward free-market principles.

The answers to the above questions by the three groups were compared to each other—those of establishment intellectuals, non-establishment intellectuals, and non-intellectuals (table 8.2). Again, it is striking that the two intellectual strata tended to converge. Overall, both intellectual groups were less materialistic and more pro-market than non-intellectuals. More of them thought education and work had a purpose other than direct material gain. They were also more likely to support market competition and equality of opportunity. Although establishment intellectuals were slightly less support-

TABLE 8.2
Socioeconomic attitudes by intellectual type, 1992 and 1999 (weighted %)

	Establishment intellectuals	Non-establishment intellectuals	Non-intellectuals
1. Education is for material gain			
(1992)	27	25	39*
2. Security is main purpose of work			
(1992)	23	21	50*
3. Support for equal opportunity			
(1992)	51	60	33*
N	230	304	1861
4. Cannot tolerate income gap			
(1999)	15	21	25*
5. Cannot tolerate unemployment			
(1999)	40	43	53
N	109	218	1493

SOURCES: 1992 Urban Social Survey (items 1–3); 1999 Six-City Survey (items 4–5).
*Statistically significantly different from the other two groups at .01

ive of equal opportunity than non-establishment intellectuals, they still were much more supportive than non-intellectuals.[8]

This section has examined data to test the competing hypotheses about convergence under modernization and divergence under distinct sociopolitical institutions. The findings provide strong support for the convergence hypothesis and lead to the conclusion that different groups of intellectuals have found more in common with each other over time.

Findings III: Political Activism

The final question concerns political activism. Conceivably, party and non-party intellectuals sharing many outlooks could still differ with regard to activism, but it was unclear whether party intellectuals would be more active than non-party intellectuals. Although party intellectuals are expected to obey the party, they are also well situated to exert their influence within the system.

Several questions in the 1992 and 1999 surveys were related to political activism. "What would you do if something happened that hurt everyone's interests at work or in your neighborhood: (a) take the lead in bringing a petition to the relevant government office and official, (b) take the lead if asked, (c) not take the lead, but support the petition, or (d) avoid trouble?" The first two choices indicate political efficacy and were coded 1; other choices were coded 0. This question was available only in the 1992 survey.

The second question in both the 1992 and 1999 surveys was about the respondent's reaction to a leader's wrong decision: "What would you do if your supervisor made a wrong decision related to work?" The respondent was asked to choose among (a) obey, (b) silently disobey, and (c) tell the supervisor he or she is wrong. The last choice shows more initiative and a greater sense of efficacy and was coded 1; the other two answers were coded 0.

The third question in both surveys was related to participation in workplace decision making: "In recent years, have you made suggestions or expressed your opinions about workplace reform, innovation, and the improvement of management?" The answers included (a) yes, often, (b) sometimes, (c) only when asked, (d) only talked to friends and colleagues about it, and

(e) never. The first two choices showed the respondent's initiative in making suggestions and were coded 1; the other answers were coded 0.

The fourth question in both surveys was related to the respondents' hypothetical action when dissatisfied: "What would be your more likely action when dissatisfied with society?" The choices were (a) talk to the relevant government bureau or official, (b) report the matter to the media, (c) complain, (d) protest or petition, (e) use illegal means, (f) find own ways to change it, and (g) do nothing, just tolerate it. Choices (a) and (b) were coded as officially establishment channels; (d), (e), and (f) were coded as unofficial channels; and (c) and (g) were coded as no action.

Finally, there were questions in the 1992 survey related to obedience before and after reform: "Currently, how many people accept their supervisor's or their supervising agency's instructions? And how many did in the 1950s and 1960s?" The answers to choose from were (a) 80%, (b) 50%, and (c) only a few activists. Choice (a) was coded 1 as more obedience; the others were coded 0.

There was evidence that intellectuals inside the system tended toward more activism. More establishment intellectuals reported themselves as active than did non-establishment intellectuals in 1992 and 1999 for the first three questions in table 8.3 (items 1–3). They were more likely to take the lead by officially presenting a petition, telling a leader that he or she was wrong, and taking the initiative in making suggestions at work. A significantly lower percentage of non-establishment intellectuals reported themselves as active. It is striking that the percentages in their case were similar to, and in some cases lower than, those of non-intellectuals. The change from 1992 to 1999 is also interesting to notice. Although the level of political activism declined overall, the gap between establishment intellectuals on the one hand and both non-establishment intellectuals and the general public on the other had widened.

In the case of channels used for petitioning (items 4 and 5, table 8.3), in 1992, the two intellectual groups showed distinctive tendencies. Perhaps predictably, party intellectuals preferred official channels to unofficial channels, but non-party intellectuals favored unofficial channels over official channels. In 1999, party intellectuals continued to show the same preferences. One could conclude that the persistent preference for official chan-

TABLE 8.3
Political efficacy by intellectual type, 1992 and 1999 (weighted %)

	Establishment intellectuals	Non-establishment intellectuals	Non-intellectuals
1. Lead petition if collective interest hurt (1992)	74*	60	62
2. Point out leader's wrong decision at work			
1992	72*	54	57
1999	58*	30‡	25
3. Take initiative to make suggestions at work			
1992	58*	41	35
1999	52**	24**	15**
4. Petition through official channels if dissatisfied			
1992	39**	18**	27**
1999	32†	23	21
5. Petition through unofficial channels if dissatisfied			
1992	16	27*	16
1999	23	22†	14
6. Most people obeyed orders before reform (1992)	94†	92	88
7. Most people obeyed orders after reform (1992)	29	33	44*
N (1992)	230	304	1861
N (1999)	109	218	1493

SOURCES: 1992 Urban Social Survey; 1999 Six-City Survey.
*Statistically significantly different from the other two groups at .01
**Statistically significantly different from each other at .01
†Statistically significantly different only from non-intellectuals at .01
‡Statistically significantly different from establishment intellectuals at .01

nels among party intellectuals indicates a lack of political initiative. If, however, the high level of activism among party intellectuals in the case of the first three questions is taken into consideration, the tendency to go through established channels suggests that those within the system can more effectively utilize those internal channels. Further, there was an interesting change over time. The gap between the two intellectual groups seemed to be reduced, with party intellectuals increasingly favoring unofficial channels and non-party intellectuals favoring official channels. This change indicates the tendency among establishment intellectuals to challenge the political center through new channels at the same time as official channels became more responsive and attractive to those outside the party.[9]

When asked whether most people obeyed orders before reform (item 6, table 8.3), almost everyone in each group agreed that they did. Far fewer people, by contrast, thought that people obeyed orders during the current reform period (item 7, table 8.3). Again, the two groups of intellectuals were similar, this time in their perception of the extent of state control over the citizenry.

It is not altogether surprising that party intellectuals, being empowered, saw themselves as more active than non-party intellectuals and non-intellectuals did. Indeed, the link between activism and a belief in democratization has not been demonstrated in the case of party intellectuals. There is, however, a plausible link between their activism, dissatisfaction with the establishment, and a desire to increase the pace of reform, as well as with their perception of loosening party control. The data thus suggest that those who controlled the state's institutional resources were more actively supporting reform (hypothesis III). They should not be pictured as an inert mass of vested interests resisting reform (hypothesis II).

Conclusion

All in all, valuable survey data strongly support hypothesis I. The two groups of intellectuals resembled each other far more than they did non-intellectuals. Compared with the latter, both groups of intellectuals were more dissatisfied with the status quo and tended to support the current reforms more strongly. As a whole, the intellectuals constituted the most pro-reform stratum, and they also inclined more than non-intellectuals toward non-materialistic values. Thus, whatever gap there may be between party and non-party intellectuals, one should also recognize a certain shared culture or worldview. This convergence in China reflected intellectual tendencies in a number of other societies. Regardless of how much governments brainwashed their intellectuals with official ideology or tried to appease and co-opt them, intellectuals often remained critical of their governments. Moreover, like intellectuals generally in industrial societies, Chinese intellectuals as a whole tended toward non-materialistic values more than the general public. Like their counterparts in other post-socialist societies, they favored the market and rapid reform more than the general public did. It should be pointed out that the degree of bifurcation between the two intellectual groups in China could not be explained simply by saying that those outside the political center were more committed to reform and democratization than those inside (hypothesis II). The outsiders were more dissatisfied with their economic prospects and were more interested in freedom. Yet even though they were often more educated than party intellectuals, they were not primarily motivated by any traditional feelings of envy and bitterness directed at those who enjoyed political power. Moreover, party intellectuals rated the credibility of the government lower than did their non-party counterparts and were more inclined to act in pursuit of their ideals (hypothesis III). Ample anecdotes show party intellectuals' support for political reform. For instance, one leading party intellectual, the deputy director of China's Environmental Protection Agency, openly advocated dealing with environmental pollution by mass political activism, rule of law, and checks and balances (see Jim Yardley, "Bad Air and Water, and a Bully Pulpit in China," *New York Times*, September 25, 2004).

The findings in this chapter show that the increasingly technocratic party elite is a group vigorously inclined toward reform. It is catching up to and perhaps surpassing the non-party intellectual elite in this regard. Though the government gives them more ideological education and privileges, the party intellectuals are somewhat more critical of the government and the party than the non-party intellectuals when asked about morale under reform, corruption, the rule of law and legal reform, the reputation of the party, and government efficiency. They support rapid reform as vigorously as their non-establishment counterparts. And they are inclined to take the lead when problems arise. They could well become a more important force for change than non-establishment intellectuals. This is the unintended effect of the socialist institutions.

The state is trying to maintain a "vassalage" relationship with intellectuals by providing "delegate resources" for them, particularly for establishment intellectuals who are also given institutional channels for problem solving. Yet it is far from clear that establishment intellectuals have been co-opted. There is a complex, dynamic relationship between intellectuals and the state even within the framework of the state itself. As the state demands higher-quality intellectuals under the new social contract, the latter in turn demand more reform of the state. This built-in tension could actually be beneficial because it puts pressure on both sides to improve and adapt to each other. But if the state fails to make the reforms demanded, this tension could become volatile.

The tension is affected by international as well as domestic circumstances.

By placing economic sanctions on and criticizing China in the post-1989 period, Western nations have aroused anti-Western feelings and nationalism among elite intellectuals, who tend to reflexively defend China against foreign criticism (e.g., Song et al. 1996). In this way, outside pressure seems to have tightened the relationship between the party-state and intellectuals.

On the other hand, a number of domestic trends have been loosening this relationship. The non-state sector is growing as the influence of the state wanes. Some of the reward mechanisms that the state utilized in the past to control elite intellectuals are now giving way to market forces. Intellectuals will be able to acquire even more resources outside the state sector in the future.

Undoubtedly, the loosening of this relationship is reflected in the activism, sense of empowerment, and critical consciousness of the party intellectuals. To be sure, the liberalism expressed by some non-party intellectuals is also a vital part of the ferment leading toward still more political change. Yet the important role in this ferment played by party intellectuals, who control resources in the party and government, should not be overlooked. This chapter shows the option of working more with party intellectuals instead of just focusing hope on critics outside the party. Working with the party elite is probably the most practical way to bring about concrete political improvement. Many popular establishment intellectuals lost their influence once they left China and became political dissidents. At the same time, too much political pressure from the West against China may push party intellectuals closer to the establishment and thereby lessen the demand for reform.

PART FOUR

Conclusion

CHAPTER NINE

Public Opinion and Political Change in an Authoritarian State

This chapter returns to the questions raised in chapter 1, namely, what the forces are that shape public opinion and whether public opinion in turn can affect political change in China. In chapter 1 I discussed several factors that were potentially important in shaping public opinion in China: political culture, economic growth and market reform, and the systemic effect of the authoritarian political environment. Now let's re-examine these factors in reverse order, together with the findings from the case studies in the previous chapters. The final section will discuss the link between public opinion and decision making.

Systemic Effect

The findings in this book confirm that China's authoritarian political system clearly has a significant role in manipulating public opinion and in curbing mass political behavior. The party continued to control public opinion–gathering, censor any open debate and criticism of the party's legitimacy, and allow only parochial opinions to be voiced. It showed effectiveness in mobilizing popular support for the current party-state political system and official ideologies. This systemic impact also was reflected in rising political conservatism and a declining sense of political efficacy in the 1990s (chaps. 2, 3, 4, and 6). All these factors are consistent with the literature on Communist politics that emphasizes the negative consequences of political control (Arendt 1951).

The more interesting and surprising findings, however, are the unintended and often counterintuitive consequences of China's authoritarian political environment. These surprises occur consistently in almost every case study throughout this volume. For example, although evidence showed that the party-state was afraid of letting public opinion be known to the outside world, public opinion surveys were nonetheless increasingly accepted as tools of research and policy making (chap. 2). Popular dissatisfaction with the cost of market reform was growing in China as the world moved toward democratization, yet support for China's authoritarian political structure and for the party was still surprisingly high (chap. 3). Media control and censorship were never subtle. However, growing media diversification and consumption clearly increased public confidence in media and nurtured citizen-initiated political participation, pro-Western feelings, a sense of political efficacy, and civic values (chap. 4). Although China's civil society was not based on participation in voluntary associations, interpersonal trust was unexpectedly high and led to liberal values just as it did in democratic societies. Even more interestingly, the Communist Party itself, while acting as a "dictator," was showing signs of a voluntary association that bred interpersonal trust (chap. 5). It is undeniable that direct and open challenges to the Communist Party were suppressed and the sense of political efficacy was declining in the 1990s. Yet voicing public opinion at the grassroots level was surprisingly common, and the channels for doing so became wider and more effective (chap. 6). Although labor unions continued to function as an instrument of party control at the workplace, they served to protect workers' welfare and job security and to facilitate solutions for labor disputes and employee participation in managerial decision making (chap. 7). Finally, while most outside observers put their hope for China's democratization in the hands of dissidents and non-party intellectuals, the findings in this volume showed clearly that demands for political change and liberalization were raised more consistently by intellectuals within the party itself (chap. 8). These counterintuitive findings make the study of public opinion in China both fascinating and worthwhile.

There are several factors that may explain why the political system was only partially successful in manipulating public opinion and mass behavior. Among the possibilities is the "backfiring" effect. According to this view, as control and mobilization intensify, the public becomes both more apathetic and rebellious. Although the rising apathy documented in chapter 6 seems to partially support this argument, there is no evidence of an increasingly rebellious public. In contrast, many other findings indicate that support for the regime and its legitimacy were growing in the 1990s (chap. 3). The second explanation for the political system's decreasing effectiveness is the retreat of the party-state. Although the very foundation of the party-state cannot be challenged, over time the state has actually reduced its efforts to control public opinion and behavior at the grassroots level. The most obvious examples of the state's retreat include the gradual acceptance of public opinion surveys, the diversification of the media market, the liberalization of grassroots political participation, and the increasing competitiveness of local elections (chaps. 2, 4, and 6). The third explanation is the growing influence of other factors, including economic growth, marketization, and the persistence of traditional values. To these we now turn.

Cultural Effects

One striking example of the persistence of traditional values is interpersonal trust, a factor that leads to another surprising conclusion about China (chap. 4). Unlike in market democracies, interpersonal trust in China is high and is based on informal social interactions such as family and neighborhood ties rather than on formal associations. Such "traditional trust" in China was just as effective in nurturing liberal ideas as the "modern trust" originating from membership in formal associations suggested by the civil culture literature (Almond and Verba 1963; Putnam 1995; Inglehart 1999). Thus the conclusion is that despite research evidence to the contrary, a non-democratic country lacking a Western type of civic culture can nonetheless generate a high degree of interpersonal trust. In an indirect way, traditional values are also linked to political change when the social elite such as the party intellectuals demand political liberalization (chap. 8). These within-system intellectuals are indoctrinated with the Confucian idea of moral responsibility and are seeking to become the driving force of further political change (Perry 1994).

Market Effect

In certain areas, economic growth and marketization are more important in shaping public opinion and mass political behavior in urban China than traditional values or even the authoritarian political system. As discussed in chapter 1, the post-Mao leaders prioritized economic and political modernization as well as market profit to such a degree that adjustments had to be made in order to achieve these goals. For example, the authoritarian tradition of withholding information because of political paranoia has given way to the need to release information for market profit and the desire to present China as a modern state under a rational technocracy. Evidence for this orientation can be seen in greater tolerance for survey research and for media diversity (chaps. 2 and 4). Further, market reform has promoted the rapid growth of the private sector. Political participation became diversified as the nouveau riche competed with the traditional state elite for political influence (chap. 6). A symbolic culmination of such power sharing could be seen in a constitutional amendment for the protection of private property approved during the second session of the Tenth National People's Congress meeting in March 2004 (http://news.xinhuanet.com/english/2004-03/14/content _1365521.htm [accessed March 22, 2005]). Finally, market reform polarized public opinion, dividing various groups based on how much they supported the regime and the extent of reform, as well as on how much they gained or benefited, or in other words, whether they were winners or losers of reform. The disadvantaged groups, which showed less enthusiasm about market reform and the current leadership, were also more likely to be involved in labor disputes. Media access became polarized based on one's economic resources, while Maoism became increasingly attractive to economically disadvantaged groups (chaps. 3, 4, and 7). All these phenomena are the results of marketization.

Modernization Effect

Finally, two other characteristics of public opinion in China are worth noting. One is its "modern" nature. Studies of public opinion in the West have shown the development of post-modern values such as environmentalism, human rights, and individual political autonomy (Inglehart 1997). By contrast, the typical Chinese value system shows a clear modernization mentality, one that ranks individual economic need on top and political freedom at the bottom (chap. 3). As market reform and its attendant economic pressures deepen, this materialistic emphasis is likely to continue. Although in post-industrial societies citizens are becoming independent minded and are more willing to challenge the government (Norris 1999), in China the paternalistic political tradition in the state-society relationship is still prevalent except among a small group of party elite and political dissidents (chaps. 3 and 8). It seems that outside pressure to speed up political reform is relevant only if one agrees that China's current "modernization" mentality is a result of manipulation of public opinion by the elite. If the current public mood is instead a true reflection of the broader public need, advocating post-modern values at this point is unlikely to make a significant difference. It would be like playing the violin to a cow (as the Chinese saying goes)—altogether the wrong audience.

Volatility of the Public Mood

In addition to the effects of the political system, culture, and marketization, another characteristic of Chinese public opinion is that it can be volatile. Changes in urban life since the mid-1980s have been everything but gradual. Automobiles have replaced bicycles, and private apartments have replaced communal dwellings. As shown in chapter 4, newspaper and television consumption exploded, growing more than tenfold from 1979 to 2002. Indeed, the public mood has experienced a great leap forward toward the very material consumption that Mao tried to fight during the Cultural Revolution. Further, the volatility of public mood is also fueled by the massive restructuring of social interest during market reform, paired with the decline of central planning. The disappearance of the traditional social safety net and job security on one hand, and the growing income gap on the other, have stirred up a large number of labor disputes and social tension (chaps. 3 and 7). Using valuable historical survey data, this book records the drastic fluctuation of public opinion. For example, income satisfaction among urban residents dropped from about 55% in May 1987 to around 15% in May 1989 (fig. 3.3). This volatility in levels of public satisfaction represented a major challenge to continued economic reform and political stability during the 1989 urban protest.

Public Opinion and Political Change

The final question is whether public opinion can influence decision making and political change in China. Studies of public opinion in the West have the advantage of examining the electoral process in order to establish the link between public opinion and policy making. In China, the obvious difficulty in studying how public opinion affects the government's decision making is the missing electoral link between the two. As discussed in chapter 1, there are no direct elections of national level leaders. Yet there are channels for expressing public opinion. One has to wear very large blinders not to see any improvement in the mechanisms that link public opinion and government decision making, including the recent development in implementing rural and urban local elections, the growing importance of the legal system, the rising political activism of the media, and the increased responsiveness of the government ombudsman system (chap. 6). Further, political mobilization can create unintended consequences. Huntington and Nelson showed that mobilized political participation could be internalized and turned into autonomous participation (1976). Some signs indicate that such a process is taking place in China. For example, the party's effort to mobilize citizens through the media has resulted in an increase in autonomous political participation and a sense of political efficacy. Party intellectuals, a group more frequently exposed to political mobilization, have turned out to demand more political opening up than others. Labor unions, an indispensable component of the party's mobilization machine, have shown their willingness to take sides with workers against management. These facts show that the authoritarian political system itself can generate autonomous public opinion and allow it to be heard.

There are at least three ways in which public opinion can influence decision making and political change in China. The first step in interpreting decision making and political change is knowing what public opinion is. Without knowing the nature of public opinion, one cannot predict the direction of political change. An incorrect understanding of public opinion will result in an incorrect prediction of political change. For example, empirical evidence in this book (chapter 3 and text box in chapter 1 on the Tiananmen Square protests) shows that public opinion in 1989 was anticorruption and anti-market reform, with a weak desire for democracy and freedom. From these facts, we know that the 1989 urban protests were not primarily a pro-democratic movement. This interpretation is different from the one based on the highly visible Statue of Liberty and the slogan "Give me liberty or give me death." Yet these findings were drawn from a more solid empirical foundation than either the sculpture or the slogan (which was printed on a poster in China in 1989). Thus, studying public opinion makes accurate interpretation and prediction of political change possible.

Second, public opinion obviously can influence decision making through mass political participation. This study shows in detail how public opinion can be heard in urban China. It shows, particularly in chapter 6, how much public opinion was heard through what channels and their effectiveness. Although the scope of issues to be heard was limited, this study provides valuable and detailed knowledge about voicing public opinion and how it changed over time.

The third way public opinion can affect decision making is protest. Even though it is not the focus of this book and is often not easily captured by survey data, protest captures much media attention and deserves more discussion (Tanner 2004; see also *South China Morning Post*, June 8, 2004). Although sporadic and rare, protest can be effective in changing decision making and forcing the government to compromise. Repression, compensation, and scapegoating are three standard techniques in handling protests in China. Repression means arresting the organizer. Compensation means at least partial satisfaction of public demands. Scapegoating means replacing the responsible official if necessary. One example is the public demand for release of information during the SARS outbreak in 2003. The leading figure, Dr. Jiang Yanyong, was put under house arrest, the Minister of Public Health was fired, and the information on the spread of the epidemic was released. This example shows how effective public protest can be in influencing decision making, even in a country where the government still arrests political dissidents.

Yet the impact of protest on political change should not be exaggerated. As mentioned earlier, protest per se does not tell the direction of change unless we know what the public's opinion and demands are. Public opinion surveys are a useful tool for gathering public opinion and facilitating the analysis of a protest. Further, the evidence in this book shows that labor disputes and protests often focus on specific issues related to pay and jobs (chap. 7). They tell little about the trend of long-term political change. The majority of Chinese citizens spend more energy on solving a greater number of problems through channels other than protest. In addition, sometimes protest may not indicate a crisis of the party's legitimacy. In some areas, the party-state is playing the role of a mediator, letting interest groups confront each other rather than fight against the state itself. For example, in the booming real estate market, the state is increasingly letting consumers deal with developers face to face. In the early 2000s, local governments issued permits for residents to protest against real estate developers. Protests of this nature have little direct influence on government decision making. In short, protest is only one way through which public opinion influences decision making. Studying the nature and formation of public opinion and the other forms of mass political participation can provide further insight in the long-term trends of the impact of public opinion on political change in China or elsewhere.

It is difficult to imagine that any regime, democratically elected or not, can sustain itself for very long without taking public opinion into consideration. The Chinese rulers, long before the invention of modern elections, compared public opinion to the river and the state to the boat—a boat that, if misguided, could easily be overturned (*shui neng zai zou, yi neng fu zou*).

Reference Matter

Description of Surveys

	Organization/ principal investigator	Month/ year of survey	Number of observations	Sample sites
Semiannual Survey	ESRIC[a]	5/1987	2576	40 cities[b]
Political Participation Survey	ESRIC	7/1987	2415	8 cities[c]
Semiannual Survey	ESRIC	10/1987	2438	37 cities
Semiannual Survey	ESRIC	5/1988	2577	39 cities
Semiannual Survey	ESRIC	10/1988	2176	35 cities
Semiannual Survey	ESRIC	5/1989	2143	35 cities
Semiannual Survey	ESRIC	10/1989	2020	33 cities
Semiannual Survey	ESRIC	9/1991	2520	39 cities
Urban Social Survey	ESRIC	6/1992	2370	44 cities
Employee Survey	ACFTU[d]	Summer 1997	54,000[e]	81 counties/ cities[f]
Six-City Survey	Peking University/ Wenfang Tang	8–10/1999	1820	6 cities[g]
World Values Survey	ISR[h]	2000–2001	118,519	96 countries/ regions[i]

NOTES: [a]Economic System Reform Institute of China.

[b]See Tang and Parish 2000, table B2.

[c]Beijing, Shanghai, Tianjin, Guangzhou, Shenyang, Wuhan, Chongqing, and Harbin.

[d]All-China Federation of Trade Unions.

[e]A subsample of 12,165 is used in this book.

[f]See All-China Federation of Trade Unions 1999.

[g]Shanghai, Chongqing, Guangzhou, Shenyang, Wuhan, and Xian.

[h]Institute of Social Research, University of Michigan.

[i]See 2000–2001 World Values Survey Questionnaire at http://wvs.isr.umich.edu/ques4.shtml (accessed March 25, 2005).

Satisfaction with Reform and Speed Variables in Table 3.1

Variable	Mean	SD	Min.	Max.
Satisfaction with economic opportunity	.44	.19	0	1
Satisfaction with political freedom	.59	.16	0	1
Satisfaction with public affairs	.39	.25	0	1
Overall satisfaction	.45	.16	0	1
Party members	.17	.38	0	1
Family income (0–10 scale)	4.48	1.71	0	10
Male	.50	.50	0	1
Years of education	10.24	3.56	0	19
Age 20 before 1949	.05	.21	0	1
Age 20 in 1949–65	.21	.41	0	1
Age 20 in 1966–76	.25	.43	0	1
Age 20 in 1977–84	.24	.43	0	1
Age 20 after 1984	.25	.43	0	1
Professional	.04	.19	0	1
Administrator/manager	.04	.19	0	1
Clerk	.09	.28	0	1
Sales/service	.05	.22	0	1
Private (geti and *siying*)	.02	.14	0	1
Manual laborer	.21	.41	0	1
Unemployed	.13	.34	0	1
Retired	.28	.45	0	1
No job and other	.15	.36	0	1
Shanghai	.17	.38	0	1
Guangzhou	.17	.37	0	1
Xian	.16	.37	0	1
Wuhan	.17	.37	0	1
Chongqing	.17	.37	0	1
Shenyang	.17	.37	0	1

SOURCE: 1999 Six-City Survey.
SD = standard deviation
N = 1820

Variables in Multivariate Analysis for 1999, Figure 4.5

Variable	Mean	SD	Min.	Max.
Support for regime (sysgood)	.59	.40	0	1
Official ideology (orthodox)	.79	.20	0	1
Nationalism (sino)	.22	.31	0	1
Pro-West (prowest)	.57	.22	0	1
Political efficacy (efficacy)	.41	.21	0	1
Political action if dissatisfied (saydisat)	.38	.48	0	1
Making suggestions at work (suggest)	.41	.34	0	1
Civic values (civsoc)	.46	.18	0	1
Media consumption (media)	.57	.22	0	1
Life satisfaction	.46	.15	0	1
Party member	.17	.38	0	1
Family income (1999)	.45	.17	0	1
Male	.50	.50	0	1
Years of education	10.24	3.56	0	19
Age 20 before 1949	.05	.21	0	1
Age 20 in 1949–65	.21	.41	0	1
Age 20 in 1966–76	.25	.43	0	1
Age 20 in 1977–84	.24	.43	0	1
Age 20 after 1984	.25	.43	0	1
Professional	.07	.26	0	1
Administrator/manager	.07	.25	0	1
Clerk	.15	.35	0	1
Sales/service	.10	.30	0	1
Private (geti/siying)	.03	.16	0	1
Other occupation	.04	.21	0	1
Student	.06	.23	0	1
Manual laborer	.49	.50	0	1
Guangzhou	.17	.37	0	1
Xian	.16	.37	0	1
Wuhan	.17	.37	0	1
Chongqing	.17	.37	0	1
Shenyang	.17	.37	0	1
Shanghai	.17	.38	0	1

SOURCE: 1999 Six-City Survey.

SD = standard deviation

N = 1820 (1650 for media consumption)

Variables in Multivariate Analysis for 1992, Figure 4.5

Variable	Observations	Mean	SD	Min.	Max.
Political efficacy (efficacy)	2395	.40	.20	0	1
Political action if dissatisfied (saydisat)	2395	.45	.50	0	1
Making suggestions at work (suggest)	2312	.54	.29	0	1
Media consumption (media)	2393	.92	.19	0	1
Party member	2387	.29	.46	0	1
Family income (1991)	2395	.47	.11	0	1
Male	2393	.51	.50	0	1
Years of education	2387	10.90	3.19	0	18
Age 20 before 1949	2395	.09	.29	0	1
Age 20 in 1949–65	2395	.25	.43	0	1
Age 20 in 1966–76	2395	.23	.42	0	1
Age 20 in 1977–84	2395	.20	.40	0	1
Age 20 after 1984	2395	.22	.41	0	1
Professional	2384	.11	.31	0	1
Administrator	2384	.08	.26	0	1
Manager	2384	.07	.25	0	1
Clerk	2384	.20	.40	0	1
Sales/service	2384	.04	.21	0	1
Private	2384	.03	.17	0	1
None/other	2384	.07	.26	0	1
Student	2384	.04	.19	0	1
Manual laborer	2384	.36	.48	0	1
Beijing	2395	.04	.20	0	1
Tianjing	2395	.04	.20	0	1
Changzhou	2395	.02	.14	0	1
Qinhuangdao	2395	.02	.15	0	1
Taiyuan	2395	.02	.15	0	1
Jincheng	2395	.02	.14	0	1
Wuhai	2395	.02	.15	0	1
Shengyan	2395	.02	.14	0	1
Dalian	2395	.02	.14	0	1
Benxi	2395	.02	.14	0	1
Jinzhou	2395	.02	.14	0	1
Wuxun	2395	.02	.14	0	1
Changchu	2395	.02	.14	0	1
Fuyu	2395	.01	.10	0	1
Harbin	2395	.02	.14	0	1

Variable	Observations	Mean	SD	Min.	Max.
Qiqiher	2395	.02	.14	0	1
Jixi	2395	.02	.14	0	1
Shanghai	2395	.04	.20	0	1
Nanjing	2395	.02	.14	0	1
Suzhou	2395	.03	.16	0	1
Hangzhou	2395	.02	.14	0	1
Hefei	2395	.02	.14	0	1
Huainan	2395	.02	.14	0	1
Xiamen	2395	.02	.14	0	1
Zhangshu	2395	.02	.14	0	1
Jinan	2395	.02	.14	0	1
Qingdao	2395	.02	.14	0	1
Zibo	2395	.02	.14	0	1
Zhengzho	2395	.02	.14	0	1
Xingxian	2395	.02	.14	0	1
Sanmenxi	2395	.02	.14	0	1
Wuhan	2395	.02	.14	0	1
Xiangfan	2395	.02	.14	0	1
Zaoyang	2395	.02	.14	0	1
Changsha	2395	.02	.14	0	1
Shantou	2395	.02	.12	0	1
Zaoqing	2395	.02	.14	0	1
Liuzhou	2395	.02	.14	0	1
Haikou	2395	.03	.17	0	1
Chengdu	2395	.02	.14	0	1
Guiyang	2395	.02	.14	0	1
Dali	2395	.02	.14	0	1
Xian	2395	.02	.14	0	1
Lanzhou	2395	.02	.14	0	1

SOURCE: 1992 Chinese Urban Survey.
SD = standard deviation

Variables for Multivariate Analysis, Figure 5.4

Variable	Mean	SD	Min.	Max.
Trust	.60	.26	0	1
Age groups:				
Age 20 before 1949	.05	.21	0	1
Age 20 in 1949–65	.21	.41	0	1
Age 20 in 1966–76	.25	.43	0	1
Age 20 in 1977–84	.24	.43	0	1
Age 20 after 1984	.25	.43	0	1
Party member	.17	.38	0	1
Private (geti/siying)	.02	.14	0	1
Family income (1998)	4.48	1.71	0	10
College education	.06	.24	0	1
Male	.50	.50	0	1
Spending time with:				
Family	.66	.20	0	1
Relative	.21	.27	0	1
Co-worker	.24	.31	0	1
Schoolmate	.07	.20	0	1
Lover	.03	.17	0	1
Friend	.39	.32	0	1
Alone	.16	.28	0	1
Close neighbor	.71	.23	0	1
Sociopolitical attitudes:				
Economic cooperation	.52	.24	0	1
Support civil society	.46	.18	0	1
Voluntary voting	.29	.45	0	1
Law-abiding	.72	.25	0	1
Political activism	.38	.48	0	1
City:				
Guangzhou	.17	.37	0	1
Xian	.16	.37	0	1
Wuhan	.17	.37	0	1
Chongqing	.17	.37	0	1
Shenyang	.17	.37	0	1
Shanghai	.17	.38	0	1

SOURCE: 1999 Six-City Survey.

SD = standard deviation

Characteristics of the 1997 Employee Survey

Variable	Observations	Mean	SD	Min.	Max.
Provincial economic growth					
(1995–97)	12,165	11.53	1.80	8.2	15.03
Provincial per capita GDP (1998)	12,165	.89	.63	.3456	2.8253
Recruited through exam	11,158	.26	.44	0	1
R's number of job changes	11,008	.53	.90	0	5
Satisfaction with occupation	11,004	.60	.21	0	1
Job preference: income	12,165	.29	.32	0	1
Job preference: security	12,165	.19	.28	0	1
Job preference:					
Party/state organization (gmt)	12,165	.26	.32	0	1
Public organization (npf)	12,165	.22	.24	0	1
State-owned enterprise (soe)	12,165	.16	.27	0	1
Foreign direct investment					
firm (fdi)	12,165	.11	.23	0	1
Private household (geti)	12,165	.07	.16	0	1
Private firm (pe)	12,165	.02	.11	0	1
Township/village firm (tve)	12,165	.01	.09	0	1
Urban collective firm (uce)	12,165	.01	.09	0	1
Reasons for dispute:					
Contract renewal	12,165	.01	.13	0	1
Resignation	12,165	.01	.07	0	1
Pay	12,165	.03	.18	0	1
Welfare	12,165	.03	.18	0	1
R's assessment of union role					
(index)	12,165	.57	.17	0	1
Ownership type:					
State-owned	12,165	.67	.47	0	1
Collective	12,165	.19	.39	0	1
Private	12,165	.01	.11	0	1
Joint venture (lianying)	12,165	.01	.11	0	1
Stock	12,165	.04	.21	0	1
Foreign-owned	12,165	.04	.20	0	1
Taiwan/Hong Kong firm	12,165	.02	.14	0	1
Firm size (log)	12,165	6.13	1.90	0	10
Technical level:					
Manual laborer	12,165	.50	.50	0	1
Technician/cadre	12,165	.39	.49	0	1

(continued)

Variable	Observations	Mean	SD	Min.	Max.
Work unit type:					
Enterprise	12,165	.09	.28	0	1
Nonprofit (shiye)	12,165	.68	.47	0	1
Party/state (jiguan)	12,165	.18	.38	0	1
Rank	11,111	2.14	1.32	1	6
Years of education (edyr)	12,165	11.66	2.71	0	19
Party member (ccp)	12,165	.33	.47	0	1
Female	12,165	.46	.50	0	1
Urban resident	12,165	.93	.25	0	1
Seniority (0 = post-1977,					
3 = pre-1959)	12,165	.65	.84	0	3
Recruited before 1959	12,165	.05	.22	0	1
Recruited 1959–66	12,165	.08	.27	0	1
Recruited 1967–77	12,165	.33	.47	0	1
Recruited after 1977	12,165	.53	.50	0	1
Age 35 or younger	12,165	.45	.50	0	1
Age 35–50	12,165	.42	.49	0	1
Age 50 and older	12,165	.12	.33	0	1
Age (1 = <35, 2 = 35–50,					
3 = 50+)	12,165	1.68	.68	1	3
Beijing	12,165	.07	.26	0	1
Inner Mongolia	12,165	.07	.25	0	1
Liaoning	12,165	.06	.24	0	1
Jilin	12,165	.06	.24	0	1
Shanghai	12,165	.06	.25	0	1
Jiangsu	12,165	.07	.26	0	1
Fujian	12,165	.07	.25	0	1
Shandong	12,165	.07	.25	0	1
Henan	12,165	.06	.24	0	1
Hubei	12,165	.07	.25	0	1
Guangdong	12,165	.07	.25	0	1
Sichuan	12,165	.07	.25	0	1
Yunan	12,165	.07	.25	0	1
Shaanxi	12,165	.06	.25	0	1
Gansu	12,165	.07	.25	0	1
Agriculture	12,165	.04	.20	0	1
Mining	12,165	.06	.23	0	1
Manufacture	12,165	.35	.48	0	1
Power	12,165	.02	.13	0	1
Construction	12,165	.07	.26	0	1
Geographic mapping	12,165	.01	.09	0	1
Transportation	12,165	.06	.23	0	1
Sales	12,165	.12	.32	0	1
Finance	12,165	.03	.16	0	1
Real estate	12,165	.01	.09	0	1
Public service	12,165	.03	.17	0	1
Education	12,165	.03	.17	0	1
Culture	12,165	.09	.29	0	1
Research	12,165	.01	.12	0	1
Government	12,165	.07	.26	0	1
Union role in improving worker					
life (bigunion)	12,165	2.31	.00	0	4
Currently working	12,165	.90	.29	0	1

Variable	Observations	Mean	SD	Min.	Max.
Had individual dispute in past 5 yrs (dispute)	11,004	.05	.21	0	1
Had group dispute in past 5 yrs (disputegrp)	11,004	.03	.18	0	1
Resolved/partially resolved dispute (solved)	355	.34	.33	0	1
Made suggestion at work in past year (suggest)	10,274	.23	.31	0	1
R's suggestion was adopted (heard)	6681	.34	.47	0	1
R saw bad labor-management tie (managtie)	10,758	.39	.22	0	1
R saw bad party-mass tie (ccptie)	10,714	.36	.20	0	1
R's firm had late pay this year (latepay)	11,004	.16	.37	0	1
R's feeling of job insecurity (losejob)	11,004	.48	.26	0	1

SOURCE: 1997 Employee Survey.

SD = standard deviation

Multivariate Analysis (OLS): Individual and Work Unit Characteristics and Labor Relations in 1997

	latepay	sat	losejob	suggest	heard	dispute	disputgrp	resolved	managtie	ccptie
Collective	0.014	-0.006	0.001	-0.008	-0.016	-0.002	-0.001	0.095	-0.029	-0.026
Private	0.036	0.021	-0.046	0.015	-0.007	0.023	0.027	0.135	-0.022	-0.024
Lianying	-0.077	-0.016	0.031	-0.008	-0.022	-0.024	-0.004	0.211	-0.032	-0.036
Stock	-0.083	0.010	-0.029	0.085	0.025	-0.007	-0.021	0.152	-0.007	-0.013
Foreign	-0.109	0.024	-0.020	-0.035	0.266	0.002	-0.012	0.128	-0.021	-0.005
Twhk	-0.024	-0.005	0.020	0.026	0.129	0.070	0.004	0.191	-0.014	0.001
Blue	0.006	-0.013	0.018	-0.014	0.003	0.008	0.007	-0.019	0.005	0.005
Shiye	0.122	-0.093	0.120	0.062	-0.031	0.027	0.015	0.002	0.055	0.035
Jiguan	0.016	-0.027	0.028	0.042	0.021	0.018	0.014	0.033	0.011	0.006
Rank	-0.002	0.009	-0.002	0.028	0.050	-0.006	-0.002	0.023	-0.006	-0.003
Edyr	-0.002	-0.004	-0.004	0.006	0.007	0.001	-0.001	-0.007	-0.001	-0.002
Ccp	0.015	0.013	-0.005	0.101	0.092	-0.009	-0.002	-0.007	-0.001	-0.020
Female	-0.016	0.004	0.002	-0.081	-0.035	-0.009	-0.004	-0.049	0.000	0.006
Urban	-0.059	-0.008	0.017	0.002	-0.101	-0.022	-0.028	-0.033	0.032	0.036
Seniority	-0.010	0.014	0.002	0.017	0.008	-0.003	-0.003	0.033	0.017	0.020
Bigunion	-0.383	0.442	-0.357	0.006	0.605	-0.202	-0.128	0.492	-0.632	-0.580
_Cons	0.381	0.454	0.610	0.042	0.166	0.164	0.138	0.161	0.700	0.653
Adj-R	0.060	0.161	0.099	0.095	0.137	0.037	0.020	0.136	0.285	0.278
N	10,812	10,812	10,812	10,205	922	10,812	10,812	355	10,681	10,637

SOURCE: 1997 Employee Survey.

OLS: Union presence on labor issues

Underlined: $p < .10$

Note: See appendix F for definitions of variables.

Notes

CHAPTER ONE

1. An English version of the Chinese Constitution can be found at http://english
.people.com.cn/constitution/constitution.html (accessed April 2, 2005).

2. An English version of the Party Constitution can be found at http://www
.china.org.cn/english/features/49109.htm (accessed March 22, 2005).

3. For the corporatist nature of American politics, see Schattschneider 1942 and
Rokkan 1966. For societal and state corporatism, see Schmitter 1979.

4. For an extended discussion of how the Chinese Communist Party sought
to co-opt and utilize the rising popular nationalism in the 1990s, see Gries 2004a,
2004b.

CHAPTER TWO

1. The materials in this chapter are based on experiences gained from the author's involvement in several public opinion surveys, such as the 1991 Enterprise
Survey by the Labor Institute of China, the 1992 China Urban Survey by the Economic System Reform Institute of China, the 1999 Six-City Survey, and the 2004
Values and Ethics Survey by Peking University. Parts of this chapter first appeared
in "An Introduction to Survey Research in Urban China," *Issues and Studies* 38, no. 4,
and 39, no. 1 (December 2002–March 2003): 269–88.

2. For example, *Beijing Qingnian Bao* (Beijing Youth Daily) lists more than a
dozen survey research organizations. Some of them are academic, some are govern-
ment-affiliated, but most are in the private sector. They are China Youth Daily So-
cial Survey Center; Gallup Ltd. China; Beijing Xin Xin Market Research Company;
Beijing Shao Hai Market Research Company, Ltd.; Guangdong Kang Sai Market
Service Company, Ltd.; Social Survey and Research Center at Peking University;
Social Survey Center of Economic System Reform Institute of China; Research
Center for Contemporary China at Peking University; Da Men Market Research
Company; Beijing Fu Bang Consulting Company, Ltd.; Horizon; Beijing Wei Lai

Zhi Lu Market Research Company, Ltd.; and Beijing Youth Daily (Jing Que Xin Wen). *Beijing Qingnian Bao* (Beijing Youth Daily), April 29, 1998.

3. For example, one anonymous reviewer of the earlier version of this chapter disagreed with the characterization that private firms had more freedom, arguing that academic institutions were the best choice due to low "transaction costs."

4. In contrast, Taiwan in recent years has become much more open to outside researchers who wish to conduct surveys and use existing survey data. The Institute of Sociology at Academia Sinica, for example, grants access to its survey data free of charge.

5. See *China Daily*, July 28, 2000. No names were mentioned in the article.

6. Examples of using existing survey data can be found in Tang and Parish 2000.

7. Budgetary issues also need to be considered in preparing for a survey. In general, a survey using the household registration method should at least include the costs of the following items: (1) sampling design (selection of residential committees and sampling distance), (2) sampling implementation (selection of households and names of respondents in each residential committee), (3) payment to residential councils for sampling, (4) questionnaire design and printing, (5) travel by the project supervisor to the site, (6) salaries for the local project manager and coordinators, (7) payment for the interviewer, (8) gifts for the respondents, (9) data entry, and (10) administrative cost and overhead charges. For spatial sampling, cost for sampling design (1) and implementation (2) would be higher, but payment to residential councils (3) would not be necessary. The cost can vary greatly depending on the difficulty of sampling, the size of the sample, the length of the questionnaire, and whether it is a single-location or multi-site survey. As a rule, urban surveys cost more than rural surveys. For example, if a sample of 1000 respondents in ten residential councils or spatial blocks in one city costs US$15,000 (or about US$15 per person for a forty-five-minute interview), this amount will at least double if the 1000 respondents are chosen from five cities (200 from ten residential councils or spatial blocks in each city). In that case, the cost is at least US$30,000 for all five cities, or US$30 per person.

8. Some ESRIC surveys also use eight large cities (Beijing, Shanghai, Guangzhou, Wuhan, Chongqing, Harbin, Tianjin, and Shenyang) in the first stage of sampling.

9. See, e.g., Nicolas Becquelin, "Without Residency Rights, Millions Wait in Limbo," *South China Morning Post*, February 27, 2003.

10. Raw data, ESRIC Forty-City Survey, May 1989.

11. In his comments on the manuscript, Stanley Rosen also suggested asking about people around the respondents in order to avoid evoking fear and dishonesty. For example, respondents' answers to questions about other people's motivation for joining the Communist Party are always more genuine than answers to such questions as they pertain to themselves.

12. This figure is weighted. For an explanation of weighting, see the next section on data comparability and analysis.

13. See the ESRIC surveys, 1987–92.

14. The "three representatives" include representing the forces of advanced material and technological production, the advancement of Chinese culture, and the basic interests of the overwhelming majority of the people. See the report of Jiang Zemin's inspection of work in Guangdong in *Renmin Ribao* (People's Daily), February 26, 2000.

CHAPTER THREE

1. For a slightly different list, see Baum 1998.

2. One may want to disaggregate the private sector because it lumped rich and well-educated owners of high-tech companies in with poorly educated corner popcorn and baked sweet potato vendors. However, what they held in common was a market mentality that fell outside traditional state-controlled channels. In a multivariate analysis, what the private sector represented was precisely this difference in mentality from public sector workers when income and education were held constant.

3. See, e.g., Chicago Council on Foreign Relations 1999 (based on surveys from 1978 to 1998 by CCFR).

4. In the same analysis, none of the occupational groups showed any difference when the administrator/manager group was the comparison group. Residents in Wuhan and Shenyang showed less preference for the U.S. economic model than those in Shanghai, Guangzhou, Xian, and Chongqing (see Tang 2001).

5. Two questions regarding the role of ideology (the relative importance of each ideology for China's economic development and social stability) were combined into an index for each ideology. Background factors were examined against each ideology index. Occupational groups made little difference and were excluded in the analysis. The anecdotal accounts of occupational difference in ideological orientation may have been explained by other factors, such as age, gender, education, and income.

6. In the same regression analysis, Guangzhou residents were much less interested in any ideology except Western culture. Xian residents thought Maoism was more important than any other ideology. Residents in Wuhan and Shenyang favored both Marxism-Leninism and Maoism, though the latter showed more support of Dengism. Shanghai residents were divided between Marxism-Leninism and Maoism on one hand and Western culture on the other (see Tang 2001 for further details).

CHAPTER FOUR

1. Materials in this paragraph are also drawn from several conversations with Lisa Rose Weaver, CNN Beijing.

2. For example, in a survey conducted by the Research Center of Contemporary China (RCCC) in 2004, 29% of the 6270 respondents trusted the media very much, 53% basically trusted the media, 14% basically did not trust the media, and only 2% did not trust the media at all. Raw data, RCCC Legal Survey, 2004.

3. City and occupation do not show any significant effect and are not included in the equation for official ideology.

CHAPTER FIVE

1. Closeness to neighbors is based on the question "How familiar are you with your neighbors?" (1 = very distant, 2 = distant, 3 = close, 4 = very close, 5 = don't know). "Don't know" is coded as the mean. The 0–1 closeness scale is then derived from the 1–4 scale: (4–1)/3. Closeness to all other groups is measured by whether the respondent usually spent the most time (3), the second-most time (2), the third-most time (1), or no time (0) with each group. The resulting 0 (most distant) to 3 (closest) scale is then converted into a 0–1 scale by dividing the amount of time spent with each group (0–3) by 3.

2. The 0–1 scale is constructed by the following method: [civil society score + (−2.041579)]/4.430983, where −2.041579 is the minimum value of the factor index and 4.430983 is the maximum value.

CHAPTER SIX

1. The most explicit forms of expressing dissatisfaction are protest, demonstration, and petition—all highly risky activities that may result in loss of one's political life and imprisonment. One may expect such activities to occur rarely under state socialism. Yet they repeatedly took place in post-Mao China, including the 1976 and 1979 protests against the Gang of Four and other radical Cultural Revolution leaders, demonstrations by college students in 1984 and 1987 demanding more democracy, and protests by people from all walks of life in 1989 against inflation, corruption, and authoritarian control. In the 1980s and 1990s there was also ethnic unrest in Tibet and Xinjiang, and strikes were held by workers in cities. Although an important topic, this chapter does not include protest activities, because participation in such activities is relatively rare in the general population.

2. E.g., Lipset 1961, 39, 61, 189; Almond and Verba 1963; Verba, Nie, and Kim 1978, 258; Barnes and Kaase 1979, 15 and 133; Dahl 1985, 64; Dalton 1988, chap. 2; Marsh 1990, 33; Conway 1991, chap. 2.

3. In a multiple regression analysis for 1999 data only, party members, the post–Cultural Revolution generations, and the upper classes (professionals, administrators, managers), and Shanghai residents felt more efficacy than others (results not shown).

4. I combined "no use" and "too much dissatisfaction" into a single item. Essentially, these two reasons for not voicing complaints are the same.

5. Individualized bargaining often takes place in work units, where networks of personal ties are the richest. Some people, such as party members and older employees, who verbally expressed opposition to using personal connections but were engaged in intensive work unit participation, should not be excluded from any account of the frequency of individualized bargaining.

6. The pattern is similar and even more extreme for work-related issues (details not shown). For work-related complaints, media contacts and personal connections accounted for a very high 26% and 22% in 1987 and 13% and 8% in 1999 of all contacts perceived as effective. In actual practice, 72% of all work-related issues continued to be voiced through work unit channels in both years.

CHAPTER SEVEN

1. Based on a Poisson regression including work unit ownership, firm size, job rank, education, party membership, gender, urban registration, and job seniority. Details not shown.

2. Interview with Tongqing Feng, China Labor Relations College, Beijing, August 2, 2003.

3. See the discussion on labor disputes and making suggestions for univariate statistics on these items. Among the 90% of respondents who were not laid off and did not retire in the 1997 survey, the rate of job satisfaction was 60%. About 16% experienced pay delays in the past year. Forty-eight percent were worried about being laid off. About one-third gave unfavorable assessments of firm-work relations and party-mass relations. See appendix F for further information.

CHAPTER EIGHT

1. Some materials in this chapter are reprinted from Wenfang Tang, *Party Intellectuals' Demand for Reform in Contemporary China*, with the permission of the publisher, Hoover Institution Press. Copyright 1999 by the Board of Trustees of Leland Stanford Junior University.

2. See, e.g., the diagram in Hamrin and Cheek 1986, 14, in which intellectuals are categorized by their relative distance from the center.

3. See, e.g., Hamrin and Cheek 1986 and Hua 1995. The first is an edited volume with chapters on Peng Zhen, Yang Xianzhen, Deng Tuo, Sun Yefang, Wu Han, and Bai Hua. Hua's study focuses on six intellectuals: Hu Qiaomu, Su Shaozhi, Jin Guantao, Wang Ruoshui, Li Zehou, and Gan Yang. Also see Fewsmith 2001 for case studies of influential intellectuals since Tiananmen.

4. For a more general discussion of the "deal" between the state and the intellectuals, see also Cheek 1994.

5. For example, some argued that the most critical intellectuals in China were non-establishment intellectuals such as political dissidents and social and cultural critics (Hao 2003).

6. For example, Ding quotes Wang Shaoguang and Hu Angang's advice (Wang and Hu 1994) for strengthening central power under reform. See Ding 1994b (p. 39, chap. 3, and p. 9). Also see Chen 1997.

7. Examples of these official intellectuals who challenged the authority of the party state include Su Shaozhi, director of the Marxism-Leninism Institute, and Yan

Jiaqi, director of the Political Science Institute, both at the Chinese Academy of Social Sciences; and Wang Ruoshui, deputy editor-in-chief of *People's Daily*, the party's official newspaper.

8. These same patterns were maintained in a multivariate analysis that examined the potentially confounding effects of age, gender, income, and occupation (details not shown).

9. In a multivariate analysis using the 1992 data only, when age, gender, income, and occupation were controlled for, political activism was the same for both non-party intellectuals and the public. There was no difference between the two intellectual groups in their use of unofficial channels. These findings are similar to the 1999 bivariate results.

References

Academia Sinica. 2001. *Taiwan Social Change Survey: General Information*. Taipei: Academic Sinica. http://www.ios.sinica.edu.tw/sc1/home2.htm (accessed April 3, 2005).

All-China Federation of Trade Unions. 1986. *Zhongguo Zhigong Duiwu Zhuangkuang Diaocha* [A Study of Chinese Workers]. Beijing: Workers Publishing House.

———. 1993. *Zouxiang Shehui Zhuyi Shichang Jingji de Zhongguo Gongren Jieji* [Chinese Working Class Marching toward Socialist Market Economy]. Beijing: China Social Science Publishing House.

———. 1999. *Zhongguo Zhigong Zhuangkuang Diaocha* [Survey of the Status of Chinese Staff and Workers in 1997]. 3 vols. Beijing: Xiyuan Publishing House.

———. 2004. *Zhongguo Zhigong Zhuangkuang Diaocha* [Survey of the Status of Chinese Staff and Workers in 2002]. Beijing: Xiyuan Publishing House.

Almond, Gabriel A., and Sidney Verba. 1963. *The Civic Culture: Political Attitudes and Democracy in Five Nations*. Princeton: Princeton University Press.

Arendt, Hannah. 1951. *Origins of Totalitarianism*. New York: Harcourt, Brace.

Bahry, Donna, and Brian D. Silver. 1990. "Soviet Citizen Participation on the Eve of Democratization." *American Political Science Review* 84, no. 3 (September): 821–47.

Barnes, Samuel H., and Max Kaase, eds. 1979. *Political Action: Mass Participation in Five Western Democracies*. Beverly Hills, Calif.: Sage Publications.

Bartels, Larry M. 1993. "Messages Received: The Political Impact of Media Exposure." *American Political Science Review* 87 (June): 267–85.

Bauer, John, Feng Wang, Nancy E. Riley, and Xiaohua Zhao. 1992. "Gender Inequality in Urban China." *Modern China* 18, no. 3: 333–69.

Baum, Richard, ed. 1991. *Reform and Reaction in Post-Mao China: The Road to Tiananmen*. New York: Routledge.

———. 1996. "China after Deng: Ten Scenarios in Search of Reality." *China Quarterly* 145 (March): 153–75.

———. 1998. "The Fifteenth National Party Congress: Jiang Takes Command?" *China Quarterly* 153 (March): 141–56.

Beijing City Government. 1995. *Beijing City Migrant Worker Survey*. Unpublished paper.

Bialer, Seweryn. 1980. *Stalin's Successors: Leadership, Stability, and Change in the Soviet Union*. New York: Cambridge University Press.

Bian, Yanjie. 1994a. "*Guanxi* and the Allocation of Urban Jobs in China." *China Quarterly* 140 (December): 971–98.

———. 1994b. *Work and Inequality in Urban China*. Albany: State University of New York Press.

Burns, John. 1999. "The People's Republic of China at 50: National Political Reform." *China Quarterly* 159 (September): 580–94.

Burstein, Paul. 1985. *Discrimination, Jobs, and Politics*. Chicago: University of Chicago Press.

Cao, Jinqing. 2000. *Huanghe Bianshang de Zhongguo* [China by the Yellow River]. Shanghai: Shanghai Literature and Art Publishing House.

Carnaghan, Ellen, and Donna Bahry. 1990. "Political Attitudes and the Gender Gap in the USSR." *Comparative Politics* 22, no. 4 (July): 379–99.

Carter Center. 1999. *The Carter Center Report on Chinese Elections*. Atlanta: The Carter Center.

Census Office, State Council (and State Statistical Bureau, Department of Population Statistics]. 1993. *Tabulation on the 1990 Population Census of the People's Republic of China* [1990 Zhongguo Renkou Pucha Baogao]. Beijing: China Statistics Press.

Center for China Social Survey. 1996. *A Brief Introduction to the Center for China Social Survey and Its Network, 1987–1996*. Beijing: Gaige Chubanshe.

Chan, Anita. 1993. "Revolution or Corporatism? Workers and Trade Unions in Post-Mao China." *Australian Journal of Chinese Affairs* 29: 31–61.

Chan, Cherris Shun-ching. 2004. "The Falun Gong in China: A Sociological Perspective." *China Quarterly* 179 (September): 665–83.

Chang, Gordon. 2001. *The Coming Collapse of China*. New York: Random House.

Cheek, Timothy. 1994. "From Priests to Professionals: Intellectuals and the State under the CCP." In *Popular Protest and Political Culture in Modern China*, edited by Jeffrey N. Wasserstrom and Elizabeth J. Perry. 2nd ed. Boulder, Colo.: Westview Press.

Chen, Feng. 1997. "Order and Stability in Social Transition: Neoconservative Political Thought in Post-1989 China." *China Quarterly* 151 (September): 593–613.

Chen, Jie. 1999. "Comparing Mass and Elite Subjective Orientations in Urban China." *Public Opinion Quarterly* 62, no. 2 (Summer): 193–219.

———. 2004. *Popular Political Support in Urban China*. Washington, D.C., and Stanford, Calif.: Woodrow Wilson Center Press and Stanford University Press.

Chen, Xueyi, and Tianjian Shi. 2001. "Media Effects on Political Confidence and Trust in the People's Republic of China in the Post-Tiananmen Period." *East Asia: An International Quarterly* 19, no. 3 (Autumn): 84–118.

Chi, Hsi-sheng. 1991. *Politics of Disillusionment: The Chinese Communist Party under Deng Xiaoping, 1978–1989.* Armonk, N.Y.: M. E. Sharpe.

Chicago Council on Foreign Relations. 1999. *Chicago Council on Foreign Relations Report, 1999.* Chicago: Chicago Council on Foreign Relations.

China Internet Network Information Center. 2004. *2004 China Internet Development Report July, 2004* [Zhongguo Hulian Wangluo Fazhan Zhuangkuang Tongji Baogao]. http://www.cnnic.com.cn/download/2004/2004072002.pdf (accessed April 3, 2005).

Ching, F. 1996. "Public Opinion Is a RiskyTool." *Far Eastern Economic Review* 159, no. 17 (April 25): 34.

Chirot, Daniel. 1972. "The Corporatist Model and Socialism." *Theory and Society* 9, no. 2 (March): 363–82.

Cho, Hyunyi. 2000. "Public Opinion as Personal Cultivation: A Normative Notion and a Source of Social Control in Traditional China." *International Journal of Public Opinion Research* 12, no. 3 (Fall): 299–323.

Connor, Walter D. 1980. "Dissent in Eastern Europe: A New Coalition?" *Problems of Communism* 29: 1–17.

Conway, M. Margaret. 1991. *Political Participation in the United States.* Washington, D.C.: Congressional Quarterly.

Crawford, Beverly, and Arend Lijphart. 1997. *Liberalization and Leninist Legacies: Comparative Perspectives on Democratic Transition.* Berkeley and Los Angeles: University of California Press.

Crespi, Irving. 1997. *The Public Opinion Process: How the People Speak.* Mahwah, N.J.: Lawrence Erlbaum Associates.

Croll, Elizabeth. 1999. "Social Welfare Reform: Trends and Tensions." *China Quarterly* 159 (September): 684–99.

Dahl, Robert A. 1985. *A Preface to Economic Democracy.* Berkeley and Los Angeles: University of California Press.

Dai, Qing. 1999. "Guiding Public Opinion." *Media Studies Journal* (Winter): 78–81.

Dalton, Russell J. 1988. *Citizen Politics in Western Democracies.* Chatham, N.J.: Chatham House.

Davis, Deborah, Richard Kraus, Barry Naughton, and Elizabeth Perry. 1995. *Urban Spaces in Contemporary China.* Washington, D.C.: Woodrow Wilson Center Press.

Davis, James A., and Tom W. Smith. 1991. *The NORC General Social Survey: A User's Guide.* Newbury Park, Calif.: Sage.

Davis, James A., Tom W. Smith, and Peter V. Marsden. 2003. *General Social Survey 1972–2002 Cumulative Codebook.* 2nd ICPSR version. Ann Arbor, Mich.: Inter-University Consortium for Political and Social Research.

De Bary, Theodore, Wing-tsit Chan, and Burton Watson, comps. 1960. *Sources of Chinese Tradition*. New York: Columbia University Press.

Deng, Xiaoping. 1983. *Deng Xiaoping Wenxuan* [Selected Works of Deng Xiaoping]. Beijing: People's Publishing House.

Dernberger, R. F. 1999. "The People's Republic at 50: The Economy." *China Quarterly* 159 (September): 606–15.

Ding, Xueliang. 1994a. *The Decline of Communism in China*. New York: Cambridge University Press.

———. 1994b. *Gongchan Zhuyi Hou Yu Zhongguo* [Post-Communism and China]. Hong Kong: Oxford University Press.

———. 1994c. "Institutional Amphibiousness and the Transition from Communism: The Case of China." *British Journal of Political Science* 24: 293–318.

Djilas, Milovan. 1957. *The New Class*. New York: Holt, Rinehart and Winston.

Donald, Stephanie Hemelryk, and Michael Keane. 2002. "Media in China: New Convergences, New Approaches." In *Media in China: Consumption, Content and Crisis*, edited by Stephanie Hemelryk Donald, Michael Keane, and Yin Hong. London and New York: RoutledgeCurzon.

Donald, Stephanie Hemelryk, Michael Keane, and Yin Hong, eds. 2002. *Media in China: Consumption, Content and Crisis*. London and New York: Routledge-Curzon.

Editorial Office. 2000. *Zhongguo Gonghui Nianjian* [China Labor Unions Statistical Yearbook 2000]. Beijing: All-China Federation of Trade Unions.

Edwards, Richard. 1979. *Contested Terrains: The Transformation of the Workplace in the 20th Century*. New York: Basic Books.

Eichenberg, Richard C. 1989. *Public Opinion and National Security in Western Europe*. Ithaca: Cornell University Press.

Esherick, Joseph, and Jeffrey Wasserstrom. 1994. "Acting Out Democracy: Political Theater in Modern China." In *Popular Protest and Political Culture in Modern China*, edited by Jeffrey N. Wasserstrom and Elizabeth J. Perry. 2nd ed. Boulder, Colo.: Westview Press.

Falkenheim, Victor C. 1978. "Political Participation in China." *Problems of Communism* 27 (May–June): 18–32.

Feng, Tongqing. 2002. *Zhongguo Gongren de Mingyun* [The Fate of Chinese Workers]. Beijing: Social Science Publishing House.

Fewsmith, Joseph. 2001. *China since Tiananmen: The Politics of Transition*. New York: Cambridge University Press.

Fewsmith, Joseph, and Stanley Rosen. 2001. "The Domestic Context of Chinese Foreign Policy: Does 'Public Opinion' Matter?" In *The Making of Chinese Foreign and Security Policy in the Era of Reform 1978–2000*, edited by David M. Lampton. Stanford: Stanford University Press.

Finifter, Ada W., and Ellen Mickiewicz. 1992. "Redefining the Political System of the USSR: Mass Support for Political Change." *American Political Science Review* 86: 857–74.

Fink, Arlene, and Jacqueline Kosecoff. 1998. *How to Conduct Surveys: A Step-by-Step Guide.* 2nd ed. Newbury Park, Calif.: Sage.

FlorCruz, Jaime A. 1999. "Chinese Media in Flux: From Party Line to Bottom Line." *Media Studies Journal* (Winter): 32–39.

Fowler, Floyd J. Jr. 1993. *Survey Research Methods.* 2nd ed. Newbury Park, Calif.: Sage.

Friedman, Milton. 1962. *Capitalism and Freedom.* Chicago: University of Chicago Press.

Gilley, Bruce. 1998. *Tiger on the Brink: Jiang Zemin and China's New Elite.* Berkeley and Los Angeles: University of California Press.

Goldberg, Bernard. 2002. *Bias: A CBS Insider Exposes How the Media Distort the News.* Washington, D.C.: Regnery.

———. 2003. *Arrogance: Rescuing America from the Media Elite.* New York: Warner Books.

Goldman, Merle. 1981. *China's Intellectuals: Advise and Dissent.* Cambridge, Mass.: Harvard University Press.

———. 1996. "Politically-Engaged Intellectuals in the Deng-Jiang Era: A Changing Relationship with the Party-State." *China Quarterly* 145 (March): 35–52.

———. 1999. "Politically-Engaged Intellectuals in the 1990s." *China Quarterly* 159 (September): 700–711.

Greenwald, Robert. 2004. *Outfoxed: Rupert Murdoch's War on Journalism* [film transcript]. Carolina Productions. http://www.outfoxed.org/docs/outfoxed_transcript.pdf (accessed March 25, 2005).

Gries, Peter Hays. 2004a. *China's New Nationalism: Pride, Politics and Diplomacy.* Berkeley and Los Angeles: University of California Press.

———. 2004b. "Popular Nationalism and State Legitimation in China." In *State and Society in 21st Century China*, edited by Peter Hays Gries and Stanley Rosen. London and New York: RoutledgeCurzon.

Griffin, Keith, and Renwei Zhao, eds. 1993. *The Distribution of Income in China.* London: Macmillan.

Gurr, Ted R. 1971. *Why Men Rebel.* Princeton: Princeton University Press.

Gustafsson, B. N., and W. Zhong. 2000. "How and Why Has Poverty in China Changed? A Study Based on Microdata for 1988 and 1995." *China Quarterly* 164 (December): 983–1006.

Guthrie, D. 1998. "The Declining Significance of Guanxi in China's Economic Transition." *China Quarterly* 154 (June): 254–82.

Gyimah-Boadi, E. 1996. "Civil Society in Africa." *Journal of Democracy* 7: 118–32.

Hague, Rod, and Martin Harrop. 2001. *Political Science: A Comparative Introduction.* 3rd ed. New York: Palgrave.

Hamrin, Carol Lee. 1991. "The Economic Costs of Intellectual Alienation." In Joint Economic Committee, Congress of the United States, *China's Economic Dilemmas in the 1990s: The Problems of Reforms, Modernization, and Interdependence.* Vol. 1. Washington, D.C.: U.S. Government Printing Office.

Hamrin, Carol Lee, and Timothy Cheek, eds. 1986. *China's Establishment Intellectuals*. Armonk, N.Y.: M. E. Sharpe.

Hao, Zhidong. 2003. *Intellectuals at a Crossroads: The Changing Politics of China's Knowledge Workers*. Albany, N.Y.: SUNY Press.

Harrison, Mark. 2002. "Satellite and Cable Platforms: Development and Content." In *Media in China: Consumption, Content and Crisis*, edited by Stephanie Hemelryk Donald, Michael Keane, and Yin Hong. London and New York: RoutledgeCurzon.

Harwit, Eric, and Duncan Clark. 2001. "Shaping the Internet in China: Evolution of Political Control over Network Infrastructure and Content." *Asian Survey* 41, no. 3 (May–June): 377–408.

He, Qinglian. 2004. "Jingti baoguo zai 'xueshu' waiyi xiade huangyan" [Be Alarmed about the Lies under the "Academic" Cloak]. *Huaxia Kuaidi*, January 17. http://archives.cnd.org/HXWK/author/HE-Qinglian/kd040117-6.gb.html (accessed April 3, 2005).

Hong, Ng Sek, and Malcolm Warner. 1998. *China's Trade Unions and Management*. New York: St. Martin's Press.

Hough, Jerry F. 1969. *The Soviet Prefects: The Local Party Organs in Industrial Decision-Making*. Cambridge, Mass: Harvard University Press.

———. 1976. "Political Participation in the Soviet Union." *Soviet Studies* 28: 3–20.

———. 1977. *The Soviet Union and Social Science Theory*. Cambridge, Mass.: Harvard University Press.

Hua, Shiping. 1995. *Scientism and Humanism: Two Cultures in Post-Mao China, 1978–1989*. Albany: State University of New York Press.

Hui, Victoria. 2004. "Confucius and Patriotism: Speak from the Heart." *South China Morning Post*. February 14.

Huntington, Samuel P. 1968. *Political Order in Changing Societies*. New Haven: Yale University Press.

———. 1991. *The Third Wave*. Norman: University of Oklahoma Press.

Huntington, Samuel P., and Joan M. Nelson. 1976. *No Easy Choice: Political Participation in Developing Countries*. Cambridge, Mass.: Harvard University Press.

International Labor Office. 1999. *1997–98 International Labor Report*. Geneva: International Labor Office.

Inglehart, Ronald. 1990. *Culture Shift*. Princeton: Princeton University Press.

———. 1997. *Modernization and Postmodernization: Cultural, Economic, and Political Change in 43 Societies*. Princeton: Princeton University Press.

———. 1999. "Trust, Well-Being and Democracy." In *Democracy and Trust*, edited by Mark E. Warren. Cambridge: Cambridge University Press.

Inkeles, Alex. 1950. *Public Opinion in Soviet Russia*. Cambridge, Mass.: Harvard University Press.

———. 1960. "Industrial Man: The Relation of Status to Experience, Perception, and Value." *American Journal of Sociology* 66: 1–31.

———. 1968. *Social Change in Soviet Russia.* Cambridge, Mass.: Harvard University Press.

———. 1974. *Becoming Modern: Individual Change in Six Developing Countries.* Cambridge, Mass.: Harvard University Press.

———. 1976. "The Modernization of Man in Socialist and Nonsocialist Countries." In *Social Consequences of Modernization in Communist Societies,* edited by M. G. Fields. Baltimore: Johns Hopkins University Press.

Inkeles, Alex, and Raymond Bauer. 1959. *The Soviet Citizen: Daily Life in a Totalitarian Society.* Cambridge, Mass.: Harvard University Press.

Iyengar, Shanto. 1991. *Is Anyone Responsible? How Television Frames Political Issues.* Chicago: University of Chicago Press.

Iyengar, Shanto, and Donald Kinder. 1987. *News That Matters.* Chicago: University of Chicago Press.

Jacobs, Lawrence. 1993. *The Health of Nations: Public Opinion and the Making of American and British Health Policy.* Ithaca: Cornell University Press.

Jacobs, Lawrence R., and Robert Y. Shapiro. 1994. "Studying Substantive Democracy." *PS: Political Science & Politics* (March): 9–17.

Jasper, James. 1990. *Nuclear Politics: Energy and the State in the United States, Sweden, and France.* Princeton: Princeton University Press.

Jennings, Kent. 1997. "Political Participation in the Chinese Countryside." *American Political Science Review* 91 (June): 361–72.

———. 2000. "Missing Data and Survey Research in China: Problems and Solutions." Paper presented at the Conference on Surveying China, George Washington University, June.

Jennings, M. Kent. 1983. "Gender Roles and Inequalities in Political Participation: Results from an Eight Nation Study." *Western Political Quarterly* 36: 364–85.

Judge, J. 1994. "Public Opinion and the New Politics of Contestation in the Late Qing, 1904–1911." *Modern China* 20, no. 1 (January): 64–91.

Karlekar, Karin Deutsch, ed. 2004. *Freedom of the Press 2004: A Global Survey of Media Independence.* New York: Freedom House; Washington, D.C.: Rowman and Littlefield. http://www.freedomhouse.org/research/pressurvey.htm (accessed March 25, 2005).

Keane, Michael, and Stephanie Hemelryk Donald. 2002. "Responses to Crisis: Convergence, Content Industries, and Media Governance." In *Media in China: Consumption, Content and Crisis,* edited by Stephanie Hemelryk Donald, Michael Keane, and Yin Hong. London and New York: RoutledgeCurzon.

Kennedy, Michael D. 1991. *Professionals, Power, and Solidarity in Poland: A Critical Sociology of Soviet-Type Society.* Cambridge: Cambridge University Press.

Ketizu [Research Group], Organization Department, Chinese Communist Party. 2001. *Zhougguo Diaocha Baogao (2000–2001): Xin Xingshi Xia Renmin Neibu Maodun Yanjiu* [China Investigative Report 2000–2001]. Beijing: Zhongyang Bianyi Chubanshe.

Khan, A. R., and C. Riskin. 1998. "Income and Inequality in China: Composition, Distribution and Growth of Household Income." *China Quarterly* 154 (June): 221–53.

Kluegel, James R., and David S. Mason. 2000. "Participation and the Foundations of Democracy." In *Market Democracy: Changing Opinion about Inequality and Politics in East Central Europe*, edited by David S. Mason and James R. Kluegel. Lanham, Md.: Rowman & Littlefield..

Konrad, Gyorgy, and Ivan Szelenyi. 1979. *The Intellectuals on the Road to Class Power.* New York: Harcourt Brace Jovanovich.

Kornai, Janos. 1980. *Economics of Shortage.* Amsterdam: North-Holland.

———. 1992. *The Socialist System: The Political Economy of Communism.* Princeton: Princeton University Press.

Kostechi, Marian, and Krzysztof Mrela. 1984. "Collective Solidarity in Poland's Powered Society." *Insurgent Sociologist* 12, no. 1–2: 131–42.

Landry, Pierre F., and Mingming Shen. 2005. "Reaching Migrants in Survey Research: The Use of the Global Positioning System to Reduce Coverage Bias in China." *Political Analysis* 13: 1-22.

Lane, David. 1985. *Soviet Economy and Society.* New York: New York University Press.

Latham, K. 2000. "Nothing but the Truth: News Media, Power and Hegemony in South China." *China Quarterly* 163 (September): 633–54.

Lee, Hong Yung. 1978. *The Politics of the Chinese Cultural Revolution.* Berkeley and Los Angeles: University of California Press.

Lenin, Vladimir Ilyich. 1987. "On Imperialism." In *Lenin: Selected Works.* London: Lawrence and Wishart.

Li, Qiang. 1998. *Zi You Zhu Yi* [Liberalism]. Beijing: Zhongguo Shehui Kexue Chubanshe.

Lieberthal, Kenneth. 1995. *Governing China: From Revolution through Reform.* New York: W. W. Norton.

Lieberthal, Kenneth, and Michel Oksenberg. 1988. *Policy Making in China.* Princeton: Princeton University Press.

Lindblom, Charles. 1977. *Politics and Markets.* New York: Basic Books.

Link, Perry. 1992. *Evening Chats in Beijing.* New York: Norton.

Lipset, Seymour Martin. 1961. *Political Man.* New York: Doubleday.

Lo, Carlos Wing Hung, and Sai Wing Leung. 2000. "Environmental Agency and Public Opinion in Guangzhou: The Limits of a Popular Approach to Environmental Governance." *China Quarterly* 163 (September): 677–704.

Logan, John R., and Yanjie Bian. 1993. "Inequalities in Access to Community Resources in a Chinese City." *Social Forces* 72 (2): 555–76.

MacFarquhar, Robert. 1998. "Reports from the field. Provincial People's Congresses." *China Quarterly* 155 (September): 656–67.

Manion, Melanie, 1994. "Survey Research in the Study of Contemporary China: Learning from Local Samples." *China Quarterly* 139 (September): 741–65.

Manion, Melanie. 1996. "The Electoral Connection in the Chinese Countryside." *American Political Science Review* 90, no. 4: 736–48.

———. 2000. "Report from the Field: Chinese Democratization in Perspective: Electorates and Selectorates at the Township Level." *China Quarterly* 163 (September): 764–82.

Mao, Zedong. 1967a. "Analysis of the Classes in Chinese Society." In *Selected Works of Mao Tse-tung*, vol. 1. Peking: Foreign Languages Press.

———. 1967b. "The May 4th Movement." In *Selected Works of Mao Tse-tung*, vol. 2. Peking: Foreign Languages Press.

———. 1967c. "Recruit Large Numbers of Intellectuals." In *Selected Works of Mao Tse-tung*, vol. 2. Peking: Foreign Languages Press.

———. 1967d. "Rectify the Party's Style of Work." In *Selected Works of Mao Tse-tung*, vol. 3. Peking: Foreign Languages Press.

———. 1967e. "Talks at the Yenan Forum on Literature and Art." In *Selected Works of Mao Tse-tung*, vol. 3. Peking: Foreign Languages Press.

March, James, and John Olsen. 1989. *Rediscovering Institutions: Organizational Factors in Political Life*. New York: Free Press.

———. 1994. *Democratic Governance*. New York: Free Press.

Margolis, Michael, and Gary A. Mauser. 1989. *Manipulating Public Opinion: Essays on Public Opinion as a Dependent Variable*. Pacific Grove, Calif.: Brooks/Cole.

Marsh, Alan. 1990. *Political Action in Europe and the USA*. London: Macmillan.

Marx, Karl, and Friedrich Engels. 1998. *Communist Manifesto*. New York: Signet.

Mason, David S. 1995. "Justice, Socialism, and Participation in the Postcommunist States." In *Social Justice and Political Change: Public Opinion in Capitalist and Post-Communist States*, edited by James R. Kluegel, David S. Mason, and Bernd Wegener. New York: Aldine De Gruyter. Pp. 49–80.

Mayer, William G. 1992. *The Changing American Mind: How and Why American Public Opinion Changed between 1960 and 1988*. Ann Arbor: University of Michigan Press.

McChesney, Robert W., and John Nichols. 2002. *Our Media, Not Theirs: The Democratic Struggle against Corporate Media*. New York: Seven Stories Press.

Manheim, Jarol B., and Richard C. Rich. 1995. *Empirical Political Analysis: Research Methods in Political Science*. 4th ed. London and New York: Longman.

Meisner, Maurice. 1986. *Mao's China and After: A History of the People's Republic*. New York: Free Press.

Metzger, A. Thomas. 1992. "Ershi Shiji Zhongguo Zhishi Fenzi de Zijue Wenti." In Yu Yingshi et al., *Zhongguo Lishi Zhuanxing Shiqi de Zhishi Fenzi* (Chinese Intellectuals during Historic Transformation). Taipei: Lian Jing. Pp. 83–138.

———. 1998. "Will China Democratize? Sources of Resistance." *Journal of Democracy* 9, no. 1 (January): 18–26.

Miller, William L., Stephen White, and Paul Heywood. 1998. *Values and Political Change in Postcommunist Europe*. New York: St. Martin's Press.

Ministry of Labor. 1985. *Zhishi Fenzi Zhengce Wenjian Huibian* [Collection of Documents on Intellectual Policy]. Beijing: Labor and Personnel Publishing House.

Moody, Peter R. 1977. *Opposition and Dissent in Contemporary China.* Stanford: Hoover Institution Press.

Muo, Rong. 2000. "Employment Still Troubling." In *Chinese Social Trends in 2000: Analysis and Forecast,* edited by Xing Ru, Xueyi Lu, and Tianlun Shan. Beijing: Social Sciences Documentation Publishing House. Pp.182–95.

Nathan, Andrew. 1973. "A Factionalism Model of CCP Politics." *China Quarterly* 53 (January–March): 34–66.

———. 1998. "Will China Democratize? Even Our Caution Must Be Hedged." *Journal of Democracy* 9, no. 1 (January): 60–64.

Nathan, Andrew, and Tianjian Shi. 1993. "Cultural Requisites for Democracy in China: Some Findings from Nation-wide Survey." *Daedalus* 122, no. 2: 95–123.

National Bureau of Statistics of China. 2004. *2003 China Statistical Abstract.* Beijing: China Statistics Press.

Norris, Pippa, ed. 1999. *Critical Citizens: Global Support for Democratic Government.* New York: Oxford University Press.

Nove, Alec. 1983. *The Economics of Feasible Socialism.* London: George Allen & Unwin.

———. 1991. *The Economics of Feasible Socialism Revisited.* 2nd ed. London and New York: HarperCollins Academic.

O'Brien, Kevin. 1990. *Reform without Liberalization: China's National People's Congress and the Politics of Institutional Change.* New York: Cambridge University Press.

O'Brien, Kevin, and Lianjiang Li. 2000. "Accommodating 'Democracy' in a One-Party State: Introducing Village Elections in China." *China Quarterly* 162 (June): 465–89.

O'Leary, Greg. 1998. *Adjusting to Capitalism: Chinese Workers and the State.* New York: M. E. Sharpe.

Page, Benjamin I. 1994. "Democratic Responsiveness? Untangling the Links between Public Opinion and Policy." *PS: Political Science & Politics* (March): 25–29.

Page, Benjamin I., and Robert Y. Shapiro. 1992. *The Rational Public: Fifty Years of Trends in Americans' Political Preferences.* Chicago: University of Chicago Press.

Parish, William L. 1979. "The View from the Factory." In *The China Difference,* edited by Ross Terrill. New York: Harper. 183–200.

———. 1989. Presentation handout on economic performance in planned and market economies. University of Chicago, March 2.

Parish, William L., and Martin King Whyte. 1978. *Village and Family in Contemporary China.* Chicago: University of Chicago Press.

Perez-Diaz, V. 1994. *The Return of Civil Society.* Cambridge, Mass.: Harvard University Press.

Perry, Elizabeth. 1991. "Intellectuals and Tiananmen: Historical Perspective on an

Aborted Revolution." In *The Crisis of Leninism and the Decline of the Left: The Revolutions of 1989*, edited by Daniel Chirot. Seattle: University of Washington Press.

———. 1994. "Casting a Chinese 'Democracy' Movement: The Roles of Students, Workers, and Entrepreneurs." In *Popular Protest and Political Culture in Modern China*, edited by Jeffrey N. Wasserstrom and Elizabeth J. Perry. 2nd ed. Boulder, Colo.: Westview Press.

Peters, Guy B. 1998. *Comparative Politics: Theory and Methods*. New York: New York University Press.

Policy Research Department of All China Federation of Trade Unions. 2001. *Chinese Trade Unions Statistics Yearbook 2000*. Beijing: China Statistics Press.

Pomfret, John. 2000. "As Change Tests China, Labor Disputes Spread." *International Herald Tribune*, April 24.

Population Census Office under the State Council & Department of Population, Social, Science and Technology Statistics of National Bureau of Statistics of China. 2002. *Tabulation on the 2000 Population Census of the People's Republic of China*. Beijing: China Statistics Press.

Putnam, R. D. 1995. "Bowling Alone: America's Declining Social Capital." *Journal of Democracy* 6: 65–78.

Putnam, R. D., with R. Leonardi and R.V. Nanetti. 1993. *Making Democracy Work: Civic Tradition in Modern Italy*. Princeton: Princeton University Press.

Pye, Lucien. 1981. *The Dynamics of Chinese Politics*. Cambridge, Mass.: Oelgeschlager, Gunn & Hain.

Pye, Lucien, and Mary Pye. 1989. *Asian Power and Politics: The Cultural Dimensions and Authority*. Harvard University Press.

Rawski, Thomas G. 2001. "What's Happening to China's GDP Statistics?" *China Economic Review* 12, no. 4: 347–54.

———. 2002. "Jinnianlai Zhongguo GDP Zengzhang Hesuan: Muqian de Zhuangkuang" [Calculating China's Recent GDP Growth: Current Situation]. *Jinjixue (Jikan)* [China Economic Quarterly] 2, no. 1 (October): 53–62.

Research Center for Contemporary China. 2004. *National Public Opinion Survey on Values and Ethics: Coding and Frequency Distribution Handbook* [Quanguo Gongzhong Sixiang Daodeguan Zhaungkuang Diaocha Bianma ji Pinshu Fenbu Shouce]. May 31.

———. 1995–present. *Beijing Area Study Codebook*.

Read, Ben. 2000. "Research Note: Revitalizing the State's Urban 'Nerve Tips.'" *China Quarterly* 163 (September): 806–20.

Redl, Anke, and Rown Simons. 2002. "Chinese Media: One Channel, Two Systems." In *Media in China: Consumption, Content and Crisis*, edited by Stephanie Hemelryk Donald, Michael Keane, and Yin Hong. London and New York: RoutledgeCurzon.

Reporters without Borders. 2003a. "Second World Press Freedom Ranking." http://www.rsf.org/article.php3?id_article=8247 (accessed March 25, 2005).

———. 2003b. "Living Dangerously on the Net: Censorship and Surveillance of the Internet Forums in China." http://www.rsf.org/article.php3?id_article= 6793 (accessed March 25, 2005).

Riskin, Carl. 1987. *China's Political Economy: The Quest for Development Since 1949.* New York: Oxford University Press.

Risse-Kappen, Thomas. 1991. "Public Opinion, Domestic Structure, and Foreign Policy in Liberal Democracies." *World Politics* 43: 479–512.

Rokkan, S. 1966. "Votes Count But Resources Decide." In *Political Oppositions in Western Democracies*, edited by R. A. Dahl. New Haven, Conn.: Yale University Press.

Rosen, Stanley. 1989. "Public Opinion and Reform in the People's Republic of China." *Studies in Comparative Communism* 22, no. 2–3: 153–70.

———. 1991. "The Rise (and Fall) of Public Opinion in Post-Mao China." In *Reform and Reaction in Post-Mao China: The Road to Tiananmen*, edited by Richard Baum. New York: Routledge.

Rosen, Stanley, and David Zweig. 2000. "Managing 'Competing Interests': Problems in Collaborative Survey Research Projects in China." Paper presented at the Conference on Surveying China, George Washington University, June.

Saich, Tony. 2000. "Negotiating the State: The Development of Social Organizations in China." *China Quarterly* 161 (March): 124–41.

Schattschneider, E. 1942. *Party Government.* New York: Farrar & Reinhart.

Schechter, Danny, ed. 2000. *Falun Gong's Challenge to China.* New York: Akashic Books.

Schmitter, Philippe C. 1979. "Still the Century of Corporatism." In *Trends toward Corporatist Intermediation*, edited by Philippe C. Schmitter and Gerhard Lehmbruch. Beverly Hills and London: Sage.

Schoenhals, M. 1999. "Political Movements, Change and Stability: The CCP in Power." *China Quarterly* 159 (September): 595–605.

Schopflin, George. 1993. *Politics in Eastern Europe, 1945–1992.* Oxford: Blackwell.

Seligson, Mitchell. 2002. "The Renaissance of Political Culture, or the Renaissance of the Ecological Fallacy." *Comparative Politics* 34 (April): 273–92.

Shapiro, Robert Y., and Harpreet Mahajan. 1986. "Gender Differences in Policy Preferences: A Summary of Trends from the 1960s to the 1980s." *Public Opinion Quarterly* 50: 42–61.

Shen, Mingming. 2001. "Analysis and Forecast of Urban Resident's Confidence during the Transition to a Market Economy." In *Gaige Fazhan yu Shehui Bianqian* [Reforms, Development, and Social Changes], edited by Mingming Shen. Beijing: Huaxia Publishing House.

Shi, Tianjian. 1996. "Survey Research in China." *Research in Micropolitics* 5: 213–50.

———. 1997. *Political Participation in Beijing.* Cambridge, Mass.: Harvard University Press.

————. 2000a. "Cultural Values and Democracy in the People's Republic of China." *China Quarterly* 162 (June): 540–59.

————. 2000b. "Response Error in Surveys in China." Paper presented at the Conference on Surveying China, George Washington University, Washington, D. C., June.

Silver, Brian. 1987. "Political Beliefs of the Soviet Citizen: Sources of Support for Regime Norms." In *Politics, Work, and Daily Life in the USSR*, edited by James Millar. New York: Cambridge University Press.

Solinger, Dorothy J. 1996. "Despite Decentralization: Disadvantages, Dependence and Ongoing Central Power in the Inland; The Case of Wuhan." *China Quarterly* 145 (March): 1–34.

Song, Qiang, Zangzang Zhang, Bian Qiao, Qingsheng Gu, and Zhengyu Tang. 1996. *Zhongguo Keyi Shuobu* [China Can Say No]. Beijing: Industry and Commerce Publishing House.

Stalin, Joseph. 1961. *Sulian Shehui Zhuyi Jingji Wenti* [Issues in the Soviet Socialist Economy]. Beijing: People's Publishing House.

StataCorp. 1995. *Stata Statistical Software*. College Station, Tex.: Stata.

State Statistical Bureau. 1982. *Chinese Economic Yearbook*. Beijing: China Statistics Press.

————. 1999. "New Regulations on Survey." *Zhongguo Gongshang Ribao* [China Industry and Commerce Daily], August 2.

————. 2002. *China Statistical Yearbook*. Beijing: China Statistics Press.

————. 2003. *China Statistical Yearbook*. Beijing: China Statistics Press.

————. 2004. *China Statistical Yearbook*. Beijing: China Statistics Press.

Stimson, James A. 1998. *Public Opinion in America: Moods, Cycles, and Swings*. 2nd ed. Boulder, Colo.: Westview Press.

Stimson, James A., Michael B. MacKuen, and Robert S. Erikson. 1994. "Opinion and Policy: A Global View." *PS: Political Science and Politics* (March): 29–35.

Sun, Li, ed. 1997. *Zhuan Xing Qi De Zhongguo Shehui* [Chinese Society in Transition]. Beijing: Gaige Chubanshe.

Szelenyi, Ivan. 1982. "The Intelligentsia in the Class Structure of State-Socialist Societies." In *Marxist Inquiries*, edited by M. Burawoy and T. Skocpol. Chicago: University of Chicago Press. Pp. 287–326.

Tang, Wenfang. 2001. "Political and Social Trends in Post-Deng Urban China: Crisis or Stability?" *China Quarterly* 168 (December): 890–909.

————. 2003. "An Introduction to Survey Research in China: A Research Guide." *Issues and Studies* 38, no. 4–39, no. 1 (December 2002–March 2003): 269–88.

Tang, Wenfang, and William Parish. 2000. *Chinese Urban Life under Reform*. New York: Cambridge University Press.

Tanner, Murray Scot. 2004. "China Rethinks Unrest." *Washington Quarterly* 27, no. 3 (Summer): 137–56.

U.S. Department of State. 2003. *2002 Country Report on Human Rights Practices: China*. March 31. http://www.state.gov/g/drl/rls/hrrpt/2002/18239.htm (accessed March 25, 2005).

Verba, Sidney. 1978. "The Parochial and the Polity." In *The Citizen and Politics: A Comparative Perspective*, edited by Sidney Verba and Lucian W. Pye. Stamford, Conn.: Greylock. Pp. 3–28.

Verba, Sidney, Norman H. Nie, and Jae-on Kim. 1978. *Participation and Political Equality*. Chicago: University of Chicago Press.

Walder, Andrew G. 1986. *Communist Neo-Traditionalism: Work and Authority in Chinese Industry*. Berkeley and Los Angeles: University of California Press.

———. 1990. "Economic Reform and Income Distribution in Tianjin, 1976–1986." In *Chinese Society on the Eve of Tiananmen*, edited by Deborah Davis and Ezra Vogel. Cambridge, Mass.: Harvard University Press. Pp. 135–56.

———. 1995a. "Career Mobility and the Communist Political Order." *American Sociological Review* 60: 309–28.

———, ed. 1995b. *The Waning of the Communist State: Economic Origins of Political Decline in China and Hungary*. Berkeley and Los Angeles: University of California Press.

Wan, Li. 1986. "Democratic and Scientific Decision Making Is an Important Issue of Political System Reform." *People's Daily*, August 15.

Wang, Shaoguang. 1995. *Failure of Charisma: The Cultural Revolution in Wuhan*. Hong Kong and New York: Oxford University Press.

Wang, Shaoguang, and Angang Hu. 1994. *Zhongguo Guojia Nengli Yanjiu Baogao* (A Study of China's National Capacity). Hong Kong: Oxford University Press.

———. 2000. *The Political Economy of Uneven Development: The Case of China*. Armonk, N.Y.: M. E. Sharpe.

Wasserstrom, Jeffrey N., and Elizabeth J. Perry, eds. 1994. *Popular Protest and Political Culture in Modern China*. 2nd ed. Boulder, Colo.: Westview Press.

Weier, John. 2000. "Bright Lights, Big City." Earth Observatory, NASA. http://visibleearth.nasa.gov/cgi-bin/viewrecord?5826 (accessed March 24, 2005).

Whyte, Martin King. 1990. "Changes in Mate Choice in Chengdu." In *Chinese Society on the Eve of Tiananmen*, edited by Deborah Davis and Ezra Vogel. Cambridge, Mass.: Harvard University Press. Pp. 181–214.

———. 1993. "Wedding Behavior and Family Strategies in Chengdu." In *Chinese Families in the Post-Mao Era*, edited by Deborah Davis and Steven Harrell. Berkeley and Los Angeles: University of California Press. Pp. 189–216.

———. 2000. "My Joys and Frustrations Doing China Survey Work." Paper presented at the Conference on Surveying China, George Washington University, Washington, D.C., June.

Whyte, Martin King, and William L. Parish. 1984. *Urban Life in Contemporary China*. Chicago: University of Chicago Press.

Wilson, Jeanne. 1986. "The People's Republic of China." In *Trade Unions in Com-*

munist States, edited by Alex Pravda and Blair A. Ruble. Boston: Allen and Unwin. Pp. 219–51.

World Bank. 1999. *China: Weathering the Storm and Learning the Lessons.* Washington, D.C.: World Bank.

World Bank Group. 2003. *World Development Indicators Online.* http://www.worldbank.org/data/ (accessed April 3, 2005).

World Values Survey Staffs. 2002. *Codebook, World Values Surveys: 1981, 1990, 1995, 2000.* World Values Survey Group. http://www.worldvaluessurvey.org/ (accessed March 25, 2005).

Wyman, Matthew. 1997. *Public Opinion in Postcommunist Russia.* New York: St. Martin's Press.

Yang, Guobin. 2003. "The Internet and Civil Society in China: A Preliminary Assessment." *Journal of Contemporary China* 12, no. 36: 453–75.

Yang, Mayfair Mei-hui. 1994. *Gifts, Favors, and Banquets: The Art of Social Relationships in China.* Ithaca: Cornell University Press.

Zaslavsky, Victor. 1995. "From Redistribution to Marketization: Social and Attitudinal Change in Post-Soviet Russia." In *New Russia: Troubled Transformation,* edited by Gail W. Lapidus. Boulder, Colo.: Westview Press.

Zhan, Jiang, and Gang Zhao. 2003. "'Now Broadcasting' Another Trump Card in Central TV's Efforts to Strengthen the Media's Supervisory Role." *Chinese Education and Society* 35, no. 4 (July–August): 95–101.

Zhang, Bingyin. 1992. *Renda Gongzuo de Lilun yu Shijian* [Theory and Practice of the People's Congress]. Beijing: Legal Publishing House.

Zhang, Jing. 1998. *Fatuan Zhuyi* [Corporatism]. Beijing: China Social Science Publishing House.

———. 2001. "The Growing Social Foundation of Public Sphere: A Case Analysis of the District Dispute in Shanghai." In *Shehui Zhuanxing Yu Shequ Fazhan* (Social Transformation and Social Development), edited by Shanghai Shehui Kexue Lianhehui (Shanghai Confederation of Social Sciences). Shanghai: Shanghai Shehui Kexue Lianhehui.

Zhang, Liang. 2001. *The Tiananmen Papers.* New York: PublicAffairs.

Zhang, Zhenzhong, Pengying Tian, Xiaomei Li, and Zhibin Sheng. 1992. *Deng Xiaoping Guanyu Zhishi Fenzi Wenti de Sixiang Yanjiu* [A Study of Deng Xiaoping's Thought on Intellectuals]. Liaoning: Liaoning People's Publishing House.

Zhe, Xiaoye. 1989. *Chengshi zai Zhuanzhedian Shang* [Cities at a Turning Point]. Booklet in *Shehui Xuezhe dui Shehui de Jinggao* [Warnings about Society from Sociologists], compendium edited by Yunkang Pan. Beijing: Chinese Women's Publishing House.

Zhu, Jian-hua. 1990. "Information Availability, Source Credibility, and Audience Sophistication: Factors Conditioning the Effects of Communist Propaganda in China." Ph.D. diss., Indiana University.

Index

Italic page numbers indicate material in tables or figures.

paternalistic politics, 5
People's Congresses, 17–19, 132
People's Liberation Army, 25
police brutality, 83
Political Bureau (Politburo), 14, 19, 79
political efficacy, 125
Political Participation Survey (1987), 34,
  126
political parties, alternative, 59
political structure: 14–20, 70; cultural effects of, 193–94; market effects of,
  194–95; modernization effect of, 195;
  systemic effects of, 191–93
political tradition, 3–6
problem solving, 135, *136*, *137*
protests, 198, 214n1. *See also* Tiananmen
  Square protests
provincial legislatures, 59
public opinion: effects of economic
  growth, 194–95; effects of media, 93–
  98; existing studies in, 22–23; influence of, 196–98; influence on policy
  making, 22–24, 26; manipulation of,
  23, 93, 191–93; modern nature of, 195;
  perceptions of other countries, 72–73,
  77; volatility of, 195–96. *See also* media; media consumption; reform satisfaction; regime legitimacy; surveys;
  voicing mass opinion

qi gong (cultivation of vital energy), 27
Qin Shi Huang Di, 5
Qing dynasty, 26

radical reform supporters, 66
Red Guards, 8
reform satisfaction, 59–70; age, 67; career
  success, 62; China's image in the world,
  60, 62, 64; crime control, 62, 64; demographics, 66–70; economic conditions,
  62, 63–64, 67, 76; economic freedom,
  60, 62; education, 67; environmental
  protection, 62, 63; family life, 60; freedom of speech, 60, 64; gender, 67; geographic location, 69; health, 60, 62;
  housing, 60, 62, 64; life priorities, *61*;
  occupation, 67, 213nn2–3 (chap. 3);
  political freedom, 62; religious freedom, 62; shifts over time, 63–64, *63*;

social life, 60; speed of reform, 65–66,
  65, *68*; variables in study, 202
regime legitimacy, 58, 70–71, 75–76, 80,
  93
religious beliefs, 83
Reporters without Borders, 82
Research Center for Contemporary
  China (RCCC), 40
revisionism, 8
righteousness and sacrifice (*yi*), 4
ritual (*li*), 4
Russian Revolution (1917), 7

SARS epidemic, 83, 198
satisfaction. *See* reform satisfaction
Secretariat, 14
separatism, 83
Shanghai, 69, 81, 91, 124, 213n4
Shenyang, 69, 72, 91, 124, 213n4
single-party system, 14, 28, 30, 70, 76
Six-City Survey (1999): interpersonal
  trust, 102, 107–8, 114–16: media consumption, 87–88; overview of, 34–35,
  201; public opinion, 124; reform satisfaction, 60, 202; regime legitimacy, 70;
  variables in, *203*; voicing complaints,
  126
social capital theory, 102
social interactions, 107–8
social organizations, 59
social polarization, 76
social responsibilities, 6
Soviet Empire, collapse of, 57
space program, 90
spatial sampling, 45
Staff and Workers Survey (1997), 36
Stalinist model of economic development, 10–12
Standing Committee of the NPC, 16
Standing Committee of the Politburo, 14
State Administration of Environmental
  Protection, 37
State Administration of Radio, Film, and
  Television, 80, 81
State Press and Publication Administra-
  tion, 80
State Statistical Bureau (SSB), 37, 39–40
surveys: barriers for Western researchers,
  39–42; budgetary issues, 212n7; data